P9-AEY-116

To my family—John, Nick, Emma and Isabelle—
and to all of the lesser-known humanitarians of the world

Jumping the Picket Fence

A Woman's Search for Meaning from the Suburbs to the Slums

Lydia Dean

Copyright © 2015 Lydia Dean
All rights reserved.

ISBN: 0990821307
ISBN 13: 9780990821304

Foreword

I believe we are all on a journey of exploration—one that will take us each on amazingly beautiful and varied paths. Mine required that I set the normal American life by the roadside to see, smell, and touch the world. Then having done so, I realized that I had work to do. These pages represent a quest, a search for a connection to humanity and a purpose within it. They also represent, at times, a daunting search within myself, one I wasn't always ready to face.

This book was written over the course of fourteen years, and during this time there were many moments when I wasn't sure I had the strength to finish it. Frustrated by the enormity of understanding how all my life experiences fit together, I would leave the pages abandoned in a folder I just called Book. And during periods when I was genuinely motivated to forge on with the manuscript, life put barriers in the way—like the day my computer was stolen at New York's Kennedy Airport, and six years of notes from our lives in Provence simply vanished.

In writing about our experiences through this vast yet sometimes harsh and complex planet, I discovered that joy could be found in the most unexpected places, in the simplest, most basic things. I would learn later, though, that even greater joy is found in sharing them. The travels and encounters were a series of risks and opportunities strung together on some thin but incredibly strong piece of universal thread. They would lead me to a place where I would be asked to learn about who I am and then offer my best to humanity. GoPhilanthropic was, in a large part, my way of doing this. It's funny how, in the moment, we can't quite see the beautiful order of things as we are living them. As several philosophers have pointed out, if you let go of the need to control how and when things happen, life will unfold like a well-ordered book.

In sum, it is my hope that these pages inspire you to follow your dreams, your life signs, no matter how scared and unsure you might be. And I hope along the way you take whatever opportunities you are given to encourage and help others to follow theirs. This story is an example of trusting what makes us tick inside, of listening to the things that tug and pull at our hearts, of keeping alive the visions that flash through our minds as we drift off to sleep. Because these are life's gifts to us, and they make each one of us unique. I now believe we can find our purposes when we let these visions lead the way.

Prologue: Zulu

Orlando, Florida
Summer 1996, shortly after getting married

John woke up one morning and told me about a dream he'd had during the night. There was a fragile look about him as he sat down. Taking a deep breath, he began to explain. "I was walking in a desert, in an incredibly dry and unforgiving refugee setting in Africa. I saw a young girl sitting on the ground. She was alone and was leaning against a straw hut in the blazing midday heat. She was dirty and hardly wearing anything, maybe just underpants. Her body was covered with severe and ugly burns, and her leg had been amputated at the right knee."

Taking a breath, he continued. "My reaction was to feel overwhelming sorrow and pity for this child. 'How could life have allowed this to happen to her?' I thought."

He went on, saying, "The setting was strange. It was like heaven but also like hell. There was destitution, but there was also a strange calm. It was as though the air was full of clarity and peace. Naturally, my immediate impulse was to help this child, to save her from her sorrow. I felt lucky in being able to do so. So I went over to her and bent down to her." Suddenly, John stopped telling me the dream and began to cry.

"It was worse than sad, Lydia—worse than tragic. It was hard to even look at her. But I got down at eye level, so I could see right into her eyes. She didn't speak to me, but I could hear what she was saying in her mind. I could hear her thoughts. Then she said to me as clear as day, 'Don't be sorry for me—look at you. Look at how you live your life. Be sorry for yourself.'"

Now sobbing, he continued. "First of all, she didn't want my pity or my help, and second, she was somehow disgusted by me—that I was in no place or position to give. She let me know I was the one who was miserable and pathetic. Then I saw someone holding a sign handwritten on the back of a legal pad. It said Zulu."

The dream about Zulu would come up again and again over the years, and John would cry every single time he retold it. He said that to him it was prophetic—a constant reminder that our lives were a search, a journey toward that place where we were whole enough to have something to offer. The child in his dream hadn't wanted what he had materially. Those things weren't the goodness he had to share. We had to be willing to offer something much deeper and more fundamental, and we had to dig down into the corners of our spirits to find it.

At the time of the dream, we were years away from living a life focused on more purposeful things, years away from GoPhilanthropic, and years away from adopting a child who would have her right leg amputated below the knee. But somehow we both knew the dream represented our time here on earth and that our search and journey had to do with getting to that place where Zulu might accept what we had to offer. And we still had many miles to log in that journey...

Disclaimer

Some names and identifying details have been changed where subject matter is sensitive, and to protect the privacy of individuals and organizations.

A Glimpse of Heaven

India will dissolve your ideas about what it is to be a human being,
what it is to be compassionate, what it is to be spiritual or conscious.
James O'Reilly and Larry Habegger

Chennai, India
Fall 2005

At 2:00 a.m., weary eyed and sweaty from the long journey, I tentatively pushed my cart through the sliding glass doors as I exited the international terminal in Chennai, India. The heat, noise, and fumes immediately battered my already uneasy state. Scanning the sea of faces, I felt a wave of relief as I spotted a man with a beaming, warm smile clutching a small sign bearing Hope Volunteers Abroad in simple scrawl. "Welcome to India, Lydia. You are the last to arrive," he shouted over the din as we piled ourselves and my bags into a tired minivan.

Raj Mihar, a gracious and overwhelmingly affable native of Chennai, would lead five of us volunteers through Hope

Volunteer Abroad's India program. For the next two weeks, we would be charged with teaching English to one hundred children who were left victim by families unable to provide for them. This was the experience I had dreamed about since I was a child, but now amid the whirlwind of sights and sounds only found in India, intimidation seeped into my very being. *What on earth have I done?* I thought. Suddenly, I felt very alone and very exposed.

Our taxi swerved in and out of the dark streets of Porur, a crowded suburb of Chennai, which is India's fourth-largest city and home to six million people. I gazed out the window in a fog of jet lag, fear, and amazement, wondering what the next weeks would have in store. Finally, we stopped at the end of a quiet road, in front of our team's guesthouse, a nondescript concrete building. Climbing out of the van, I noticed a small shrine with the Hindu elephant god, Ganesh, lord of success and destroyer of evils, placed next to the entrance gate. Gazing further, I could make out a great heaping mass of dirt and garbage next to a line of sleeping cows on the sidewalk.

We climbed a narrow staircase in the dark and entered the house. Raj groped around clumsily for lights and, whispering, gave me a quick tour of our Spartan quarters. We walked through a small room that smelled strongly of spices, onions, and garlic. A chipped and worn countertop housed a tattered two-burner gas stove. A couple of baskets exposed bunches of coriander, curry leaves, potatoes, and eggplants.

He led me by boxes of drinking water stacked along a wall to the conference room, which was papered with posters of flags from all over the world, a Hope Volunteers Abroad logo, and some poster paper with TEAM GOALS scratched out in sloppy handwriting. I quickly scanned the words written— LOVE THE CHILDREN, SERVE, HELP OTHERS—basic statements fundamental to why volunteers had come. "From the last team," Raj explained. Centered in the room was a big brown table bordered by red plastic chairs where we would eat, hold team meetings, read, generally live. *Lonely Planet* guides to India, phonics flash cards, and children's books were heaped on a counter in the corner of the room.

I entered the bathroom, which consisted of a bare concrete floor and walls of faded and dirty chipped paint. A small, baby-blue plastic mirror hung delicately over an old sink, where a line of ants busily headed toward the cracked window. A single tap was mounted high—cold water only. This was the shower. Raj advised me not to use any of the electrical outlets. "Not safe," he said flatly.

Mumbling something about a morning meeting only a few short hours away, Raj bade me a quick farewell and pointed to a room I was sharing with a woman named Cheryl. I rummaged in the dark through my bags in search of my sheet and pillow, then collapsed onto a hard cot, stalked by mosquitoes. I fell into a fitful sleep with great startling claps of thunder and lightning outside, brief flashes of light exposing a bare-bones room and the snoozing lump of my fellow volunteer.

Sizzling sounds and potent curried aromas woke me in the morning. Cheryl's bed was empty. Pulling a brush through my hair and quickly tying it up on the top of my head, I took the few steps into the main room, where I could hear the sounds of voices. "Hi, I'm Liam," said a young, energetic Asian man with big, round, sweet eyes full of positive spirit. "I'm from Toronto—in banking," he added awkwardly.

"Lydia," I replied as I reached out to shake his hand. "I'm actually from Canada too—but then I moved to the United States, married, and now have a family. But we live in France," I said even more awkwardly. *God, that never flows well,* I thought to myself. *I have got to get a better spiel.* And I had left out the part about having English parents, meaning that I wasn't really 100 percent Canadian. And yes, I had an American passport, but I didn't feel American—could I add that? I had always stumbled over the simple questions that had to do with, where are you from? My mind would spin with the variations of what that could mean: Where am I from originally? Where am I living now? Where do I feel I am from?

Who could know that my children would have an even worse time with this for their own reasons? But none of that mattered now, in India.

Over a breakfast of tiny, short noodles, spicy tomato chutney, and ruby-red pomegranates, I acquainted myself with the rest of the team. Middle-aged Ryan also introduced himself as a banker, more formally than Liam had, yet his warmth came through in his every breath. This was his first trip abroad, and his trepidation was evident. I felt his pain, from the careful manner in which he dished himself his first Indian breakfast that morning, to the way he grabbed my elbow crossing the crazy Porur street that afternoon. Manny, sweet and innocently kind, was a border-control officer and had been on several volunteer projects around the world. My roommate, Cheryl, was divorced and in her sixties with two daughters about my age. A true free spirit at heart with an infectious laugh, she reflected a deep wisdom enhanced by years of travel. I felt immediately comfortable with her, and the feeling seemed mutual.

Scanning the faces of my new friends, I wondered what internal dialogues had brought each of them to this scrappy guesthouse a million miles away from their normal lives. Had they, like me, dreamed of escaping the monotony of everyday life in search of something more meaningful? Had they questioned what it was they were meant to do in life, give in life? Did they feel as vulnerable and clueless as I did sitting in this red plastic chair? *Ryan does at least*, I thought. I knew that.

Later that morning, we set off for the orphanage, crammed into a jeep blaring new age Indian pop music, sandalwood incense burning on the dash next to a small Hindu statue of Shiva. Over the course of our stay, trips in the van would have each one of us gasping and crying out in fear every split second as we swerved, often violently, to avoid obstacles in the road. If we weren't swerving, we were braking suddenly in front of massive potholes, making sudden stops that jerked us forward and sent bags of school supplies and water bottles flying. I gripped the seat in front of me, trying to stabilize myself. It felt like two hundred degrees in the van; we were literally on top of one another. I made the mistake of opening the window, which only exacerbated the earsplitting noise of music and honking horns and wafted in inches of dust that caked my sweaty skin.

On that first day, our jeep was held up by what looked like a fantastic, colorful parade. Throngs of young men were singing and banging on drums around a donkey-driven wooden cart entirely covered in a dazzling display of fresh flowers. "Is it a wedding, Raj, or a religious festival?" I asked.

"No, this is a funeral," he yelled back over the noise. Looking closer, I noticed the small brown toe of the corpse on its way to the crematorium. I quickly realized that there was no insulation from the realities of life in India. It was all to be seen on the streets—birth, daily ablution, celebration, death.

After pushing past the busy life of Porur, we finally entered lush countryside surrounded by green rice fields and banana trees. We arrived at Reaching Stars Orphanage after only one hour of driving, yet we were all exhausted and filthy. Anticipation was in the air as we pulled up to a roughly built, unfinished cinder-block building. None of us knew as we turned that last corner that what we would experience in the coming days would affect us each deeply—four out of the five of us would change our life courses dramatically.

Some of my fellow volunteers had brought overstuffed bags of school supplies—what collectively amounted to mass amounts of paper, pens, notebooks, balls, toys, and medicines. Piling out of the van and slinging large bags over our shoulders, we set out to mount a steep set of stairs, finally landing in a big, bare room lined with tattered couches. At the top, I was relieved to meet a young man who whisked away our heaping bags of supplies. Hot and sweaty, we dumped ourselves onto the worn couches, and I began to take in what would be our surroundings, fumbling for my water bottle.

Where the hell am I, and why have I put myself here? My mind wandered to John and the kids, picturing them at home in France in front of the big fireplace, doing homework or playing on the terrace as the late-afternoon sun set. The cocktail of emotions had fear strangely coupled with a sense comfort, like I was lost, yet in the place I was meant to be. Taking a deep breath, I sipped my water, slipping into that part of me that had learned to trust.

Peering around the corner and into another dark room, I spied the corner of the bag of supplies I had dragged up the stairs. Curious, I took a few steps to get a better look. "Holy shit," I mumbled to myself as I noticed what appeared to be hundreds of heaped bags of school supplies—thousands of notebooks and bags of pencils and pens, more balls and toys. *What a little bounty for this small orphanage. What is it all doing here? It doesn't look as if anyone is using any of it. Why is there so much of it?* I wondered. As my mind started to question this a little further, Anuj and Jyoti, the

Indian couple who had founded the orphanage, walked in the door.

For the next hour and with limited English, Anuj and Jyoti described the humble beginnings of their program. It had all begun when the couple had been made aware of a handful of orphaned children in a nearby village a few years back. They hadn't had much, but they had decided they could take a few in on their veranda, feeding them an evening meal. Word had spread quickly, and soon the floodgates had opened, homeless children drifting in from all over the area. Within the course of three years, Anuj and Jyoti had taken in over a hundred children. Forced to quit his day job in order to care for the growing crowd, Anuj had been afraid he would not be able to provide. It was "the hand of God," he said, that had brought Hope Volunteers Abroad to their doorstep and, over time, began channeling support through paid volunteer vacations such as ours. Eventually they had earned enough money to purchase some land and build the small, simple structure that now housed the children full-time. They explained that they had no funding whatsoever from the Indian government.

Motioning us to follow her, Jyoti proudly guided us through the newly constructed but rough and dark rooms. For her, it was clearly a huge step up from the veranda packed with kids, yet I could tell from glancing at the other volunteers that they were are all silently gasping. The walls were stacked cinder blocks, and the floors on the ground level, where the children slept, were made of packed dirt. By day the building became a school for the children, yet there were

no desks, and the only light came from one or two weary fluo-
rescent bulbs on the ground floor. We passed a dingy corner
with two cots. Jyoti described how they had taken in an old
homeless man and, more recently, a disabled person.

As we toured the outside of the building, Jyoti pointed
to the neighboring field. "This is where they use the toilets,"
she stated flatly. Continuing on, she walked us around the
back to their outdoor kitchen. A turkey and several chickens
ran around the perimeter. All the meals were cooked in a
thatched, open-air structure over an open wood fire. The
diet consisted of an assortment mainly of fruit, vegetables,
rice, beans, and lentils. To eat, the children seated themselves in lines outdoors and, due to a shortage of plates, the
first round hurried to eat and rinse their plates to be handed
off to the next. A water pump sat next to an aluminum con-
tainer holding drinking water. Two cups dangling from the
side were shared by all one hundred kids.

Hearing the giggles of children not far away, I felt a sudden impatience to get on with what we had come to do. But
the simple reality was that I wasn't quite sure what that
was. The first forty-eight hours had been a clear indicator
that none of us was prepared to know what a child would
or would not need, given their difficult backgrounds, in a
country that was so foreign. *Am I here to do my part in a
world with endless problems? Sure, great—but how far is two
weeks going to get with that?* Simple yet haunting questions
began to creep into the back corners of my consciousness.
There was a much more complex reason, a more real reason, but I was far from knowing what that was.

Anuj ushered us into one of the dark rooms on the main floor and told us to seat ourselves on the two benches at the front of the room. Scanning him up and down, I tried to make sense of the mixed signals I was getting from him: impatience, boredom with us, like it had become just a bit too routine to welcome a group of white foreigners here to do something good. No, I couldn't put my finger on it, but something told me that there was more than met the eye.

In lines of two, one for the girls and one for the boys, the children filed in to greet us, some bearing wide, toothy grins, others hiding shy smiles. They sat down in perfectly neat rows and stared at us with open, expecting eyes. The heat of the room then became suddenly extreme, and I sweated profusely, feeling channels of water run down my back, my calves, my forehead. I tried to discreetly sop up my rivers of sweat while swatting away the hovering flies and mosquitoes. The children just stared at us, appearing oblivious to the heat and bugs. One by one they came up and shook our hands, individually introducing themselves.

From ages two to sixteen, some proudly sported their introductions in English, others eked out their hellos in Tamil, and some said nothing at all, simply holding out their dusty hands, staring wide-eyed. While they appeared relatively well groomed and healthy at first glance, a few even wearing black shoes and pulled-up socks to match their tattered school uniforms, I would later notice that many of them had oozing open sores on their heads, arms, and legs. Most scratched incessantly at heads full of lice. Their clothes, especially the young ones' clothes, fell off their bony bodies, with gaping holes here and there. The girls' backs were bare as all of the dresses lacked working zippers. Collectively they hacked, snuffled, and sniffed, especially the little ones, who toddled around, diaperless and dirty, noses streaming. A baby the size of a newborn, who I would learn later was five months old, sat listless in the lap of a girl no more than six. I locked my gaze on this dot of a child, staring at her minuscule little wrists, her hips protruding in a way babies' hips didn't in my world.

After a few days, we fell into a loose routine that began with breakfast, followed by the hair-raising ride from Porur. In the mornings, the children completed their lessons in Tamil. Our jobs in the afternoons and early evenings were to teach English classes to small groups of fourth and fifth graders. They were already starting out in the world with major disadvantages and life obstacles, raised in poverty, many without parents. At least if they were sent off into Indian life with a proficiency in English, they would have one leg up from the bottom. A chance. Maybe.

While teaching English seemed a relatively simple task to perform at the outset, it quickly proved incredibly challenging. Some spoke, read, and wrote easily, while others had trouble expressing their names and sounding out simple English sounds. Reaching them at their individual levels took some planning and coordination. Our team was not given any direction or curriculum to follow, and I wondered where the last group had left off. But luckily, the children were mostly all ravenous to learn, always eager to come and set up my red plastic chair before them. "'Scuse me, miss— 'scuse me, miss," they shouted as they rushed around fussing about, brushing off my chair before the lesson.

With my bright-eyed and animated fourth graders, Pondichurai, Sureth, and Sancheth, sitting before me, I began each lesson by pulling out three long, sharpened pencils. Eyes widening, they tentatively reached out and took the cherished items like prized Christmas gifts. I briefly wondered about the dark back room full of school supplies, the thousands of pencils stocked in overstuffed bags from the United States. With their papers delicately balancing on knobby knees, they carefully printed out words and eagerly repeated phrases. They learned quickly and passionately. My two fifth graders, however, were not as studious. Vijay struggled to get through the writing of his name, discouraged each time as he could go no further than the *J*. And Rajethswari, either overly tired or very bored, rolled her eyes back in her head in blatant apathy. Smirking, she passed her time playing with the lice that fell on her paper. But I knew she was bright and had an inkling that she was much further along in English than the others, so I fought and toiled each day to spark her attention.

At the end of our lessons, I let them draw, dream, and imagine with colored pencils and crayons. There was such little opportunity within the orphanage for the luxuries of expressing themselves individually, and they impatiently awaited the handing out of the white paper when our class was over. Watching them color, I wondered where they had come from, what they had endured so far in their young lifetimes. I thought of their mothers—if they were alive, if the children missed them, how they might endure the pain of separation. Scanning the children's worn faces, I wondered what they dreamed of, what they feared. I began to question which part of our time together was more important, the learning or the dreaming. When the lessons were over, they would shove their precious drawings into my hand before running off. Silently, I would thumb through their pictures, feeling as though I was crawling into their little minds and hearts. Despite their sheltered existence and limited occasion for new experiences, their creations radiated joy and hope—worlds full of oceans, ice creams, planes on which to discover the world, homes filled with families.

At the sound of the four o'clock bell each day, the children were ushered out of their uniforms and into play clothes. For the girls, this meant a combination of dresses, both Western and Indian styles, all in a questionable state—zipperless, torn, and graying at the hems. Even so, there were older girls with an obvious flair for fashion who managed to find style in the rags, swishing brightly colored scarves around their necks. Complementing the scarves with a proud strut, off they marched to the snack line, ready to take on the world.

But for most of the children, typically the smaller ones, changing meant grabbing whatever clothes were left and available, almost always several sizes too large. One boy walked around permanently clutching at his waist in an attempt to keep up his shorts.

Having changed and visited the field to use "the facilities," the children lined up on the ground outside for a snack of assorted fruit combined with either chickpeas or lentils. They each took turns using the two metal cups. While the children ate in tidy rows on the ground, we retreated to the upstairs room, sipping from our purified-water bottles and snacking on packaged food from our backpacks. We took turns scrubbing our hands raw.

From six o'clock on, we had free rein to play with them however we wanted. The younger ones gravitated to the open-air top floor, where they could play freely without being pestered by the older children. If they were lucky, a faint breeze would take the edge off the weakening afternoon sun.

There was one activity that the children prized more than anything else—reading books. The most favored by far was *Beauty and the Beast*. "Beast, beast!" they would yell as the books were placed down on the gravel, where they were hungrily grabbed at and dispersed within seconds. It was with sheer panic that the children got the prized books in their hands, and then off they went, forming little groups huddled around children who could read. The glossy photos of iced cakes and round chocolates had them lurching at the pictures with fists clenched as though stuffing the food into their faces. They relaxed into contented trances taking in the melodic sounds of the stories, lounging on each other's laps.

Every afternoon like clockwork, one of them would upend of a huge bucket of broken plastic pieces that had long since seen better playful days. I silently wondered what on earth the kids could do with such a motley collection of bits of broken toy pieces. Within minutes, however, busted airplane wings became swords, legless babies were propped up, anything with even one working wheel became a mode of racing transport. Small pieces of plastic were, with the swish of a small hand, magnificent arrays of fruits and cakes.

I was tentative during the first few days at free time, more comfortable with the structure of my organized classroom with measurable accomplishments. "'Scuse me, miss, 'scuse me. Have some *tea*." I was abruptly forced out of my comfort zone one afternoon by a group of young girls—an upside-down hat (pretend teacup) was lovingly shoved into my hand.

"And some *cake*," another said boisterously, shoving a make-believe plate into my hand. I was suddenly a welcomed guest at an intimate tea party with fellow girlfriends, each with a baby tucked under her arm. Others soon joined our party, with their babies on their laps, all tenderly primped and poked, fed and put to bed every other minute.

Out of the corner of my eye, I saw a little girl no more than three years old creeping closer and closer to me. "What's your name?" I asked gently. But she just turned her head coyly and leaned into my arm. I was surprised by the heat of her touch—clearly a full-blown fever. Touching her hair, I attempted to pull her into our girlie play. Gingerly, she sat her almost weightless self in the center of my folded legs and then, comfortable with her perch, drifted in and out of sleep as I stroked her cheeks. So I found myself among my new girlfriends at a tea party sipping the best tea India had to offer, eating plate-loads of cakes and candies. Taking in the girls with their stuffed babies and me with mine curled up in my lap, I felt a rush of joy I had never quite felt. It was so unexpected—and for the briefest of moments, I felt like I had been given the quickest glimpse of heaven.

Out of nowhere, the skies opened up, thunder and lightning only minutes away from shaking their angry fists. My little fevered friend leaped from my lap, running for cover while I glanced around the yard, worried about how we could possibly gather up the hundreds of flash cards and dozens of books and toys that had been distributed. But in the time that it took me to find the bag that we stored everything in, I was greeted with little hands bearing cards stacked with perfect tidiness, books ordered properly and placed neatly in the bag. "Thank you, miss; here you are, miss," they said. I was amazed at their appreciation and sense of orderliness, even in a hurried situation.

We all ran for shelter as the rain began to pour and the sky filled with lightning. All one hundred of us crammed into the three tiny upstairs rooms, almost pitch-black without electricity or sunlight. The kids groped for the bag of books I had brought in from the outside. "Bag, miss—'scuse me, miss—books, miss—books, miss." It was a panic of bodies, movement, jumping, shoving—utter chaos. Where one body ended and twisted, another began. I saw only whites of eyes, heard shrieks of joy and fear as lightning bolted down and rain beat on the concrete roof in a deafening roar. Kids continued to play as they would have outdoors, yet in a dark and microscopic space. A dented ball was kicked around while pairs of friends felt for lice in each other's hair. But many were scared, and they huddled to help one another. I put my arms around whomever I could reach.

The wind picked up, whipping rain through the doorless entryway and sending the whole moving mass to the back of the room. I felt a hand forced into mine and then another tugging at my other side, pulling me back into the pushing heap of bodies. The lightning afforded me a brief look at the girls who had now tucked themselves under my arms, one a fourteen-year-old and the other my little fevered friend from the tea party. She would somehow find her way to my side throughout my stay at Reaching Stars.

Out of the madness, I heard the anxious scream of the five-month-old baby. By now I knew her cry and went frantically in search of her, weaving in and of the craziness, stepping over bodies hoping that she was in the safe arms of an older girl or staff helper. I found her in the lap of a five-year-old who was rocking her, almost violently, in an attempt to stop the crying. The girl quickly dumped her in my arms and, relieved of the responsibility, ran off. The baby had gobs of mucous blocking her nose and running into her mouth. I desperately looked around for anything I could use to clear her nose. As I pulled out the end of my shirt to use as a rag, another child came by, peered into the baby's face through the darkness, and pinched the oozing mess from her face with her fingers. Then she slipped away as quickly as she had appeared. Once again I was left astonished and speechless at how the children naturally looked after one another. I found a slice of space to shield the baby from the shoving swarm and resumed a gentle rocking. The baby soon settled down and went to sleep.

The storm finally subsided, and children began to curl up and sleep—some alone along a wall, others in the middle of the room with arms cupped over their ears, others piled up in little mountains. Literally draped one on top of the other, they slept as if the storm had sucked away all of their remaining energy.

As the sun began to set, our volunteer group crawled into the van to head back to our guesthouse. We were dripping with sweat and caked with layers of mud from the storm. Drained physically and mentally from the afternoon, nobody reacted to the hair-raising ride home. Silent and reflective, we battled our own internal wars of whys and what-should-bes. The whole scene had rattled me—the suffocating disorder of it all had made me feel so uneasy, the way it had felt to be in India in general. At times it was horridly crowded and messy, with so many people stuffed into such small places doing so many things at once. But sitting there in that crowded, hot, and dirty room with a sweet baby in my arms among a frenzy of children, I had suddenly felt like India was a big, warm, and welcoming family. There was joy in the madness, more so than I ever could have expected.

That night we ate our vegetable curries and naan, quietly planned our next day's lessons, and retreated to our beds. Drifting off to sleep, I tried as hard as I could to find a neat, sorted place to assimilate what I was witnessing, but it wasn't possible, as if life wouldn't allow it. So far it had been a series of disturbing highs and lows that I hoped would lead to some clarity about what was, at the end of the day—or the end of our lives—really important.

I returned home to France, my home away from home at the time, and in my comfortable brown leather chair, hot coffee at my side and children tucked sleeping soundly into warm beds, I thought about India. I thought about my fevered friend, the girls at the tea party, and Rajethswari, my little student—would someone notice her latent brilliance?

I pictured the next group of volunteers getting their tour from Jyoti, teaching their classes, scrubbing their hands silly at snack times as though it would take away the discomfort of the reality of what they were seeing. I thought of the dark room full of supplies and the strange eeriness that surrounded Anuj. What had I actually accomplished, if anything, at the orphanage? Friends and family asked what it was that I had come away with. How had it changed my life? Yet I could only think of the children at Reaching Stars, and of all the other orphanages filled with poor yet amazingly hopeful and capable children who dreamed of more than they were living. A better question might have been, what would they come away with in life?

2

What Have I Become?

*When you want something, all the universe conspires
in helping you to achieve it.*
Paulo Coelho

*Orlando, Florida
Fall 1999*

In India I felt like someone had turned on a light switch in my subconscious that I didn't even know was there. But looking back, I see that the grueling, unhappy steps it took to get to that point were as important as what transpired afterward. Eight years prior to setting foot off the plane at the Chennai International Airport, I was twenty-eight and living in Orlando, Florida. My firstborn, Nick, was three, and Emma had only just turned one. A few months earlier, we had moved into a beautiful house on Lancaster Drive in historic downtown Orlando, a well-established area, conservative and pristine. We had a lovely, rambling colonial home with a white picket fence and towering oak trees overlooking a lake surrounded by other lovely homes with towering oak trees and picket fences. The streets were red brick, and on most afternoons, you would see nannies pushing strollers around the block. My husband, John, said our home was the house he had always dreamed of having. I could hear him saying to himself, "Don't you just love it?" every time we pulled up the driveway.

No...no, I don't, I thought quietly to myself. In fact, it felt like I was wearing someone else's shoes—ones with sharp-pointed toes, straps that pinched, the kind of shoes you can't wait to kick off into the back corners of your closet at the end of an evening. I loved John and the children madly, but I hated my life and all of its pretty and comfortable trappings right then. I hated our big house and all its comfort and perfection, the lawn and bug services. I was horrified at what we had spent on window treatments, a phrase I hadn't known existed a few years before.

In the short period of time between finishing college and starting a family, John and I had managed to achieve financial security beyond what we had expected so early in life. Both of us had been raised in families that had struggled in their early days. Our parents had fought hard to provide for us, with John's mother juggling two children and working as a single mom for several years before remarrying, and my parents having taken the boat over to Canada from England with fifty dollars in their pockets. Both sets of parents were from the post-Depression era, a time when butter and jam were luxuries and your future depended more on earning a solid wage and less on what you *liked* to do. Our homes might have differed dramatically in culture—John's distinctly American, mine European—but they were similar in that they were rooted in constant encouragement to make something of ourselves—come hell or high water. If our parents were dead set on providing us something, it was the educational tools needed to make our way in life. We both knew from a very early age that we would be individually responsible for our futures—our respective roads would need to be paved with hard work and tenacity.

John had been self-employed since childhood, starting with a paper route that had him busy after school and out of bed early on Sundays, even on the darkest of frigid upstate New York winter mornings. Later, in his early teens, he built a lawn business, and while other kids were running on the high school sports fields in the afternoons, he was mowing lawns, sometimes five in a day. We met during my sophomore year of high school in Pittsford, a small suburb of Rochester, New York. I recall how he always smelled like freshly cut grass. Handsome, blond-haired, blue-eyed, and well-built, he had a fire in his gut to live life to the fullest. "I'm going to be a millionaire," he told me boldly at the age of fifteen, while we kissed on the swings at the Thornell Road Elementary School playground. "I'm going to thrive on any scrap of opportunity thrown my way...I could make something out of toenail clippings," he would say. And I believed he would. I loved how he approached everything with such a great sense of impatience—he simply couldn't wait to get going in life. But alongside his drive for opportunity, he was also an artist at heart, a guitarist and a songwriter. Music was where John connected with his spirit, and any pain he might have carried with him came through in the tender lyrics in his songs. I imagined that he would then tuck his pain into his back pocket as he mowed perfect lines in the lawns of the neighborhood.

Parts of John's childhood had been difficult. Sucked into the black hole of alcoholism, his father had been unable to cope with the responsibilities of family life, and so he had left, never to return, when John was only seven. John had taught himself over the years that he would be anything but this. He might not have been able to control the past, but he could chop the wood and stoke the fire for his own future.

My dreams were of a different sort, filled with worldwide adventures and freedom. "Not me," I would say. "A backpack and a passport are all I need to find happiness." Combined with my desire to see all the exotic corners of the globe was a deep fascination with the world's caretakers and spiritual leaders—Mother Theresa, Gandhi, and others whom I believed represented the best of humanity. Captivated by their commitment to simple yet fundamental ideals, I found in them an endless source of fascination. Somehow they had the ability to cast a light on what was not always so clear to the rest of us. Yes, I wanted to travel and explore the world, but I wanted to understand these truth seekers more. My life would be a search—a quest, I hoped, to understand what it was they knew.

John and I might not have had similar visions for our futures, but we had the common trait of being big dreamers, passing endless evenings staring at the stars from either of our rooftops, chatting about all that we could do with the years that lay ahead of us when we would be unleashed from the boring suburbs of Rochester, New York.

We continued to date through college, painting houses in the summer months to support ourselves during the school years. After finishing our studies, we married in a small church on Main Street in Geneseo, New York, and later moved to Florida, where John got a job as a sales rep for the Yellow Pages. I went to graduate school at the University of Central Florida and, only a few credit hours short from getting my master's in public administration, threw in the towel when I was offered a job at a local executive-recruiting firm. Despite the job being completely commission based and offering no salary or benefits, I took it, mastering the art of recruiting very quickly. Within months I was making a very decent salary—so good that John decided to join the firm a year later. We bought and renovated our first home at the age of twenty-three and had Nick only a year later. A year after that, and only months after delivering our second child, Emma, we left the recruiting firm to hang our own shingle, Dean Search Consultants, identifying and placing senior management for major insurance companies.

It is a sort of fairytale love story that began with him asking me to the prom before I was barely becoming a woman, and continues now, as I write this and approach my forty-fourth birthday. I never dated anyone else, yet I always gave myself the personal freedom to move on should the spark between us fade. It simply hasn't.

But looking out over the lake on Lancaster Drive a few years after getting married, I was far from living the dreams

I had envisioned for myself at fifteen, far from knowing myself or how I could possibly build a life around who that was. Somewhere between my childhood years, when I dreamed of traveling the world, and my college graduation, my humanitarian interests had taken a back seat. It had been ground into our heads and hearts by everyone, from teachers and professors to parents and grandparents, that the important parts of life revolved around landing a good job, having children, and saving for retirement. Our achievements and successes would be rated on securing these things, saving these things. Over the years, I had disconnected myself from what it was that made me *me*, and an empty, hollow feeling lodged itself into my gut. Each day I woke up and dragged myself into my office, listening to the whispering voices echoing from deep inside me, telling me, "Lydia, you are in the wrong place, doing the wrong thing." I was in a place that felt entirely foreign. I didn't know who I had become.

Wandering around, a shell of my former self, I behaved normally but was quietly wilting in some sort of slow death. I was listless and flat, which spilled into every aspect of my life—personally, professionally, and socially. I couldn't seem to relate to friends, what they spoke about, complained about, or dreamed of having. *This can't be it,* I thought. *There must be more.* I jogged endlessly around the brick streets of Orlando, staring at others, wondering what made them happy. I hung out at play dates with the neighborhood mothers. They all seemed content and comfortable; they laughed easily. I tried to join in, to not take things so seriously. I got my teeth bleached and went to the salon and sipped wine like the others while getting my hair lightened. Nothing changed. I felt ugly and miserable inside. Blaming John was an easy place to park the unhappiness. I had found myself living in his world, and I resented him for it—yet deep down I knew that I had only myself to blame.

Sometimes I would surf the Internet for Peace Corps or humanitarian jobs, knowing all the while that it was totally illogical with the children. I felt like George Bailey in one of my favorite movies, *It's a Wonderful Life*. His bags were packed, but he would never be able to leave. I tossed and turned at night, unable to find solace in sleep. Sometimes I would sneak away and lie down in my walk-in closet and stare at the ceiling. The soft new carpet against my bare legs and the cool quiet would give me brief moments of relief from the constant sense of dissatisfaction with everything around me. *I have a good life, don't I? Why is it not feeling good? Why am I not feeling good?* I began feeling guilty—and not just slightly guilty, but terribly guilty for not appreciating what I had around me, for not feeling like it was enough. Guilt lodged itself in places all over my body—in the back of my head, on my shoulders, in the pit of my stomach. It became my best friend. I could always count on it being there. We passed the time together, enjoying endless, pointless banter.

A friend suggested that I find a therapist. "We all need them; we all have them," she assured me.

"Let's explore your past, Lydia," the therapist said as she smoothed the wrinkles from her skirt and glanced at the clock.

"Look back?" I barked. "I don't know what the hell is wrong with me, but I have a gut feeling it doesn't have to do with looking backward. I am dead sure of one thing, and that's that my answers aren't behind me—they are in front on me. I just need to get *out of this place* and find them!"

Life has this funny way of blocking you from forward motion if you try to skip steps. And if by chance you get a hall pass along the way, you will find yourself catching your toe on your own jean cuff running up the stairs when you least expect it. I may have wanted to run out the door of that therapist's office to the nearest airport and book a flight to Timbuktu, but it wasn't going to be that easy. Instead I was to take a mental journey that took me back in time, to a place I both missed and feared returning to.

I was sitting on my mother's bare legs, and it was prickly where she had shaved, and the hair was just coming in on her upper thighs. I have no idea how old I was—maybe three or five. We were on our wooden deck in Canada, and she was wearing a crisp white cotton skirt, and her legs were a deep golden-brown. She was stroking and patting my back as she spoke to someone else, a girlfriend most likely. She tipped her head back and laughed heartily, then chuckled—they must have been poking fun at somebody, but only kindly. She loved a good laugh.

I was playing with the rings on her strong fingers, marveling at how they could spin around with such ease—yet it was completely impossible to get them over her knuckles.

I would always give it a good try each time, knowing it was futile. I imagined that those rings would stay on for her lifetime—time would tell that they wouldn't. After fiddling with the rings, I traced the length of her fingers with mine, finding my way to her nails—hard as rocks and perfectly rounded at the tips. I always loved her hands. Strong and gentle, feminine and capable. On her lap I was safe and happy. I could have stayed there forever.

I remember grilled-cheese lunches with real cheddar cheese on wheat bread, plus tomato soup and magic bars, which we had nicknamed "goo." Sunday dinners meant roast beef, Yorkshire pudding, which she almost always burned on the bottom, and treacle tart. She would take time in the early evenings to prepare hot-water bottles for our beds so that our feet would be warm during those bitter northern nights in Ottawa. I could tell how much she loved me and my older sister, Helene, by the way she would wrap us in towels after our baths. She was always a little hurried when she did it, drying us roughly, then wrapping the towel a bit too tightly, but it was done with care and a kiss on the forehead. I would lie to my teacher and the nurse at school about being sick, so I could go home and be with her in the afternoons. I could then curl up on the fuzzy green couch that smelled slightly musty and doze while she sipped tea, knitted, and watched soap operas. It was the only time of the day she ever sat down. To come home from school in the mornings would not have been nearly as relaxing, though I would have been able to watch her dance to Abba or Neil Diamond or Roger Whitaker on the record player as she vacuumed. It was only after she had cleaned and baked a little something for us to have after school that she would sit down properly and enjoy her "cuppa." And there was nothing better than to be snuggled up on that green couch with her in a time of my life when stress and responsibility had not yet been born. There was just comfort, time, and my mother.

When I was really sick and the fever felt as though it was eating me up as we sat and waited for the doctor, the very hair on my body hurting, she stroked my knee, easing the pain. It was as if, in her touch, she herself felt the pain and took some of it on herself. She made everything feel better—the discomfort of sickness or the uneasiness of hurt feelings. She was the kind of mum who was aware of everything—aware when we were feeling down or when we were up to something naughty. As we grew and at times strayed from what we were supposed to do, she never held our faces to the fire or made us feel too bad about it. Like the time I lied about having been caught showing my "parts" to the next-door-neighbor's son. Years later, when I started smoking cigarettes by the side of the house after school, she knew but never let on. Some things she would let go, just like that. Maybe it was that she trusted us to right our own wrongs, or perhaps it was that she knew that stepping a bit out of line was part of life, and that it was OK not to be perfect.

While her life with my father was not always happy, the finances often tight, I felt she was at peace when she was with us—her girls. I loved sensing her excitement as we prepared for the long journeys back to our family in England, how she would dress us up in our prettiest dresses and our shiny black patent leather shoes for the flight. We got to wear our silver bracelets with our names engraved on them.

I can only imagine her need to be with her own mother, father, and sister, to be nestled and comforted by them and the smells of England, the freshness of the green manicured gardens. I knew she felt something deep for her own mum because I could see the pain on her face as she started to receive letters in which the handwriting became increasingly less legible, the thoughts not so concise. I would watch as she would fold the letters ever so carefully and put them back in their envelopes, quietly sliding them into her top drawer.

Perhaps it was because my childhood felt like a carefully wrapped piece of cake in a napkin that the shock and crumble of my family hurt so badly. My mother and father finally divorced after a not-so-tidy breakup sometime near my fifteenth birthday. It left us all lost and devastated. They had not been happy for years and had slowly drifted apart. A year later, Mum moved away, creating a new life with a new man. I would come to love him dearly later in life, but not then. When I saw her, she was in a world I didn't know, her words entangled in what must have been her own grief over the loss of her family and the guilt over needing to leave. I moved in with my father and swallowed much of my pain, wanting to put on a good face for her. I was thankful for all of the afternoons on the green couch, wanting to convince myself I was strong enough to let her go, to let her focus on herself and her own happiness.

My sister left for college, John following suit the year after, taking with them any remnants of the emotional comfort of my life before the divorce. I would come home from school to an empty house and smoke Marlboro Reds and sip black coffee. When that no longer filled the void, I busied myself after school working two jobs, slipping my running shoes on afterward to soak in the solace of the outdoors. While I struggled during this time alone, it made me recognize the beauty in childhood, the power of a loving, united family. How was it that so much goodness, so much of everything could come from that one source—all of those things that were no longer there? But looking back, I see that, had they not been taken from me, I might never have known their true value. I might not have spent decades supporting children who had been denied this. Sitting at the foot of the stairs in my father's house, staring at the dust balls wedged between the wall and the ugly carpet, I decided I alone was responsible for my own happiness. It was time to pick myself up, dust off, and move on.

"Maybe I should quit working," I said to John one day. "Maybe it's as simple as that." I knew nothing about my own motherhood despite now having a three- and a one-year-old. How did that happen? Both had been in day care since six weeks old, since the days when they couldn't even hold up their heads. In our mad rush to success, I had insulated myself from basic maternal experiences and had developed an awkward sort of insecurity toward my newfound role. I was afraid of something I couldn't put my finger on—loss of control, a lack of predictability, a sense of loss for my own childhood and youth. *And how does one measure accomplishment in a day of mothering, anyway?* I had always wondered guiltily.

"Honey...do what you want. You are clearly not in a good spot," John said, genuinely concerned. While he loved where we were and what we were doing, he knew something was terribly wrong with me, and he felt so helpless.

"But I'm scared. What if I can't do it right? What if I suck at being a mother?" I sobbed.

"You'll be fine," he said as I spilled into his warm arms, sucking in the sweet smell of his skin that somehow made the world feel better. "You'll figure it out."

God, how I envied his strength. While I questioned everything, he marched along with what seemed like such a surefootedness. Would I—could I—ever feel sure like this, like he did?

I quit working, tugged it off like a dirty running shirt, and left John with the business we had so painstakingly launched and nurtured together. I turned my back on everything I had built for myself professionally, and it was the easiest thing I have ever done. And little did I know that all the children needed from me was time, time for me to tap into my own maternal instincts. I brought Emma home from the day care she had been attending, and together we took some baby steps into a world that was completely new and scary to me. Thankfully she was patient and forgiving, her big blue eyes staring at me expectantly. "Don't look at me for answers," I would chuckle at her. "I am just as clueless as you!" We sat on the floor of the playroom and read, listened to Mozart, and let the world go on without us.

On many days the children and I would spend hours within the cool walls of the downtown Orlando library. We wrapped ourselves up in its quietness—tucking ourselves into corners with piles of musty-smelling books around us. I perused every level, every aisle, running my fingers down the spines of books as if searching for some unknown treasure. Over time, I noticed my hand being drawn to stories relating to travel experiences, around-the-world trips, sailing and mountaineering adventures. Tromping out of the library with Emma slung on one hip, a heavy overstuffed bag of books on the other, and Nick trailing behind in his little black cowboy boots, I would spend the remaining afternoon hours sitting on the cool tiles of our porch, escaping into my own world, holding onto the pages for dear life while the kids played in the yard.

I traveled within those books with dozens and dozens of courageous men and women who gave up the normal life to see the world, to experience the wonders of other cultures in faraway places, to feel the earth's edges. I felt as though I had crawled into Leila Hadley's suitcase during *Give Me the World* as she left her New York job to travel the world with her young son. I rode seventy-eight thousand miles on the back of Ted Simon's Triumph motorcycle as he ventured around the globe and into his own soul in *Jupiter's Travels*. I sailed with eighteen-year-old Tania Aebi in *Maiden Voyage* as she circumnavigated the world alone in a twenty-six-foot sailboat. I hiked the Sahara with five other female Peace Corps workers in *Harmattan*. The *Traveler's Tales* series was consumed like candy along with anything else that fell into the category of adventure-travel journals. With Pico Iyer, Paul Theroux, Brad Newsham, and so many other brave and free-spirited souls, I got a glimpse of the beauty that comes from freedom.

They reminded me at times of my father, who was also an explorer at heart. After receiving his PhD in photon physics at London University before moving to Ottawa with my mother, he often traveled to faraway places, sometimes for extended periods. It was hard on my mother, I am sure, and my sister and I missed him when he was away. But we also knew he was doing interesting things in interesting places, and we were proud of that. I remember excitement mounting as the date approached for his return from wherever he had been. Once home he would open up his suitcases, releasing wafts of foreign smells. He never came home empty-handed. He would hand us little gifts one by one—hand-painted wooden dolls or books revealing faraway lands. But more importantly, like many of the authors I was reading, he combined his deep love for exploration with a mind that constantly questioned things. My father taught me a lot about the world and about life. He encouraged me to search for answers. "Ask the whys, the hows, and the what-ifs, Lydia." Maybe that was what I was beginning to do.

Looking back, I realize that, there on that porch with those books in my hands and the children at my feet, I found small grains of who I truly am. The authors had found the meaning in their lives through their experiences on the road, and I knew deep down that, similarly, my answers were not going to be found on Lancaster Drive.

"Listen to this," I would say to John, reading him exciting sections from various books. He was patient with me and listened to my narrations of varied excerpts, a snapshot from Tibet, a snippet from someone's crazy journey, simply because he knew it brought me joy. Perhaps for brief moments he saw the spark return of the girl he had fallen in love with ten years before.

At the end of one of Ted Simon's books on his motorcycle adventures was a small bio. Next to it was an e-mail address. For some strange reason, I felt the urge to send him a note and let him know just how courageous I thought he was and how much I had enjoyed his books. The following day, I found a response in my inbox. I don't remember the exact words, but it was short and sweet and read something like, "Glad you enjoyed my experiences...all the best in yours. Ted."

I was shocked, paralyzed.

Yours? What did he mean, *yours?* The words sunk into the very cells of my body, and somewhere deep down, they spoke to me.

Over the course of a few months, I became gradually more ravenous for life out there, wherever that was. I ached to be out of my element and pined to be set free on an unfamiliar road where I knew I would find whatever it was I was looking for. I just knew I was supposed to be doing something else. I was so ready and willing to do what that something was; I just needed to find it.

One day on a run, out of nowhere a flash of energy rushed through my body, scooping me up and catapulting me out of the semireverie state that had become my existence and into reality. It suddenly dawned on me that I was not a passive bystander to my life. I could do better than to sit on my porch and read about all of this. I had the power of choice and action, and I had been standing in my own way, blocking my own road to happiness. *Could it really be that easy?* I ran home full speed like I had won the lottery. The time had come to get off the porch, out of the library, off my ass—time to live. I hadn't a clue exactly what that meant at the time, but I knew for sure that it had something to do with a backpack and a passport.

"What are your thoughts about going away for a bit?" I blurted out to John, who was sitting on the couch watching CNN. I was still breathless from my sprint home.

Giving me one of his critical looks, he asked carefully, "What do you mean by *a bit*?"

"Well, I don't know...like a few months...a year maybe?" I said boldly, panting as I filled a glass with water. "We could...see the world...we could...go around the world," I continued, a bit more tentatively.

He stopped and looked at me—straight into me. "Look, Lydia. I know you are searching and have been really unhappy. You know I would do anything to help you, but why does it have to mean risking everything we have done? Why does it have to be so drastic? It's not smart. It's so all or nothing. Why can't we just take a vacation somewhere far—anywhere? We can go as far as you want!" he said.

I could feel the positive vibes of the awakening I had felt on the run draining out of my legs, my stomach sinking at the thought of where this discussion was going to go.

"Because it is so much bigger than that, John. Don't you understand?"

He was happy with what we had. I knew he was, and that made it all worse. I knew what it meant to him to have carefully, methodically built a secure world for himself and his family. In being self-employed, there was a safety in trusting himself—things could only go wrong if he messed them up himself, and he wasn't going to be that man, the one who failed. Not only that, but he was becoming the father he hadn't had at any early age. He coached Nick's Little League team, he sang to the kids in the car, he tucked them into bed. The whole thing was working, the perfect castle, the American dream. Logically, to him, this was no time to scrap it all over some nebulous search for meaning or adventure. I was fast becoming a threat to everything he cared about.

"Lydia, I just don't understand why this doesn't work for you. It's not as if I haven't tried to accommodate your needs. I feel as if you are undermining all that we have built." He sat up and flicked the TV off, impatience clearly mounting. "The way I see things, nothing seems enough for you." His voice became louder. "Things are just starting to get rolling here at work. I'm finally seeing the results I have worked my whole life for. Why do we have to do this NOW?"

The words echoed out the kitchen, through the patio, and out into the neighborhood for all creation to hear. I imagined all the other moms sitting outside during their playdates stopping at the sound of his words, hearing his sheer frustration and rising anger with me. Then I watched in shock as he took one of our cream leather couches and upended it, flipping it over onto its backside. Books then came flying off the bookshelf. *My precious books,* I thought. *How could you?*

"The only people who seem to get it are those who have taken the chance to live what I am talking about—the ones who have somehow broken free from the mold of normal, the ones in those books you are throwing across the room. I feel pathetic coveting them! Someone is banging on our front door—screaming through the keyhole, demanding that we wake up. I've been trying to keep my thoughts at bay, John, trying to keep that banging, screaming voice on the other side of the door, but I can't help but hear it. I want to do more than travel—this isn't about taking longer vacations. What are we really doing this all for? Is it just to...to... exist? There is more out there; I know there is. There has got to be. I admit I am fumbling around in the dark, searching for what is missing, but please, please trust me. We have to look for more. Please come and look with me," I sobbed. "Please."

I stood there, paralyzed with emotion—my body clenched with fear and outrage, watching as books slid across the room, pages crumpling, spines cracking as they landed facedown with the force of what I knew to be anger toward me. As Tania Eibi's *Maiden Voyage* ricocheted off the edge of the upturned couch, I realized that it wasn't just me who was fragile. It dawned on me that our living room floor, now littered with broken books and upended furniture, reflected not just my inner turmoil, but his as well. Was what I was asking for, this search, worth putting him in such a vulnerable spot? Was it worth stripping him down to his naked insecurities as well as mine?

Now. The word rang in my ears so loudly I wanted to burst into a million pieces. How could I make him understand it had to be now? And not just for me, but for him, for us, for our family.

Then it was as if the doors to my heart opened and everything I had been carrying inside of me came flowing out. And there was no stopping it. The furniture was already flying—what did I have to lose?

"It has to be now because I can't go on anymore like this. I can't do this anymore," I finally said.

Taking a breath he asked, "You can't do what anymore?"

"This life we have. I don't want it. There is more. I just know it." There it was, the plain truth that I had been carrying around for months, years. I fumbled across the room, which now looked like a war zone, to find him, to find his great strong hands, to find my way into his big sweet soul. I needed to make him understand I wasn't doing this to take anything away from him.

And then terrible silence grew between us. For what felt like an eternity. Separately, we started to question whether our marriage could take the pressure of this search I was on.

Later that week, walking around the trendy café-lined streets of Winter Park in a daze of emotion, I found myself at the foot of the church where Nick and Emma had been baptized. Running inside, I stumbled into a pew and, burying my head in my hands, unleashed all of my sadness. The cool, still air in the church felt so good, and I just wanted to stay there forever, sobbing. Looking up to the altar and above, through the beautiful stained glass windows, I did the only thing I had not yet tried. I begged for help, begged for answers. Not having been raised in a religious family, I didn't have the right words, yet I felt there was nowhere else to turn. "God, please, if you are there, please listen to me. Tell me, what am I supposed to do? Where did I go wrong? Please help me—show me the way."

Miraculously, a single thread of hope weaved its way from John's heart to mine, keeping us intact at this dreadful, fragile time. I often wonder where this thread came from. It might have been simply the love we had for one another that pulled us through, the pure, uncomplicated form that we had felt at fifteen on the school grounds. Maybe we were being granted one of the hundreds of wishes we had made under the stars at night. Or perhaps he simply thought about my words during the somber days that followed that awful conversation. Had he asked himself some of the hard questions I had thrown at him, questions I didn't even have answers to myself?

Finally one night he said, "OK. I'll go to the ends of the earth to give you a slice of what you believe is out there, whatever that is." And unbeknownst to either of us, that was exactly where we needed to go. He was willing to set aside everything he had worked toward, everything he wanted and feared altogether to save our marriage. "But can we take a small step first? How about the summer away...six weeks but no more," he said, looking deep into my eyes, pulling me into his arms. "Where do you want to go?"

"Costa Rica. Let's go to Costa Rica," I said, as though it mattered where we went. I sighed from the very depths of my being and tasted relief and gratitude beyond what I could have expressed at the moment, and I believe he felt it too. His willingness to offer us this time was a saving grace that picked us up and plopped us on the road we needed to be on. Neither of us knew where we were going exactly, but we were going there together, putting our trust in each other and the big world that awaited us.

3

Fertile Ground

We must let go of the life we have planned, so as to
accept the one that is waiting for us.
Joseph Campbell

San Jose, Costa Rica
Summer 2000

I woke up on that first morning in Costa Rica to sunshine
streaming through the windows. Walking out onto the balcony of our hotel, taking in the stunning views of the Central
Valley outside San Jose, I took in the sweet, cool morning air,
my senses exploding with it. Precious little voices of children
echoed as they made their way to school, a beautifully familiar sound in such an unfamiliar setting. I was a kid in a candy
shop, a horse set free; it was Christmas morning times one
hundred. Relief came over me in waves as it sunk in that I had
escaped the box that I had confined myself to, the one that
had driven me, and poor John, nearly crazy. Planted in a lush
foreign land with the man I loved and my children at my side,

I had been given a golden ticket, and I was going to make the most of it. There were endless things to learn and do in our six weeks ahead, and I was giddy, high on life at the prospect of living in the unknown. It wasn't exactly the year of around-the-world adventures that I had dreamed of and read about, but it was a gift, a beginning. Grinning ear to ear, I tiptoed back into the room where John, Nick, and Emma still slept soundly after the late night of travel. I had the urge to wake them up to tell them how monumental this was, how great it felt. *No,* I thought. *We just need to live this thing together.*

Over the following days, we planned out the next stop on our journey. We knew we didn't want to stay in the city of San Jose any longer—Costa Rica's jewels were in her misty mountain rainforest and rugged coastlines filled with jumping monkeys and sleeping sloths. We traveled north-west to Tamarindo, which was at the time a remote yet popular surfer destination on the Pacific coast. Pulling into the somewhat scrappy town, I knew right away that we had landed in the right place. There were only dirt roads, deeply pitted with potholes and ditches, empty tropical beaches, and a noticeable lack of footwear.

The first thing on our agenda was to hunt for a small rental house. The community seemed pretty contained, so I figured we could find one by chatting with folks who ran the local tourist shops and cafés. After a few stops, we pulled up to a little hotel run by a middle-aged Californian couple. Cozy and adorned with simple, colorful fabrics, the hotel oozed serenity, and as we entered, I had a deep longing to drop my bags and curl up on one of their beds for the rest of my life. Sweaty from the drive, we followed the cool breeze heading out toward a terrace at the foot of the beach where guests were enjoying lazy breakfasts only a few feet from the breaking surf. I took off Emma's shoes, set her down in the warm sand, and watched as she toddled off, screeching with joy, Nick following her lead.

A deeply tanned and lean middle-aged man was just coming in from a morning of surfing—one of the hotel staff indicated that he was the owner. "What can I do for you?" he asked, eyeing us up casually as he brushed sand off of his feet.

"We are looking for a small place to rent for a few weeks—do you know of any?" asked John.

"I sure do—we've got a small, one-bedroom place right down the road that's empty," Jeff said warmly. His crystal clear blue eyes continued to scan the both of us. Feeling a little self-conscious, I got the impression we were coming off as a little city-uptight to him.

"The thing is, it's got to have very reliable Internet and phone lines—I can't live without them," said John flatly.

As Jeff wandered to grab his keys, I could see a smirk begin to spread across his tan face. "Well, this is Costa Rica... nothing is predictable here," he said.

John had done his research before coming. He knew connectivity was going to be an issue and was concerned.

While it was clear that that this trip represented the saving grace to what had felt like a crumbling marriage, he was nowhere near ready to let the business, and our security, be compromised in the process. "There is no need to take any chances with shitty phone lines," he had said. "I'll rent a satellite phone just in case." When the phone arrived it looked like such a massive contraption. I was bugged by its enormity, its hard black box sitting next to the other simple belongings we were packing—colored pencils, journals, and bathing suits.

As we entered the sweet little bungalow completely surrounded by massive green jungle growth only steps from the beach, I knew we would be staying on. The soothing echo of waves crashed in the distance, and a howler monkey bellowed from the front porch. It was simply perfect. Jeff turned to leave as John was unpacking his computer, adapters, and the sat phone, cords tumbling everywhere. "Just holler if you need anything. If you don't mind me saying, though, my advice to you while here, if you really want to make the most if it, would be to just let go," he said as he bid us farewell.

I could feel John's rising frustration over the course of the next few days as Jeff's words hung in the air. *"Just let go...who the fuck does he think he is?"* I heard him mumble a few times as he hooked his laptop to phone lines for dial-up Internet that only worked intermittently. As his angst grew, I knew what he was thinking. I could read it on his face. He had toddlers to think of, a mortgage to pay. He had a wife on his hands who had been on the verge of a breakdown for the past year, a wife who wasn't happy with the perfect life he had built and who had now dragged him to the jungles of Central America. A wife who was threatening the secure world he had carefully created. I knew he was thinking, *Just let go, my ass.*

A part of me felt bad, responsible for putting him through the frustration and stress, but I also knew that we all needed something that was there, deeply needed it. I may not have been sure of what that was exactly, but I was damn sure that our answers were not inside our house or on the porch in Orlando. It felt too right to be here. With a spring in my step, I continued to unpack our bags and embraced the freedom of the weeks ahead.

I'll admit to it feeling a little strange at first, having all day with the children for weeks on end. While I was used to time with them, it hadn't been empty time. There had been a normal lineup of toys, neighborhood friends, and libraries to occupy ourselves with. You can quickly forget all the layers of entertainment when they're there, the buffers you have that fill your time and space, and I secretly wondered whether the days might end up with me dreaming of having Barney on the television. But the pang of fear was short-lived, and the days ticked by naturally with the howler monkeys howling and the ocean crashing in the distance. Emma toddled around, chasing and catching all the poor creatures that moved in her line of sight. I would find her with massive toads or green geckos in her hands. One day I caught her frozen in silence, mesmerized by a praying mantis on the hood of our rental car. Sweat dripped down the sides of her little red cheeks as she stared, motionless under the searing sun. When she would tire of her bug and reptile explorations, she would curl up in a ball and drift off to sleep to the sounds of the ocean and jungle.

In the small suitcase of entertainment I had packed for the kids was a cassette tape of children's songs. The one of Old King Cole became a favorite for Nick—he would listen, losing himself in the song for hours and hours, singing and acting. He marched around the little kitchen, his personal stage, in a world where he was both performer and audience. Sometimes he would take off by himself, crossing the red dirt path in front of the house and wandering a short distance to the beach. I would often find him there, alone, standing on a piece of driftwood, facing the waves, tufts of blond hair flying in the wind. Holding a small stick in his chubby little hand, he would sing his heart out into the ocean as the surf crashed around him, waving his arms about like a conductor. He might have appeared alone out there physically, but it was it was as if he were singing to a whole world that was listening and responding. The birds flew, the surf pulled in and out, the wind blew—all taking place in his own grand and natural music hall.

From day one we were swept away by Costa Rica's beauty. Green seemed greener than anywhere else, and at every turn we faced the most vibrant colors of bougainvillea. We snuggled in easily to the lush jungle, rolling hills, rugged empty coastline, cloud forests, and towering palms. It felt comfortable to be small against such greatness. Coffee plants covered the mountains; cows, chickens, and dogs owned the roads; grass was still cut by hand with a machete. Luscious pineapple, mango, papaya, and banana plants dotted the landscape.

Some mornings our only accomplishment might be to walk the muddy, potholed roads into town for basic groceries. It could easily be a several-hour outing, as there would invariably be iguanas or monkeys to spot. Afternoon hours melted away on the worn futon as we listened to rain pounding on the roof. I read the same five children's books, the only ones we brought with us, over and over, making up silly endings that had us reeling with laughter. Sometimes we took leisurely horse rides into the rainforests, through hidden villages and pastures. Emma wore the same T-shirt the whole time we were away, and Nick just his swim trunks and cowboy boots. My hairdryer and makeup stayed neatly packed away in my case—a wrap and a tank top were all I bothered with.

Slowly I began to feel myself relax, to breathe again. It didn't take too long for John to do the same either. By the second week, I noticed him sticking his head out from his makeshift office on the terrace to see what we were giggling about. He would quit his work early in the day with the lame excuse that the jungle buzz made it too loud to concentrate.

One day I was surprised to find him crouched over a giant lizard. Normally he was headlong into a call at that time of the day, describing the ethos and corporate culture of AIG Insurance Company to a potential candidate. AIG was our biggest client, a leading insurance company known for hiring highly driven, type A, results-oriented professionals. John had a lot riding on this placement. He had recently flown to New York City to meet with the head of HR, and the pressure was on to fill the position. But instead of clinging to his phone, he was outside, admiring the activity of the jungle.

"Holy shit—I just saw an Iguana chasing a rat! I wonder if he got 'im," he said.

Itching to move on and explore further, we traveled to Manuel Antonio, a verdant, hilly coastal area home to a national park well known for its immense collection of rainforest wildlife. Strapped into our little rental car, which was now caked with mud, Nick and Emma sang away to the same Old King Cole cassette tape as we made the long and bumpy ride down the Pacific coast, stopping for local bags of snacks, fried plantains and freshly cut pineapple. Once in Manuel Antonio, we tucked ourselves into a simple little hotel on the top of the hill for a couple of days. The area was almost eerily quiet and peacefully free of tourists. As we contemplated what our options were for a longer-term stay, we were introduced to Barry, a middle-aged American who had left his tanning salon business in the United States to get an early jump on buying and selling rainforest real estate. Keen to get a last-minute rental during the low tourist season, Barry pounced on the chance to take us on a tour of his properties—he had recently purchased two villas further down the a steep and rocky road from our hotel. "You can't see it now in the low season, John, but the villa biz is just beginning to boom here. It's a fantastic investment—giving the hotels a sure run for their money," he shared excitedly as he guided us down the rocky road.

At the time, tourism in Costa Rica was in its infancy. People were only beginning to buzz about its beauty, and villas were quickly becoming an alternative to the traditional all-inclusive resort spots. The two men walked quickly ahead, lost in a passionate discussion about houses and investments. It was great to see John with such a spring in his step—nice to see him come alive. Houses had always been a draw for him—a passion. I could remember evenings as teenagers when he would bore me to tears with stories about the historical houses he had grown up around in Saratoga Springs. He had known them all as the local paperboy, taking careful interest in how folks were renovating, how much they invested, and what the houses sold for afterward. But it wasn't just the financial piece that got his juices flowing. It was the process of making a home the most beautiful it could be—of bringing out the best in something that mattered. He looked at details that most people never noticed—the styles of crown molding, shapes of eaves, curves of banisters.

By the time Nick, Emma, and I caught up, Barry and John were taking in the sweeping views of the Pacific on the balcony of one of the villas. We bargained hard and landed a great last-minute rental deal, and by the afternoon, we were unpacking our bags again. The kids had already found a perfect perch for afternoon monkey gazing. John had set to work arranging his little office on the top floor of the house, next to the hammock and underneath a large palm tree that made clapping sounds in the strong ocean breeze. He seemed a little more at ease, yet I saw waves of discomfort come over him whenever we talked about home, about our future.

Over a candlelit dinner that night, after the kids were tucked into their beds, I found the strength to probe. "How has it been for you here?" I asked.

Taking a sip of his wine and a deep breath, he said, "Well, actually, it has been the oddest combination of feelings. I have to admit to feeling a certain panic over losing a grip on the business at the beginning, losing the edge I feel I have—you know, that step ahead I feel we have been given. I am deathly afraid of giving that up."

I wondered about this fear he talked of, this death grip he described. I wondered how much of it was a logical concern for being a bit out of pocket and how much of it came from a more profound place—from his dad walking away from him, his mother, and his newborn brother. At the age of seven, he had watched from the top of the stairwell as his dad stumbled out the door, never to return.

"Each day we have been here, it is as though that tight hold gets a little looser," he said to me that night while the nighttime jungle seared. "Thank you for doing this. The world didn't crumble because we left—in fact, it feels strangely safer. It might just be OK to *just let go*." We both burst into laughter at that.

"Well then," I chuckled. "Maybe Jeff had your number all along."

"Let's get out on the water," John suggested one afternoon, nearing the end of our stay. Speeding off into the vast open space, I looked back upon beautiful Costa Rica, all signs of human life fading away in the distance, the green of the mountains taking over and the clouds meandering in and out of the tops of the hills. I could feel the power of the sea and earth underneath us as we crashed through the waves.

Somewhere out on the ocean swells, we were cut loose from all that tied us down. During our few weeks in Costa Rica, the restlessness from the previous years had come to a complete standstill, and I began to understand silence in a way I hadn't before. The earth felt grand and beautiful, and stillness had replaced guilt. I felt very, very thankful for that. John pulled me in close while I tucked my head into the safe nook of his arms. At that moment I loved him more than I ever thought possible. The smell of his sweet tanned skin, the strength of his body—our paths met again like they had in the beginning. We became one, floating, flying freely. I shut my eyes and let myself melt into him, salt water splashing hard into my face.

4

The Door Cracked Ajar

All endings are also beginnings. We just don't know it at the time.
Mitch Albom

Orlando, Florida
Fall 2000

Looking back, I see that the trip was so simple, almost trivial compared to the depth of the journeys that were to come. It wasn't wildly off the grid, but it offered us the space and time we needed to just be. Trapped in what had felt like such a deep freeze, we took the six weeks as a thawing out, a stripping down. It was at least a step, a breath of air, a small baby step in the right direction. When we returned to pretty Lancaster Drive, I stole away to my room, feverishly banging away at an ancient Macintosh computer and piecing together chapters into a book I had no idea I would write. Getting the words out on paper was the only way to preserve the experience.

At the end of our trip to Costa Rica, we made a rather bold move and bought the house that Barry had rented to us in Manuel Antonio. Maybe it was my way to physically hang onto a world outside our lives in Orlando—one way to keep a foot lodged in a door that had been cracked ajar. "We'll rent it out," I suggested to John. "We will make our money back in no time from vacation rentals. I'll do it all— the marketing, the website, the bookings. You won't have to worry about a thing." But I knew it wasn't going to take much to convince John on this one. Barry had him sold on the business opportunity on the first day we had met him. And I don't think either one of us was looking forward to going back to the same ugly place in our relationship that we had left behind before the trip. Buying the house, and a minibusiness for that matter, seemed like a win-win.

That fall, from the stool in the kitchen, I brainstormed the design of the website and mapped out a general sketch of a marketing plan for our villa rental. On our dial-up Internet, I explored the new world of e-commerce, advertising the house on every villa site I could find, a novel thing at the time. Within a few months, my inbox was full of requests to rent the house, the calendar packed with names of families planning to come. We hired Raoul, a sweet Chilean man living in Quepos, the closest town outside of Manuel Antonio, to manage the maid service and maintenance of the house and to meet and greet the guests. Exchanging e-mails with Raoul on a weekly basis became my link to a larger world, an outlet from which I created a new normal.

I lived virtually and vicariously through the varied experiences of the families and couples who rented the house—their shock and amazement in discovering the monkeys prancing through the house, their horror at having to get their rental vans up our steep, rocky hill. "You have to rev the engine as much as you can, hit the gas, and go for it," I would say. "There is a mossy spot in the middle somewhere where you might spin your tires a bit, but don't let off that gas, and you will make it."

Travel had awakened part of me that had been sleeping and brought me such tremendous solace and liberation that I was happy helping it do the same for others. Apprehensive mothers would e-mail me questions about traveling to Costa Rica with children; retirees who now had the time and resources to explore were tentative and needed some hand-holding. I encouraged, rallied, and seduced them into testing the limits of what felt comfortable, all the while knowing that they would return feeling different, hopefully feeling connected to something bigger and broader and maybe just a little more beautiful than they had imagined was out there. Also, it was no minor detail that I could manage the whole project from the kitchen stool while being a mother and wife. It naturally weaved together so many parts of myself, and for the first time in my adult life, I felt pangs of joy for what could be considered a "job."

Costa Rica quickly became a home away from home. We were forced to keep an active eye on the management and upkeep of the house, but it was no hardship to make the visits during the year. These brief jaunts offered us sweet exotic escapes into a private world that was our own. When we were there, nobody invaded our space, and time was unadulterated, uncontaminated—it was our own. Little by little we made a small group of friends, a somewhat wild bunch also drawn in by the sense of adventure. Some were people bootstrapping new businesses, or just folks attracted to the surf and yoga life, the carefree days of living off of four dollars a day on the beach sipping Imperial beer. Seeds of living a dual life, of having a home in the United States yet feeling most *at home* when we were far from it, were planted in these early years.

Within minutes of parking the rental car at the house on the hill in Manuel Antonio, John would chuck his business bag in a heap on the floor, pour himself a splash of rum, and stomp around looking the house over—inspecting things that needed to be fixed. He and Francisco, a wonderful Costa Rican man Raoul had hired to take care of things while we were not there, would tour around making their to-do lists, John enjoying the time to roll up his sleeves. "John, you were not born with those massive hands to tick away at a computer," I would say. "There is no doubt that those are a mason's hands." He happily chipped away at the house projects, singing out loud as he worked and driving up and down the windy road to Quepos in his swim trunks and flips-flop, wind in his sun-bleached hair, to pick things up at the hardware store. He radiated a special type of joy, one I didn't sense he received even after a big recruiting placement. Just as it had been with mowing lawns in his teen years, or with painting houses in college, the unique combination of physical work, the outdoors, and the satisfaction of making a property look its very best brought him a deep sense of fulfillment.

One might have thought, myself included at the time, that this would have been the perfect balance of what I wanted and what John needed. But since that initial summer away, we were both sensing a shift, an odd feeling that had less to do with needing to escape our normal lives and more to do with an inner tug, a pull to wander farther down the road. It became more and more strange to refer to Orlando as our *normal life*. We found ourselves spending our time thinking about things outside of Orlando, imagining other adventures, other what-ifs. Fear over leaving what we had built for ourselves and what we had achieved wasn't weighing in as powerfully as the beauty of what else might be out there. Over wine in the evening or on runs around the city, we reminisced about the summer, the peace, how great it had felt to be together as a couple and as a family. There really was not a whole lot left standing in the way of stretching our wings a little more.

It was John who came up with the plan to move to France for a year. My father had purchased an ancient village house in the South of France that we could lease for a very reasonable price. In our college years, we had visited it and fallen in love with the little Provençal village of Rognes it was nestled in. Having been raised in Canada, I had learned French at an early age, and John had loved the French classes he had taken in high school. Truth be told, the idea to go to France seemed so simple and right that I don't think we spent much time considering any alternatives. We could rent out our house in Orlando, transport the business, and spend a year in Provence. Roughly three hours after the thought had even come to mind, it was decided—it was that easy, we thought.

Unfortunately, though, it proved much easier said than done to leave our lives for a year in Provence. Months ticked by with little movement on finding a renter for our house. "Lydia, I have crunched the numbers a million times, and there is simply no way to go unless we offset the mortgage with a renter. There is just no way," John said.

Then two and a half months before our expected leave date, just as we were planning on bagging the whole idea, a nice young family offered to buy our house. "We have been waiting and waiting for a house on Lancaster Drive, and we know you only wanted to rent...but would you consider selling?" they asked.

"Sell?" I asked later that evening. "Where would we go when the year in France is up? And besides that, John, this is the house you always dreamed about having."

Restless nights were spent grappling with the decision to go or not to go, to sell or not to sell. And just when we thought the stress of the decision was going to foil the plan, a strange calm came over us, as if a protective blanket of hope and strength was laid upon us, giving us the confidence to walk through another foreign door. The decision then became crystal clear, yet the future entirely unknown. "Let's go," he said. "Let's just do it. I have a feeling we aren't meant to live here anyway."

I almost couldn't believe what I was hearing. "Are you sure? Are you one hundred, two hundred percent sure?" I asked. But neither of us could deny that it was looking as if a chapter in our lives was undoubtedly over.

"Yup, Lyd. It's time. Let's do it. There's no way I could convince you to come back here after a year in France anyway," he said with a grin.

Within a few weeks, the house and car were sold, and only our furniture and most precious belongings stored. We hugged our loved ones goodbye, and even though we felt scared and insecure, we flew across the ocean to plant ourselves in the heart of a Provençal village.

5

Only a Year in Provence?

Leap and the net will appear.
John Burroughs

Marseille Airport, France
May 2001

"How are we going to get all of these bags in a taxi?" I asked, gazing at the mountain of full-sized suitcases we had brought. In packing up our lives, I hadn't known if and when we would be back, so I had packed well beyond what we needed—early reader learning books, snowsuits and boots, basically all of our collective wardrobes, even a jogging stroller. John and I walked out of the airport each blindly pushing carts piled high with our bags, the children lagging behind in a daze of jet lag. We found the largest taxi possible and crammed ourselves into the car without an inch to breathe, at which point the driver promptly told us it would be seventy euros for the ride.

"Seventy euros!" I said, shocked.

"*Oui*, madame, look at all of your zings..." he said, rolling his eyes. I was too tired to bother about the price and at the same time disgusted that I had packed so much.

Forty-five minutes later, our car drove into Rognes, a simple town near the Luberon mountains and surrounded by vineyards. It was deliciously peaceful during the lunch hour. Through open windows we could hear the faint clinging of silverware on plates, lulled chatter of families sharing a meal. Barely squeezing itself into the narrow road, our taxi inched between the two rows of village houses, finally stopping in front of a faded green garage door at 5 Rue Montée des Callats. We spilled out of the car, a mess of bags and bodies, and stared up at what was to be our home for who knew how long. The *maison de village* stood three stories tall, was hundreds of years old, and had rugged exposed stone inside and out. While we had both been to Rognes before, nothing could prepare John and me for that singular moment of exhaustion mixed with equal doses of excitement and fear on that morning we arrived. Deep down I knew this was a true stepping out of the box—the very thing I had been pining for, yearning for—yet a sense of doubt crept into my thoughts. We were a boat floating freely on the ocean without a map or compass.

After fumbling with an oversized key that looked like something from medieval times, we climbed up the winding staircase inside, lugging our bags alongside us, breathing in our new surroundings, soaking in what was to be our new life. The kids ran down the length of the hallway, thrilled to be free from the confines of the cramped car and plane, and found the room they would be sharing. Since the house was still freezing from being closed up all winter, I wandered around, opening the old, creaking shutters as I went, letting the warmth of the spring sunshine fill the rooms. There was a strange sense of time standing still inside these stone walls—a silent promise that nothing would change from one visit to the next, regardless of the time that passed between.

Gliding my hands over the plaster walls, cracked in some places, I took in the expanse of tall ceilings and richly colored, ancient wooden beams, stopping to gaze across the rolling hills outside on one of the small terraces. "What on earth have we done?" I asked. It would become an all-too-familiar question for the next ten years.

John poured himself a glass of wine from the bottle of rosé that had been left for us. Beaming and grinning ear to ear, he said, "I don't know, but I like it already."

The house was located in the heart of the village, only a few steps from the butcher, boulangerie, patisserie, pharmacy, and doctor's office. From the terrace on the top floor, we could smell the luscious aromas of the *boucherie* cooking meats throughout the day. The morning after we arrived was Wednesday, the weekly market day for Rognes. We strolled the length of the main street that ran through the center of the village, still in a post-travel daze, placing this and that in a wicker basket I had found dangling on a hook in my dad's house. I was nowhere near ready to plan a proper meal, happy to simply pick what tempted us at the moment—aged salami, bright juicy tomato, fat green asparagus, tender rounds of chèvre cheese topped with peppercorns and herbs. Stretching a bit farther around the corner, past the market and village café, we found the *cave* of the local wine co-op, where we filled a wine jug with locally made rosé for a mere dollar a liter.

Our first significant accomplishment was buying a car—we knew that even if we stayed a year, it was the only option for transport. We agreed on a cute white convertible VW Golf that had seen better years but was very affordable and gave us the thrill of fresh air in our faces during the day and star shows at night. Driving the winding narrow roads through the Luberon, exploring the hilltop villages perched over limestone cliffs, we picnicked under olive trees and stuffed ourselves full of figs, apricots, and cherries on long walks in the countryside.

"OK, Lyd," John finally said. "It's time to settle in here— let's get the kids squared away with school." We had allowed ourselves a couple of weeks to adjust to our new reality, but it was time to begin to build the structure of a real life. After filling out some papers at the Mairie de Rognes (town hall), we set off to the little building perched on the side of a hill— L'École Maternelle. On the kids' first day, we sat quietly on a bench outside the school and watched as the two of them tentatively approached the playground, looking over their shoulders at us as they went.

"Go on, go on," I ushered them, waving toward the playground. "Off you go," I attempted to say confidently, praying they couldn't pick up on the quiver in my voice. "How will they adapt?" I turned to John nervously.

"I don't know. Naturally, probably, like kids do. What could be the worst? I mean, seriously—this is such a fabulous opportunity. I think we just have to trust it will all work out," he said, wrapping his arm around my waist.

Deep down I knew this myself, that they would gain so much from this experience, but I was also sure that for the next little while, they would be lost in a sea of foreign sounds. It reminded me of that first day of infant-survival swimming class we had enrolled Emma in at only eighteen months old. When the instructor took her little bare body from me, naked except for a pair of purple-and-pink swim diapers, I thought I would die from panic. The two of them gently entered the pool, with the instructor holding Emma for a few minutes before gently letting go of her, forcing her to find her own way to air. "Sometimes it is easier to turn your back, flip through a magazine—better yet, go out for coffee. I know it is hard," she said, looking over her shoulder. But it had only taken a matter of days before my tiny dot floated effortlessly on her own, first on her back, big eyes fixated toward the blue sky, then rolling over onto her stomach, twisting her head toward the air once again, finding her own way to survive. Yes, infant survival. That's exactly what this felt like, but this time it was both kids at the same time.

Amazingly though, we sat back, awestruck at the speed with which they adapted to and absorbed the language. After only two weeks at school, Nick came home and sang a Mother's Day song to me in French with the most perfect little accent that it made me cry. *"Je t'apporte, Maman, une petite fleur des champs..."* He had found comfort and the beginnings of the language through music and poetry, something that was naturally emphasized in the early years of primary school in Provence. Being two years younger, Emma soaked in the language even faster, adding French words to her growing list of English vocabulary. The two toddled off to school quite happily in the mornings, coming home filled with stories of the new friends they were making, reporting back on the fantastic spread of hot delicacies they were served at lunchtime.

Little by little, my own rusty French came back, inch by painful inch. While my family had lived in Ottawa, my parents had sent my sister and me to a French-immersion school—Le Phare, it was called. All of our classes from kindergarten to grade five were taught in French. By the time we moved to Rochester, New York, we were both essentially bilingual, yet the US system waited until high school to get going on foreign languages. Being only ten and twelve at the time, my sister and I would not use that French again for years. While this gap hadn't wiped our comprehension by any stretch, neither one of us quite regained that carefree, easy dialogue that we had achieved as children, and I would be living in France for years before feeling that comfort again. Poor John had only the few years he had been taught in high school, so he had the tallest mountain to climb of all of us. In those early days, though, it didn't seem to faze him much.

Settling in was made easy by the pure kindness of our neighbors, who extended themselves to us, sought us out, welcomed us into their homes. As Christmas approached and our next-door neighbor Marie-Jo was preparing her family recipe for foie gras, she called me over to show me how it was prepared. *"Tu fais comme cela,"* she said as she meticulously pulled out tiny, thin veins from the livers with a paring knife as her mother had taught her to do.

Everyone wanted to know just what on earth we were doing coming from America to this little town in Provence. *"Mais pourquoi ici?"* they would demand, embarrassed at their self-perceived lack of efficiency and antiquated bureaucracy.

No matter how hard we tried to explain that Provence was a must-see for many in the States, they just couldn't grasp what it was that we were searching for outside of our country of have-it-all.

We were invited in for Sunday lunches, several-coursed affairs where afternoon hours melted easily into early evenings, the sun setting gently in the background wherever we were—a garden terrace or in front of a cozy stone fireplace. The meals were always simple yet unbelievably delicious—everything locally grown and handpicked at the market. Salads tossed in olive oil, vinegar, and salt from the Camargue; tomatoes sliced with fresh mozzarella and basil; vegetables I hadn't known existed, like endive and fennel, baked with garlic and cream; chickens roasted on a spit. I felt like a child at each meal, tasting things for the first time, my senses exploding from the freshness, the flavors. Whether a Sunday lunch or a Friday evening meal, the whole luscious experience would begin with the apéritif—a light *vin de pêche,* a sparkling rosé or pastis served alongside home-grown olives *casseés,* small toasts topped with *brandade de morue* or *anchoïade.* Time virtually stood still when apéritifs were served, daytime chores and activities set aside to appreciate that divine gap between the active busy life and the sacred moments of sharing a meal together. A virtual collective sigh took place when that drink was poured, and it continued through the heavenly spread that always followed. Net sum, food and wine had never tasted this good to me—it was comfort, beauty, and satisfaction all wrapped in one.

One day walking to the car after dropping the kids at school, I passed a tall, beautiful Nordic-looking blond woman in a running outfit. *"Bonjour, excusez-moi. Vous faites du footing?* (Hello, excuse me. Do you jog?)" I asked rather boldly.

She must have been surprised because she stopped abruptly and turned to me, staring at me up and down. *"Oui, oui,"* she said, in what was clearly not a French accent. "I have noticed you and your husband—you are not from here? I have a son, Roman. He is in the same class as your son."

Louise, I learned, was Danish and married to Gilles, a Frenchman who worked as the public relations officer of Patrouille de France, comparable to the US Blue Angels, in nearby Salon. She explained that she had two close friends, Nicole and Natalie, with whom she ran on a regular basis. Would I like to join? "Yes!" I said, almost overly eager. *It would be great to meet some other women,* I thought to myself, already picturing a little running group meandering its way through the colorful vineyard paths. Truth be told, it had been a long time since I had felt that deep camaraderie with other women. More simply put, it had been a long time since I had made a friend. There had been several other moms in Orlando whom I saw on a regular basis, but it had been such an awkward time period for me. The years of burying myself in my work, the months of breaking down and feeling like the odd, ugly duckling, then the escape to Costa Rica that nobody really understood. I wouldn't say that it had brought out my best side. I am not even sure I would have wanted to be friends with me during that time.

Since arriving in France, we had met many local villagers, mainly neighbors and some old friends of my father's from his early career days in Ottawa. We also met Jean-Louis, father to young Maël, who also attended the village elementary school. Jean-Louis was a Shakespeare professor, but he also loved to paint, do bodybuilding, and play guitar. This unique mixture of life passions resonated comfortably with John. They became fast friends, spending hours together lifting weights and passing the guitar back and forth between sets. They even played out together at a local restaurant, Le Brassero. It was wonderful to see John play again, the one thing that tapped into his soul yet was forever overshadowed by his drive to build a secure life. I too longed for the companionship of those with similar interests and was thrilled at the prospect of meeting Louise and her friends for a run.

"Meet me at the foot of Caire Val at eight o'clock tomorrow morning," she said, waving as she opened her car door to leave.

"OK, super!" I responded. Caire Val was a wooded area at the base of a small mountain ridge five minutes' drive down the narrow, windy country road outside Rognes. We had hiked there a couple of times as a family, enjoying the sweeping views of the valley and admiring the tidy rows of olive trees from the top of the ridge. I drove back through Rognes that morning, stopping briefly to pick up a fresh baguette for lunch, a spring in my toe, giddy about my running date. But opening the shutters of the village house that following morning, I was greeted with a brisk, crisp wind and angry skies pouring rain. "Shit," I muttered. "I wonder if they will show with this crappy weather."

I sat shivering in the parking at Caire Val while the rain pounded on the car, leaking in through the small tears in the leather roof. After about ten minutes, just when I was starting to wonder whether they were going to come, I heard the faint hum of a car pulling up next to mine and three car doors closing seconds after. The introductions were very brief, partly from not wanting to linger under the awful rain, yet I sensed Louise's friends were not jumping at the chance to add me to their nicely established running trio. Within no time we were running at a steady pace through the flat section that preceded the steep ascent up the ridge. I could tell by the way they ran that they knew each other well—there was a strange synchronicity to the way they moved, Nicole often taking the lead, Natalie safely sandwiched in the middle. Louise's long legs could have easily put her in the front, yet even in the little time I had been around her, it was clear she had a kind and nurturing spirit about her, and it didn't surprise me that she provided the back support.

"We didn't think you would show up in this bad weather," Louise admitted with a grin on her face as we rounded the last corner before the hill. "My friends here were wondering just how tough this little blond American could be."

The bad weather had certainly taken the edge off my excitement at potentially making friends, and that feeling was now compounded by small waves of intimidation rushing through me, as if I was being tested.

Their pace quickened, and the path steepened. I had been a runner most of my life—not an amazingly fast runner but a loyal and decent one. When my parents had divorced and I had moved into my father's house after my mother moved away, I would run to pass the empty time, to escape the reality of what had happened to our family. Running had never failed me; the fresh air and scent of the earth, the sound of my pounding feet were things I could count on wherever I was, in whatever weather the universe decided to deliver. I drew my strength from the trees around me, serenity from the birds, clarity from the wind. Today would be no different, I told myself as my feet dug into the muddy path, lengthening my stride.

They chatted easily and quietly as they put one foot in front of the other. Their effortless conversation was all a little too fast for me to understand clearly—plus I was focusing on my footing on the rocky trail, telling myself over and over that I was not going to stop, no matter how steep it got. I heard Natalie mention divorce, and Nicole spoke of teenage children, Louise listening intently. I admired their camaraderie, the ease with which they exchanged their words and glances despite the rigorous trail. This was a result, I would learn later, of having shared endless life ups and downs on those trails—marriages that failed, jobs that came and went, parents who passed, children who challenged. They may not have been able to fix each other's problems over the years, but they could listen to one another, through tears of joy or pain, offering each other slices of their own strength. They were partners in their life journeys, and there was much to be said for that.

Roughly an hour later, we arrived back at the cars, the sun just beginning to peek through the edge of a cloud. "Lydia—*tu cours bien* (you run well)," smiled Nicole. She hadn't said a word to me on the run, but I had caught her looking at me, not so much in a critical way as I had thought she might, but with more of a silent, inquisitive look. Natalie had warmed as well and was asking about recipes and life in the United States. By the end of the run, it was clear that I had passed whatever test I had been put up to. Years later, Louise and I would laugh about that fateful day we ran Caire Val: "If you hadn't shown up, I don't think we would have ever become close friends," she would say. "I knew if you could run that awful hill in the lashing wind and rain just to gain friends that you were worth getting to know."

The months slipped by easily with the changing seasons, continuing to bring treats of all forms. On my evening walks after having dinner and tucking the kids into bed, I saw great earthy fields transform from gorgeous red and yellow spring flowers to tall wheat and corn, rows of carrots, cabbage, and lettuce. Later came breathtaking rows of lavender and the sweet faces of sunflowers. Nuts dropped in the road beside brambles of blueberries and blackberries. I watched as the vineyards transformed from month to month, their trimmed, budding stumps proudly growing into miniature trees brimming with fruit.

In the afternoons and after dinner, John would chip away at the search business, lining up his calls with the times zones in Manhattan. It paid for our daily living and provided a structure to his day, yet I noticed over time the effort becoming more halfhearted. Just as he had been in Costa Rica, he was easily distracted over being somewhere full of new things to take in and discover. Daily life was filled with menial and humbling challenges, but they kept him occupied. Signing up for car insurance and Internet and getting from one village to another without getting lost were huge tasks that often required enormous amounts of patience. These projects presented him with an odd and unexpected sense of accomplishment—something he wasn't getting from his normal business life. Every day there was something novel to learn, infusing our little household with a newfound spirit of fun, energy, and excitement. I kept up with the Costa Rica villa bookings, pleased to be adding my part to the family income. There was something gratifying about doing our work virtually, ingraining in us a sense of freedom yet connectedness. The world wasn't such a vast and expansive stretch, so *out there* anymore as it had seemed on the porch in Orlando.

As important as it had been to immerse ourselves in a French social world, it had been equally important to have a circle of close English-speaking families who shared similar challenges. We met Gary and Fiona, an English couple renovating an old olive mill in nearby Pelissanne. They had two children, adopted from Vietnam, near the same ages as Nick and Emma. There was also Darren and Julie, an American family with a son, Sawyer, exactly the same age as Nick, and a daughter, McKenna, only one year older than Emma. These friends took the place of family, and without them, life would have felt out of balance. On weekends and holidays, we shared laughs over our daily mishaps. There was a bit of needed bitching and moaning, but we all knew what a gift it was to be there. On those evenings, we served ketchup without shame and had cheese with wine before dinner instead of after. We chatted about how our children were adjusting at the village schools, about the strictness of the academic system, the lack of peanut butter, the harshness of the tax administration, and above all, the beauty of the experience. The key became to not lean on these relationships for survival. Looking back, managing this delicate balance between immersion and familiarity was critical, and if tipped too far toward the familiar, we would have become at risk of insulating ourselves—that horrible, scary concept that had driven us abroad in the first place. We had to constantly remind ourselves that we were there to move beyond our comfort zones.

One evening, sipping local wine on the terrace, John and I looked back on how we had been living in the States and wondered what all the rush had been about, the mad race to success. "Can you put your finger on what exactly we were trying to get ahead of? What was it we were so hell bent on achieving?" I asked. "Get ahead? Ahead of what exactly?" Neither one of us had any good answers, and it was nice to finally be in a place where we could consider these questions, chat about them between ourselves without threats ending in tearful and angry arguments or couches upside down. We weren't coming to any decisions, but between our time in Costa Rica and now France, we had found some sort of safe middle ground. The fact that our relationship had been in such a fragile spot the year before had frightened us both, and it was such an incredible relief to be beyond it. We were so thankful to have made it through the storm.

"I guess at some point we need to think about whether we are staying," I finally said one day. Our one-year-in-France anniversary was approaching, and while selling the house in Orlando had afforded us a margin of time to consider where we were in life, it was time to consider the next step, to carve out some sort of general plan for what we wanted for the future.

6

Transformation

When I let go of what I am, I become what I might be.
Lao Tzu

It all changed on September 11th. I went to the school to pick up Nick and Emma, and I was stopped by a friend, a parent of another child. She ran up to me and grabbed me by the arm. "I am so sorry for what happened in New York...the buildings," she said with deep concern in her eyes. I hadn't seen the news that day and was clueless about the horrifying events taking place. I grabbed the kids and sped home. Turning on the TV, we froze in fear and horror as we took in sickening smoky scenes. John and I spent the following days on the couch in our village house stunned, tearful, and shattered. Several of John's insurance clients had been affected; tragically, some had family members or colleagues in the buildings. We grieved alone, far away from friends and family. The business came to a full stop. A seeping realization that awful things could in fact happen hung in the air for weeks. We went through the motions of our daily routines, but something profound had shifted. At the age of thirty, we were getting our first clue, the first genuine sinking appreciation, for just how short and fragile life was.

Over time I could see in John's eyes that he was chewing on something, an idea of some sort. I wasn't sure what it was, and at the time, it didn't feel right to probe too much. During the hours he would normally be working, I found him thumbing through the *immobilier* (real estate) offerings. At first I thought it was a comforting way to spend the time, but the wrinkle in his forehead and the way in which he picked incessantly at his eyebrows communicated that more serious intentions were brewing. Piles of bent, dog-eared listings were strewn about the various tables in the house, on his nightstand, and on the lounge chair on the terrace. Abandoned *cabanons* (stone cabin) listings were circled, as were ancient village houses or ruined farm houses.

One afternoon he skipped up the final flight of stairs with a rolled-up listing in his fist. "Just come with me. Let's just look," he panted. "It's an uninhabited retirement home—a *maison de retraite*—eight kilometers away in the countryside past Lambesc. Look, it even has a small vineyard and fruit trees. You love fruit trees, Lydia!"

Two days later, after dropping the kids at school, we pulled up to a massive neglected building behind a small patch of vineyard. Gray clouds hung low in the air, and drizzle collected on the windshield. "Good Lord, this thing is huge," I said, taking in the view out of the back, the exposed smoky-blue rocks of the Luberon mountains peeking through the pine trees. A cool breeze brushed past my face, carrying with it faintly sweet, earthy aromas. Looking down at my feet, I noticed that the scrubby grass that bordered the property was in fact clumps of thyme and rosemary. While we waited for the real-estate agent to arrive, we wandered around the property and, despite the light rain, took in the sweeping stretches of rolling hills surrounding the house. In the far distance I could make out the small red door of an ancient stone building that I recognized as La Chapelle Saint Symphorien, a stunning twelfth-century chapel that stood proudly at the foot of the hill that the old village of Vernègues stood atop.

The house was three stories high, and even from the outside we could tell that it needed a tremendous amount of work. Faded, faint gray paint chipped away from the windowsills and shutters, and a dull, brownish mold crept down from the edge of the clay tile roof. I found my way around to the side of the house. Peering through a small windowpane thick with smudged dirt, I spotted what looked like a kitchen, massive but institutionally outfitted with metal workstations and a large industrial sink. "Whoa. This place is weird—what did you say it was, John? An old-folks' home?"

"Yup," said John as he took a turn looking through the window. When the agent arrived, we got the full story. The family who owned much of the vineyard land in the sur-rounding hills had built the house as their family home, but later they had run into financial trouble. In lieu of selling the property, they had leased it out as a retirement home but had been later forced to shut it down due to a lack of maintaining proper health and safety codes. The elderly residents had often been found, sometimes clad in a night robes or pajamas, wandering the roads aimlessly. Villagers had complained, and the home had ultimately been denied its lease renewal.

"It has been on the market for some time and has not moved—it is too big for an average home and obviously needs to be gutted," the agent said to us in French. "Nobody is really willing to put in the time and money for the renovation. As you will see, it will be a big job. This is why it is selling for such a good price," he added, opening up the back door.

The first thing I noticed was the smell—a pungent mix of urine, mold, and old people. Trying to hide the hand over my nose and mouth, I walked ahead of the agent and John, making my own way through the damp, rambling building. Everything was metal—the cupboards, closet doors, railings. Massive, ugly fire alarm boxes lined the hallways alongside exposed pipes; electric EXIT signs hung over every door to the outside. I winced at the dark brown, blue, and pink porcelain toilets and bathroom tile. *Stark, smelly,* and *institutional* were the only words floating through my head.

John paced crazily around the house—I could tell by his stride, more like a march fueled by motivation, that he was excited. "Lydia, wow...this has such potential," he said. "Just think about what we could do with this..."

Oh, God, here we go, I thought to myself as I continued through the empty halls, now echoing with John's lively voice and footsteps. Joining him in one of the bedrooms, I wandered over to the window; desperate for some air and light I unlatched the shutter. Pushing hard, leaning my shoulder into it, I was surprised that it wouldn't budge. "The vines must have grown over the front facade," John said as he motioned for me to move, his strong arm forcing open the shutter. Cool, wet air brushed by the both of us, and a slight ray of light pierced the gray skies, casting an unexpected hue of warm yellow across the empty room. Approaching the edge of the window, we both took a quick gasp of delight as we took in the view of a little vineyard down below.

I couldn't deny that something was fluttering in the pit of my stomach; the whole spirit of the place had unexpectedly become intoxicating. Together John and I paced through the rest of the rooms, shoving open the vine-covered shutters as we went, letting the light and air filter through the dusty rooms, as if giving them the breath they had been desperately waiting for.

Le Mas de Gancel, as it was named, reeked of neglect in almost every respect, but to us at that moment, on that morning, it represented a small haven, a retreat with potential that reached out and would not let go. We didn't need to say much as we drove the windy roads back to Rognes in the rain. The flicker of excitement in John's blue eyes said it all—I knew that face so well there wasn't a need to speak. Something had happened back in that house; the strange mixture of challenge, comfort, and hope represented a step, a project, a move that simply felt right for us both.

We stayed up late on the following nights scratching numbers and figuring out how to make the investment work. "Shit. John, this is going to be a real stretch financially." We would basically have to put every penny we had into it and more. And knowing the effort and time it would take to renovate the place, John would have to hang up the search business completely. While John had put it aside since September 11th, we had never fully discussed closing the doors entirely. He had been making calls to contacts in the insurance world who had died, quit, or been displaced to New Jersey after the attacks—it was too difficult to continue. It was becoming clear that we weren't going back to the States. Abandoning the safety of earning an income felt like yet one more massive leap away from the old world we had left, and I was surprised at John's easy willingness to cross that divide.

I leaned over in the bed and stared at my sleeping husband, a lump with a happy grin still pasted to his face. Then he opened an eye. "We'll make it work," he said and rolled over.

Our basic idea was to create a vacation rental for the tourist season in Provence. The positive results we continued to have with the villa in Costa Rica offered the grain of confidence we needed to push through those final doubts before purchasing. Once the house was finished, it could take groups of ten to eighteen with its nine bedrooms. I did my due diligence, researching what else was on the market for larger villa rentals, and it was pretty clear that it could potentially be one of a few in the region. The income-generating weeks would last from May to September, maybe October if we were lucky, just long enough to bring in the income needed to pay the mortgage, yearly maintenance costs, and whatever we would need for day-to-day living. "Here we go," John said, clinking his glass of champagne to mine after signing the papers. "To a new a job—to the next chapter."

In order to conserve funds, we decided to be our own general contractors, putting together a team of local craftsmen— electricians, a plumber, a tile layer, a pool builder, and masons. They were a bit of a motley crew, definitely rough around the edges, but they were soon to be like family as we passed the cold months together in a half-demolished retirement home. The mistral wind blew hard, but the contractors' loud and echoing chatter, bickering, and laughter filled all of the empty corners each day. Dust and plaster thickened by inches on the floor as Gancel was transformed, metamorphosed from a foul-smelling old-folks' home into what we hoped would be a warm and inviting Provençal country house.

John immediately found his stride, completely embracing the switch from businessman to mason and contractor. Energy pumped through his veins as he popped out of bed every morning, eagerly pulling on his ripped jeans and work boots. It was as natural to him as me leaving the executive-search business, as though life had been just waiting for him to find the right moment to take the plunge.

It immediately brought back fond memories of renovating our first little house on historic Ridgewood Avenue in Orlando, a project that had been nothing of this magnitude yet had brought us so much joy. On the weekends or when the clock hit five, John would rip off his work clothes to dive into whatever project he had going—the early-evening hours slipping away with the setting sun. But the flood of memories went back even farther, to before we were married with our first house, back to the long, hot summer college days when we had painted houses to earn money for the school year. PERFORMANCE PAINTING, we called ourselves on the flyers we stuck in mailboxes around town. HONEST, PROFESSIONAL, RELIABLE. CALL FOR YOUR FREE QUOTE TODAY! it had stated.

We had worked for College Pro Painters the previous summer, John as the foreman and me on the paint crew, long enough to gain the confidence to go it alone with our own company the following year. The independence and freedom were a thrill to us both—it felt more natural to have control over what we did and how we did it. While our friends logged their hours checking at the Gap or waiting tables and flipping hamburgers at Bill Gray's, we pounded the pavement, knocked on doors, and excitedly tempted people: "Your trim is looking a little dull; we can be in and out in three days, and it'll look like new."

Looking back, I could see that having our own little business and working together at such a young age had been a test, both personally and to our relationship. At the beginning, I had had a terrible time moving my ladder around myself, and John had made it clear at the outset that he wasn't going to coddle me—I would simply have to find a ladder I could move easily without his help. It was out of the question for me to manage on my own with a normal thirty-foot ladder. The tall aluminum ones were so long, they swayed horribly in the wind as I tried to move them, and we both had visions of me taking out the windows of the houses next door. Tucked into the back of my dad's dusty garage was a little wooden one, smooth to the touch from years of use and light as a feather. "This is just perfect," I said, screeching with joy, knowing that with it I could pull my own weight.

That ladder and I became one that summer—together we lived through hundreds of serene and horrifically scary hours. Second-story houses were the death of me, and I dreaded landing a job where there were multiple levels. For the most part, I got to stay close to the ground, as I had the perfect excuse that my ladder didn't extend far enough. But many of the two-story houses had the dreaded middle roof, one that I could reach easily. Once on top of the first level, I could, in theory, extend my ladder on that middle roof to get to the next story. "I can't do that side, John," I had said flatly at one house. "There is no flippin' way I am climbing up that high to do that window and peak."

"Yes, you are—and, yes, you will," he had snapped back, staring at me with his deep-blue eyes. "Buck up and get the job done, Lydia. At any rate, I've got to do the other peak, and we have to finish this house today."

I stood there in a maze of shock, anger, and frustration, yet I remember him looking over his shoulder as he walked back to his ladder, his face hiding a more tender message. *You can do this*, it said. *I know you can. Just try...*Hands and knees shaking, up I went, bucket in one hand, taking deep breaths to calm myself, eyes fixated only on the window above me. Sliding my boots onto one smooth, round step after another, I mustered the strength to do what I didn't think I was capable of doing.

Our days, often ten hours long, would go by with only the sounds of lightly whispering wind and faintly ringing top-forty songs coming from the paint-splattered radio plugged in somewhere around the side of the house. Working on our new venture in Provence, I laughed at the thought of that radio, remembering it was never where I wanted it to be when I finally made it up to the top of my ladder with the assortment of tools I would need for the next two hours—sandpaper and a five-in-one scraper stuffed in one pocket, window putty in the other. John and I would each carry a five-gallon bucket of paint in one hand, with a brush and roller pad balanced perfectly on the side, up to the tops of our ladders. I am not a formidable size by any means, and it required a certain amount of stamina to climb up a ladder with one hand and balance all that crap in the other. Once I got the whole load to the top of the ladder, there was no going down to move the radio closer to my ladder. "Shit...the radio is still on the other side of the house," John or I complained at least two times a day. But before long, the sound of the wind in our ears would force us into our own peaceful thoughts, and the radio would be quickly forgotten.

By the end of the summer, with John's pushing and prodding, that ladder and I had learned to carry our own, and I was proud. Our bank accounts had been topped off with money we had earned on our own steam, on our time. We each sported well-defined upper-body muscles, and our shoulders and the backs of our legs were a deep golden brown. It was clear there was a link between our

Performance Painting days and now—it was all too familiar and comfortable, as if the puzzle pieces were slowly being pieced together.

We lived in the house as it was being restored, and after long days of work, we were often without heat or hot water. Our hands quickly cracked from the sanding and scraping, and I forgot what it was like to be clean and feel pretty. Our knowledge of French *gros mots* (swear words) flourished, as did the daily misunderstandings due to a combination of language and cultural differences and restoration know-how. *"Non...tu ne peux pas faire cela!"* the masons bellowed as we wanted to put wood floors in the kitchen. We insisted, and of course the floors buckled and had to be replaced soon after. Renovating Gancel was a long and draining process, filled with the pleasure of accomplishment and the pain of physical and mental exertion, much like painting days had been so many years ago. Relating this to friends and family at home was nearly impossible. They had all read *Under the Tuscan Sun* and *A Year in Provence,* and they wouldn't be fooled. I could whine all I wanted about our dwindling funds or the cold days, but we were living a dream—it just wasn't always an easy one.

Fortunately, the tensions of the project would easily melt away with the fading sun as we trimmed the vines, getting them ready for the next season. The children were completely oblivious to the stresses. "What's for dinner?" they would yell as they smashed old tiles with hammers.

"Uh...cheese! And, uh...fresh bread!" I would say, looking around the kitchen countertops littered with sand paper and dust.

"Great, Ma...camembert or chèvre?" they would yell back.

There wasn't a need for television, and we didn't own video games. There were tools everywhere, pieces of wood—ideal raw materials for their inventive minds. Both kids also spent endless hours singing in the hallways, finding the corners that offered the perfect sonic balance. Nick would always begin, Emma later joining in, sliding her voice in between his. At the end of a day, they were happy to bundle up and roast marshmallows outside over a bonfire; it didn't matter to them that their hot water had to be heated on the stove for their baths.

I would go to school to pick up the kids, and the other Provençal mothers would admire my American white teeth but truly wonder at the ripped jeans and paint-splattered hair. "What do the Americans know about renovating in Provence?" I imagined them scoffing. Luckily there were the rugged and rocky runs on the trails with Nicole, Natalie, and Louise, with whom I unloaded my insecurities and doubts. They were wonderfully supportive, accepting our naiveté yet respecting our drive and motivation to get beyond what we knew.

Over time, my friendship with Louise had moved well beyond running, with our families getting together regularly. Friday evenings were often spent together in front of their fireplace or ours, Roman, Nick, and Em curled up together to watch a movie. While John and Gilles talked endlessly about stones and renovating, Louise and I slowly began to share our personal histories. I learned that her mother had passed away from cancer when Louise was only fifteen. It had been a terrible loss, one that she had attempted to escape by pulling on her running shoes and running for miles along empty roads in her native Denmark. I shared the troubles John and I had lived through in the previous years, my own need to escape the world I felt so trapped in. One evening after several glasses of wine, I found myself talking about my childhood dreams, my fascination with Mother Theresa and Gandhi, my almost primal need to smell and taste India.

Louise listened intently, her big blue Danish eyes taking in my every word. "What are you looking for, Lydia?" she asked quietly.

"I don't know, Louise," I said. "But I know deep in my heart I am going to find what it is I am searching for."

Little by little the house became what we had envisioned, glowing with the warmth and charm we had hoped for. After seven or so months, the main crew of masons had finished the bulk of their work, leaving just the odd electrician or carpenter to stop by for minor projects. I bought bedspreads at the Pelissanne's Sunday market, hung soft linen drapes in the bedrooms, and placed a small, leather-bound guest book that my mother had given me on the shelf of our library. In the spring months, the final touches on the pool were made, and the lavender we had planted in front of the house began to sprout. Gancel had transformed, and there was no doubt we had too. John had comfortably reconnected with his passion for using his hands, our lives had become intricately connected with the outdoors, and we had made some genuine friends. And I was as far as I could imagine from the packaged world I had needed to escape.

As we headed into these final stages of Gancel's renovation, I dove into marketing it as a vacation rental, retracing many of the same steps and methods that had been successful in Costa Rica. We took two dozen photos and listed Gancel online as a vacation rental, and as we had hoped, it quickly appealed to the Americans visiting the region. As we began to book weeks for the upcoming rental season, we were forced to plan where we would go when we had to be out. I found myself imagining traveling to all the places I had always wanted to go—Egypt, Morocco, Vietnam, Africa, India. The conversations I had begun to have with Louise were still fresh in my mind; the thought of slipping deeper into the earth's corners tugged at me inside. More was at work here, I knew it—yet I couldn't grab onto one crisp or clear thought that could shed light on the bigger picture. One thing was for sure, though—the wind had changed direction, and our little boat was shifting course, whether we realized it or not.

7

A Tiny Flame

Come forth into the light of things,
Let Nature be your teacher.
William Wordsworth

Still reluctant to plan our future and not wanting to think of anything but living in the moment, we spent any extra dime we made from renting Mas de Gancel or the house in Costa Rica on traveling. During the high-season weeks and on weekends, we crammed ourselves into the little white VW, venturing to easily accessible countries—Spain, Italy, Austria, Switzerland, Germany. We traveled to England to visit my sister, Helene, and her family. When we could, we stretched further, to North Africa and Asia. Emma was a magnet to languages, and Nick's warm spirit left a trail of new friends everywhere we went. Traveling continued to have a combined effect of opening us up individually and uniting us as a family. Having built a new life for ourselves with control of our own time, the world was now at our doorstep, and we were hell-bent on discovering it.

Our English friends Gary and Fiona had traveled extensively as a war photographer and a TV news producer. One afternoon over a lazy Sunday lunch of slow-cooked lamb and lentils, they introduced the idea of visiting Cambodia. "It's magical," they said. "Siem Reap is where you want to go. The ancient temples of Angkor Wat and the kindness and warmth of the culture are really something to experience. Cambodia has had a difficult past, but the place is a must-do in a lifetime."

For months afterward, I read everything I could about Cambodia and neighboring Laos and Vietnam. I learned of the perplexing blend of variables that created its complex tapestry—its rich spiritual history alongside harrowing years of war, both recent and past. During Pol Pot's Khmer Rouge regime, unspeakable crimes were committed, leaving gaping, painful holes in their current population. I had learned about the Vietnam War in school, yet for the first time I read through haunting firsthand accounts from the perspective of the Vietnamese. Images of Southeast Asia began to weave their way into my thoughts, on my runs and in the early hours as the sun cast its light on the apricot tree outside our bedroom window. By the end of the year, I knew we had to go.

The grumbling sounds coming from John's stomach dragged me out of a thick, muddled sleep. A quick look at the watch...4:30 a.m. "John, we need to get up soon," I whispered, trying not to wake the kids. He groaned and headed for the bathroom. I slipped on the shirt and pants I had left in a heap by the bed the night before and stopped briefly to gaze at my sweet babies, who had somehow, without me knowing it, grown into spirited and inquisitive individuals. John reappeared looking pale and disheveled. The air in Bangkok during the prior week must have somehow seeped into his stomach. We slipped out the door, carefully locking it behind us. I tried to dodge a pang of fear for leaving the children alone in the hotel a million miles away from home for the couple of hours we would be away. *What if they wake up?* I pushed away the wave of anxiety and quickened my pace. Travel had us doing all sorts of things we wouldn't have done at home. Trust, faith, and gut instinct seemed to be taking the driver's seat.

The day before at the airport, we had begun to line up with all of the others at the counter to apply for a tourist-entry visa to Cambodia. Out of nowhere a man swept in, dressed in what looked like official clothes, and approached us at the end of the line. He spoke no English. Singling us out he snatched our passports and cash required for the visas and disappeared—for a long time. "What on earth is this guy doing, John?" I panicked. We waited and waited and began to worry about the consequences of him not return-ing. My mind ran through the list of horrible eventualities. Cambodia had just recently opened up to tourists, finally finding peace after decades of war, poverty, and genocide. Until the late nineties, it had not been a safe place for trav-elers to venture, as Khmer Rouge guerrillas still occupied certain areas, and land mines lurked everywhere.

There had been several occasions during our travels when we had genuinely feared for our safety, and during those moments, I had had only myself to blame. I would hear my mother or John's mother in my ear quipping, *Is it entirely necessary for you to take the children there?* Then in my other ear, I would hear a small voice more loudly: *Just go...there is stuff out there you have got to get to.*

Cab rides were most often the sources of our harried memories—as any traveler does, we put our personal safety in the hands of a total stranger. You have no clue where you are; jet-lagged and normally with some cash in your pocket, you are exposed, to say the very least. At the exchange of a few dollars, you simply have to trust that your cabdriver is a good person and will get you from A to B.

There had been a time in Costa Rica where tourists were being robbed in taxis and rental cars, and travelers were told to be extra careful. We had flown in very late one night and had more bags than usual, as we were going to stay for a longer period of time (and why on earth did I need all of that stuff?). Our cabdriver had had to pile the suitcases on the roof of his shabby rusted car as we stuffed ourselves into the back seats. The stories and warnings of tourist attacks were fresh in my mind, and I immediately took note as the driver chose to take the dark side road to the hotel, driving around the back of the airport instead of on the main highway.

At some point on the road, at a spot completely pitch black with not a car or house or business in sight, the driver slowly brought the car to a stop. Not saying a word, he parked the car and got out. My body went numb as fear swept through every inch of me, my heart pounding so hard I swore I could hear it. John's body language told me

I wasn't the only one who was scared, and he took a stance prepared to defend. I glanced at the kids, who had fallen asleep—if we needed to run, it was going to be a challenge. "Why on earth did he stop?" I whispered to John.

"I have no idea, but this isn't good," he responded. The cabdriver moved to the back door, and John and I braced for God-only-knew-what. But he didn't reach for the door or open it. Instead he fiddled with the old ragged string he had used to tie the bags to the roof—they had come loose—then climbed back in and drove on.

Our man at the Siem Reap airport returned, beaming a kindness we would later find common among Cambodians. Grinning from ear to ear, he handed us the passports and visas—all in order, stamped a million times—with exact change in hand. He apologized for having pulled us from the line and explained he had selected us because he'd noticed we had children, and he had wanted to give us preferential attention. As with so many situations we had encountered on the road, I was being reminded to trust more.

"Are you going to be OK?" I asked John as we nestled into our tuk-tuk taxi, leaving our sleeping children in the hotel. But I knew the answer. He would have to be on death's door to be anywhere else right now. Like me, he was captivated by the moment as we whizzed by tiny huts, which bore small fires cooking predawn breakfasts. The magic in the soft cool air had us somewhere beyond thought or realities of stomach pain. I tucked myself under his warm arm and breathed in the smoky humid air.

The streets of Siem Reap were flooded with water from the night's rain, and our tuk-tuk created a wake that flooded the sidewalks on either side. We weaved through the outskirts of town, past a bizarre mix of old markets and funky deco bars. Almost oddly out of place, the town had a Euro-chicness about it, with modern restaurants playing trendy casual lounge music for wealthy tourists sipping cocktails in the evenings.

But it wasn't all pretty—begging children carrying tiny infants slung around their waists tugged at our shirts selling postcards. Countless men with missing limbs lined the streets, sitting on straw mats and exposing the devastating and ongoing consequences of land mines. Cambodia was still considered one of the poorest countries in the world, and the horrors committed in the not-so-distant past left a heaviness lingering in the dense air. Fragility definitely hovered, but so did the ring of hope for a bright future, resonating in the whirling noises of hotels being built to support a burgeoning tourist industry. Newfound peace and tourism, with the Angkor temples at their epicenter, were helping pave a new road for Cambodia.

Entering the south gate of the temple complex, we could barely make out the grand stone snake heads lining the road that had the previous day been the playground for a pack of monkeys. At this hour we couldn't see, but we could feel the weight of the great jungle trees around us. The tuk-tuk stopped, and the driver motioned for us to get out. "John, it's pitch-black...how are we going to see the temples?" I mumbled as we piled out. The driver took off down the road, leaving us alone in the dark. Silently we turned to face the silhouette of Banteay Kdie, a sprawling, mainly unrestored monastic complex. Behind its majestic entrance was a path leading to a sea of black jungle growth.

Angkor Wat in Cambodia had become a premier historical site in Asia. In 1992, the UNESCO World Heritage Committee declared the whole city of Angkor a World Heritage site, and now visitors from all over the world were pouring in. While some argued that the temples rivaled the Great Pyramid and Taj Mahal in artistry, it was the spiritual element that visitors came away attempting to describe. The architecture and bas reliefs found at Angkor revealed a time immensely rich in mythology, cosmology, and spirituality. Certain temples were thought to represent the universe in stone, an earthly model of the cosmic world linking the mundane to the divine—terrestrial versions of the heavens. Only recently had they been cleared of land mines, and the guide books still advised sticking to the marked paths.

"Coffeeeee, madam! Bracelets, madaaam!" I jumped ten feet, startled by the small figure of a barefoot girl wearing a scrap of a purple dress hanging off her shoulder. She was persistent and energetic, following us all the way into the temple entrance. "Coffeeeee, madam! Bracelets, madaaam!" she repeated even louder. I could barely make out her sweet features in the premorning darkness but caught a clear glimpse of bright eyes flashing with hope that I might buy something from her. Or was it desperation? I stopped, gently shaking my head no at her. After one last feeble attempt at showing me her wares, she dropped her head and shuffled back to a dark hut, unsold bracelets dangling from her slight hand.

The air was filled with searing jungle noises as we meandered down the path into a world hundreds of centuries gone by. Inside the falling stone temple, with only the light of the moon to lead our way, we surrendered to our senses, to the cool walls, the darkness, the lingering incense, to the history-filled roots pushing their way through the massive slabs of stone. Tremendous silence sat alongside deafening noise from the jungle. The dark outline of John's body slipped away as we took different routes through the maze of dark hallways filled with shrines and heaps of stone and growth. The temples were such a strange union of spiritual, historical, and natural worlds in perfect symmetry, as if heaven and earth were reaching for one another.

Our friend Gary had encouraged us to visit the temples at sunrise when the light was particularly special, the heat of the day yet to penetrate. We had already toured some of the temples on our first day at high noon and were so wrapped in astonishment over the grandeur of it all that it was hard to imagine it could get better. It had been a hot and steamy scene with vendors selling grilled corn, cut fruit, and small sacks of green curry. Hordes of tourists milled, with flashes of orange-robed monks flying by on the backs of motorcycles.

As vivid shades of orange and purple began to stripe the sky with the awakening sun, we wandered back out of the darkness into the sunrise toward Srah Srang, overlooking the lake. "Coffeeee, madam!" the young girl tried again, this time looking straight into my eyes. For a brief second, time seemed to stop as our eyes locked onto one another, communicating a language that transcended thoughts or words, the jungle searing all around us. A million shades of color now splashed themselves across the dawn sky. Several groups of tourists zoomed up in tuk-tuks and descended with cameras in hand. The girl quickly shifted her focus to her new crop of tourists. I watched quietly as they waved her off like a fly and made a beeline for the lake, snapping and chatting loudly as they went. The scene had changed, and I wanted to go, to leave and preserve whatever it was that I had felt.

The following morning we relived the magic all over again, this time with Nick and Emma. Leaving such an astonishingly spiritual place without sharing with them the experience at sunrise would have been a crime. This was why we had brought them—to inspire them to venture out, to connect in new ways, to feel things they had never felt before. I wanted to let them wander aimlessly through the broken corridors as we had the previous day at Banteay Kdie, guided only by a faint light, jungle sounds, and scented air. John gave them firm orders to not wander outside of the temple; there were still risks of land mines.

Instead of entering the temples, I sat on an ancient stone slab and watched as the children silently weaved in and out of the timeworn chambers, peering wide-eyed through windows, gently patting the massive roots of the trees as if offering their respects. As they disappeared into the mass of tree limbs and stone, I took a few deep breaths, gently sucking in the foreign smoky air. My mind drifted to the girl who had been selling the bracelets. I wondered where she was, what she was doing. In Cuba and Egypt, we had also seen children working or begging during the day instead of going to school. In Morocco, Nick was dumbfounded at the boys his age and younger lined up on the floor in the mosaic-tile factories. At first I think he thought it was cool that they didn't have to go to school, but when he realized that they had to spend full days chipping tile with raw and calloused hands on the dusty ground in the sweltering heat, it sank in that perhaps this wasn't such a luxury.

Logically, when traveling with the kids, we avoided the areas where the more disadvantaged populations lived— really remote villages or slum areas. These decisions were based on both our own unfounded fear and ignorance. It's amazing that a decade later we would be traveling straight to them. Like it had been for John and me, it was of course a shock for the kids to see extreme poverty for the first time, yet they seemed to see past the surface more easily. They soaked in normal life—people working hard, children laughing and playing, music echoing from tin homes and corner cafés. At times they were oblivious to the fact that, in many cases, these people were surviving below the poverty line; to them they were just people. They were free of the layers of emotions and classifications on how people lived, free of any pity we might have felt when we were confronted with it.

On one of our summer weeks away from Gancel, we stumbled on a tiny and charming yet crumbling artist gallery in Cuba, deep in the heart of Old Havana and off the main city roads. Stepping inside to admire the work, we met a woman. Her name was Maria, and many of the paintings in the gallery were hers. Our conversations with Maria led from one topic to another, and before we knew it, we were sipping thick and fragrant coffee in her tiny two-room apartment with her elderly mother. Nick and Emma and Maria's son, who was about the same age, were outside tending to a hurt pigeon in the road.

Maria described the difficulties of life in Cuba, the things that she needed but would have to save for months or years to acquire—bras, artist paints, sanitary pads—simple luxuries to her. While she spent her free time painting, her day job was a government position that barely brought enough in for food. As we chatted, I scanned her living quarters, the cracked walls, her laundry hung to dry yet covering every square inch of the minuscule apartment. Maria radiated tremendous warmth and kindness, and she insisted that we come back, that we stay in her home. "Come and have dinner with me, then leave the children with me for an evening, and I will send you two lovers off to the best spot in Havana for music!" she said as though we were dear friends. She had so little yet so much to share.

Once home, we tried to send her things in the mail but never heard back and doubted they arrived. One of her paintings still hangs in the dining room at Gancel and remains a reminder to me that it's on the back streets where the richness in life can be found. There was much to be learned from Maria, from the dignified way in which she took on her life challenges. Living closer to the fundamentals, or the lack thereof, she must have known just that much more about what really mattered. Why was it that I was the one who felt humbled in these brief encounters? It made me think of how, in Costa Rica, a hard-working woman raising five children in a tin-roofed cinder-block house, had pinched my cheeks like I was one of her own clueless kids—as though I had much to learn yet about life, its hardships, its wisdom.

The trips had begun to stir up my early childhood humanitarian interests, but those interests continued to float out in the wind, unattached to anything concrete. It was as if I was a young student sitting in a classroom, with nothing to offer but hungry to learn. The world was my teacher. Instead of finding life answers, I just seemed to gather more questions. I continued to write about it all, scribbling in my journals at each day's end.

Sitting on the stone that early morning, surrounded by the power of towering trees, I was suddenly flooded by an intense rush of gratitude. With my feet sinking deeper in to the dark Cambodian sand, I could feel the power of the earth beneath me. At that moment, I knew there was no need to worry about the unanswered questions. I only had to continue to listen, continue to honor the lessons and the goodness that the world was offering. Something in me had altered—as if a tiny flame, a simple candle like those found in a dark and dusty corner of a temple, had been lit in my soul, connecting me, grounding me to something much greater. As the plane took off a few days later, I felt I was leaving something behind. I knew I would return again.

8

Anything but Paradise

The truth knocks on the door and you say,
Go away, I'm looking for the truth,
and so it goes away.
Robert M. Pirsig

More and more, we found ourselves returning from our foreign trips a little bit antsy, and for what, I didn't know. Day to day life in Provence had become calm and predictable, like a new normal of sorts, but we were not ready for normal again. "I am starting to wonder if we will be ready to settle down in any one place," I stated to John one day. He admitted to wondering the same. All the moving around had instilled a comfort zone with respect to homelessness, and that familiar nudge to keep moving poked at our backsides.

Mas de Gancel was now full of tourists, week in and week out, and way more often than our originally anticipated three summer months. The house was now fully booked for at least six months, beginning in May and running through the end of October. We hired a bilingual American woman who lived in the nearby village of Alleins to manage the property and meet and greet the guests as they arrived. There wasn't much to do, or so we thought, beyond getting out of everyone's way.

John was anxious to sink his teeth into a new project of some sort, so we let our hearts wander back to the jungle once again, to Costa Rica, to the place where things were just a little bit wild and unpredictable. He had been kicking around the idea of starting a boat business, a catamaran day tour out of the Quepos marina. He had always had a love for boats and sailing, and Manuel Antonio was an ideal place to give it a try. Once the business ideas started to swirl, the temptation was just too strong. It was as if life was pulling us toward something, an undercurrent that was almost out of our control. Giving into it now felt as easy as slipping on an old shoe. And so, just as we had done two and a half years before in Orlando, we hugged our dear friends in Provence goodbye, and with open hearts and minds, once again—and this time with a dog named Jengo—found a faith within ourselves to not be afraid of what lay around the corner or across an ocean.

Manuel Antonio, Costa Rica
Summer 2003

I woke up in our jungle nest and took my steaming cup of coffee to the terrace to take in the sounds of Manuel Antonio— the croaking, chirping, buzzing made by thousands of insects, monkeys, birds, and geckos. An old diesel public bus chugged up the Manuel hill; the surf crashed somewhere in the distance. Precious sounds of pattering rainwater hitting millions of giant leaves echoed next to the pounding hammers of workmen as they built yet another luxury home in the mountainous jungle. Not one day went by without the relentless sawing and searing of new development. I looked down from the balcony and watched groups of Costa Rican men, perched on precarious cement foundations, pouring more cement. The whole community feared that the weak ground soil would fail to support the weight of all the new homes—our uninsurable structures that could slide down the hill in the next mud slide or earthquake. This week alone, there had been three earthquakes.

The rapid growth and development mirrored the tourism industry that had continued to expand since we had purchased the house a few years earlier. Our guest book was filled with pages upon pages of families who had vacationed there, sharing special memories of exploration together. I wondered whether they had felt the same rush of excitement that I did gazing out at the Pacific through the rounded wooden windows, some days seeing splashing specks from dolphins and whales in the distance. Did they love the feel of clean, cool terra cotta tile and natural rock on their feet, the smell of hardwoods in the doors, furniture, and ceilings filling the air? It was easy to get swept away on vacation here, easy to forget or ignore the development—the greed. Easy to not see our part in it.

I considered why we had come, what it was that drew us to the point where we would give up an idyllic lifestyle in the French countryside. But while Provence had shown us beauty in so many forms, had taught us the goodness of simple things, it also represented old Europe, with enormous amounts of conformity and regulation. To get anything done, you needed endless amounts of formal paperwork—some argued that the administration in France was among the most rigid in the Western world. The word *interdit*, meaning *not allowed*, had been among the first ten French words we had learned. How I had grown to loathe that word. If we were going to truly settle there, we would have to be willing to accept this. There was a price to pay for all the rich wonders of Provence.

Costa Rica was the antithesis for foreigners who essentially made their own rules or paid to get around existing ones. Like others, we came for freedom and the opportunity to live where there were no measuring sticks or standards. But while the liberty freed some, it destroyed others. The history in the expat community was not pretty by any means. Marriages split, people resorted to the endless amount of cheap cocaine and alcohol, ruined families and tortured souls lined the road like corpses. When people failed, it was on a horrific scale—yet when they succeeded, it was tremendous. Multimillionaires sped around in their fancy SUVs, jockeying the jungle, buying and selling plots of land to those who weren't satisfied with their two-week vacations— to people like us. It was common to make bets on how long people would last when they came to stay longer term. Very few of them made it past the three-month mark. I couldn't help but wonder how we would turn out, whether we might be tempting fate. Taking a sip of my coffee, I pushed the fears away, spying a toucan in the distance. I couldn't imagine things not working.

My first goal was to put together the semblance of a normal life for the family, school being at the top of the list. There were not many options in Manuel Antonio. We could put the children in the local Costa Rican school and have them immediately immersed in the language and life. Had we not just done the same thing in France, I would have taken this route, but I knew it would be too soon to shock the kids like this again. I was proud at how they had integrated in Provence, but to ask them to do the same thing two years later in Spanish seemed overly ambitious and unfair.

The other option was a private school in Quepos, but children were required to have proficiency in Spanish in order to enroll, ruling it out as an option. Michael, a friend of ours who had recently moved his family from New York City to Manuel Antonio, had faced similar school challenges as the other expat families lacking a solution for educating their children. With critical mass to start a small school, Michael set out to launch his own. He hired a teacher and rented a couple of rooms at a nearby hotel. They followed the American curriculum but added basic Spanish for the newcomers. It was all rather loose and relaxed, which of course fitted in easily with the mentality of those moving there. We wanted good education for the children yet valued varied experiences over traditional methods of teaching. This alternative thinking and the fact that we had all made our way to this rather remote spot in the world were commonalities among our families. Michael's school plan sounded decent enough as a starting point, so we decided to go with it.

Over the course of the next several weeks, we strung together a basic life routine. John dove into researching the boat business, securing a loan to do it, and buying a car. After financing and purchasing the boat, he planned on hiring a captain to run it. The coastline near Manuel Antonio was stunning, and while there had long been a simple daily sailboat tour, the area needed something bigger to take larger groups—a catamaran. We had images of sunset trips, with nice wine and local tapas. Our assessment was that it would take about six months to get the boat and captain in place and to secure the permits and insurances. From there, we thought, it would be clear sailing.

I signed up for yoga classes in town and frequented the laid-back Café Milagro at the top of the hill. I befriended Adrienne, a warm and gregarious co-owner of the café from Colorado, who had moved to Costa Rica ten years prior. We were the same age and shared much in common—namely an insatiable passion to explore the world. We would meet at sunrise at the top of the hill, halfway between our house and the café, and jog down to Nature's Beach, chatting about the ups and downs of building a life abroad.

In the afternoons when the kids came home, we found ourselves with vast stretches of empty time, which we mainly spent monkey watching from the balcony. Placing the outdoor teak chairs in strategic positions outside, so we could be comfortable for long periods of time, we would spot three different types of monkeys—howlers, white-faces, and titis. The white-faced monkeys acted like they owned the house, trampling around wherever they wanted, screeching and making mean faces. They just loved to play, taking running leaps onto the big African palm and sliding down its leaves. A myriad insects were admired during any given day—bright-blue cicadas, gigantic grasshoppers, leaf-carrying ants, butterflies ranging from magnetic blue to fiery reds and oranges, and millions of tiny white moths that stuck to the side of the driveway wall. Iguanas of alarming sizes skittered across the road and hid in the bushes. Emma caught toads the size of mutant grapefruits.

We had to move in and out of the house as renters came and went. We were not in a position to turn rent down, given that we were about to launch a new small business. Normally we would move into an inexpensive hotel somewhere on the hill and resume the normal daily activities, yet I began to find the routine mildly disruptive. "God, this is feeling a little familiar," I complained to John one day over breakfast. "Did you ever count the number of places we moved to or lived out of during the weeks that Gancel was rented?"

"Nope, I never bothered," he responded unemotionally. "We chose this wacky lifestyle, and like any, it has its ups and downs. In my mind, there is no room to complain about it." He was right. Displacing the entire family every few weeks was the sacrifice for our life of freedom and adventure, and we were reliving this in Costa Rica, for better or worse.

"Lydia, I've booked a boat ride down in the marina with a fisherman to get a feel for the water and what might be an appropriate route for our catamaran tour," John said one day.

As we waited in the searing sun on the dock for the boat to arrive, a man who ran a fishing-tour operation approached us. "I couldn't help overhearing your discussion about launching a cat tour. You do know that there is another catamaran owner planning on launching its tour in two months," he said matter-of-factly, as he loaded coolers of beer into his boat.

I looked at John. His deep-blue eyes sharpened and looked right through mine. We were speechless.

The fisherman pointed to a mast in the distance. "It's being worked on right over there in that cove."

Disappointment hit us like an unpredicted mistral in Provence—we were in shock. Our confidence in the idea had stemmed from the fact that nobody else was on the radar. There was definitely not enough room in the market for two boats offering the same tour. The tourist market was growing, but it wasn't that robust. "What the fuck?" mumbled John. We walked down the boat ramp and continued to wait for our boat ride, which now seemed utterly pointless.

"I don't know what to say," was all I could muster.

"I do," John said. "We have just moved all the way from Europe for no reason at all."

Later in the day, John went to see this rival cat in the marina, tucked behind a tiny village smelling of fish and rotten mangoes. After John had been gone only a short while, I heard the sound of him skipping up our stone steps. "I found a big boat all right, Lyd—but it's a hunk of shit," he said, panting as he burst through the door. "Someone is fixing it up, but it won't be ready to sail anytime soon." Relieved, he spent the following days surfing the Internet for possible boats to buy, but renewed disappointment settled in as he realized he couldn't afford what he wanted with the budget we had. He knew that if he pushed the limits of this budget with me too much, I would crack. Gancel had been a stretch for us financially, and while it came out beautifully, we had felt the financial strain. I was not excited about taking on another big loan right now.

"This reeks of becoming a huge stress, John...I'm not liking the feeling that we are going to risk everything for a boat. We don't even know how to sail for God's sake," I said.

"The plan is to find a captain, Lydia...don't get off course here. Don't get all dramatic on me now," he spat back. "Besides, there's no wind here—we'll be motoring most of the time anyway."

"I'm not talking about wind, John; I'm talking about security. Look—we have just finished a massive project. Why does everything have to be so big with you...why can't you just think...I don't know...smaller?"

Taking a breath and sliding his body next to mine on the couch, he looked me in the eyes, trying to calm himself and me at the same time. "I've looked at the numbers a hundred times, Lydia. We can bypass getting the loan altogether if we sell this house."

"You have got to be kidding me!" I ranted. "Are you serious? Sell the house! You know I have my heart in the place.

There is nowhere else on earth—well, besides Provence—that I feel so connected to. The thought is just unbearable." Just as the words flew from my mouth, I got a sudden flash, a memory of the sacrifice John had made in selling the house on Lancaster Drive, but I flung the thought away and stormed out, slamming the door behind me. Pounding the ground down to the beach, I finally came to a stop at the water's edge, the ocean breeze slowly sweeping my anger away. After letting my feet sink into the wet sand for half an hour, I came to the conclusion that, somewhere along the line, we had made an unspoken pact between us that no house, no material thing, was going to get in the way of living life to its fullest. I would have to just let it go. Returning to the house I found John staring at the floor. He hadn't moved from the spot on the couch. "OK," I said. "I'm all right with it."

Days crept by, and, despite having come to what felt like a humble compromise, I began to feel a little off. I created a nice little box in my head to house the growing fear, an uneasy, eerie feeling that we were heading down a wrong road. My desire to live an uncomplicated life in Costa Rica where we could connect more with the earth was quietly developing into something far from it. We were, in fact, living in a superficial world with other expatriates, searching for some sort of similar idealized life in the jungle where the focus was on making wild money and living life on the edge. But it seemed there was nothing to do about it but continue to put one foot in front of the other.

Word quickly spread around town that our house was for sale. Hungry and aggressive expat real-estate agents swirled. Within hours, an agent called to show it to some Americans in town, whom he claimed "had coin to drop and were ready to do it." The people walked in, took a quick glance around, and asked how much "she pulled in" in rental income per year. They wanted to buy something ready to make cash. It made my stomach turn. *Don't talk about her like that,* I thought to myself, *like she's a whore.* I screwed up my numbers, subconsciously or on purpose, giving them low figures. They lost interest quickly. Within minutes, I heard the car doors slam and chuckled at the wheels of their SUV spinning as they tried to make it up the wet cement on the hill. Then I cringed at the thought of telling John what I had done.

The weeks crept along, and things became increasing challenging. The realities of daily life in Costa Rica set in. Even our sunset hours at the beach lost their charm when a large German tourist approached me as Nick was changing into his swim trunks behind a tree. Emma had already made her way to the water's edge. "There is a crocodile about two hundred meters away," he said.

We had been hearing about this mysterious croc since we first started coming here several years before. Word was he hung out in a pool of seawater that collected at the end of Nature's Beach road, an entrance to one of the main beaches in the area. I ran there most days with the dog yet had never seen him. We had seen the warning sign on our first trip there but hadn't thought much of it. I was certain the croco-dile story was some fabrication until now. But apparently the croc was indeed very real and was assuming the spot-light. There were rumors that he had eaten six dogs. Locals had captured him and moved him away several times, but he kept coming back. I tucked my new fear of swimming at the beach in my back pocket, along with all my concerns about how life was unfolding in Costa Rica, and headed back home. *How on earth are we going protect ourselves here?* I wondered.

I began to worry about Nick. He seemed to have lost his regular spark and was floundering at school. I wondered if it was the general lack of structure in our lives. Getting him to focus on his schoolwork at home became a constant fight, and the teacher mentioned that his reading was sluggish and that he was quick to be distracted. This news hit us hard, and that horrible wave of concern that we were going to pay the price for moving the children from a good school situation in France washed over me. They were both very happy in Europe, where the system was predictable and structured. Here the materials were sparse and the curriculum all over the map. A newsletter was sent home stating that the school would likely close due to finances. It was run on a shoestring, and they had been in the red for two months. I was quickly reminded that nothing here was for sure, that you could not rely on anything but yourself. Left with no other option, I prepared to consider homeschooling.

It was the wet season, and it rained and rained and rained. Storms came through, and the jungle rumbled incessantly. Everything got wet—things around the house felt damp. All the books and papers curled at the edges, and the cushions on the living room couch had a moist feel. Appliances didn't do well in the climate. The fridge froze all the food we put in it and made a gurgling, digestive sound every time we opened and closed it. The dryer down in the bodega ran nonstop for some reason. We put some towels in it one day, and I found it still running at 8:00 a.m. the following morning. The VCR stopped working, as did the digital cameras and watches. The humidity even warped John's beloved new guitar. But the rain wrought more significant havoc—it brought dengue fever. The boat broker John had been working with came down with it. The broker admitted that he had just been joking with some buddies that the fear of dengue was completely hyped up, that nobody ever got it. He now claimed he had never in his lifetime felt so awful.

More unsettling events continued to occur. Adrienne jogged me by the house that her friends had been building. Wandering in and out of the work site, we chatted about the great view and what a neat house it would be when it was soon finished. Later that week, after lots of rain, we jogged by again, but the house was no longer standing. Only a few stray cinder blocks remained. "Ade...where is the house?" I asked.

"It slipped down the hill in the night," she said.

John lived on the Internet, shopping for boats. Each day he paced, pined, and picked at his eyebrows, a sure sign he was stressed. He found potentials in Jamaica, California, and Australia. We looked into the horrific price to ship a boat from Brisbane to Costa Rica. If it was the right boat it would be worth it, but the whole thing was starting to take its toll on me, the undertaking weighing heavily.

Renters had booked our house last minute for two weeks, so we needed to quickly find a place to live. I searched for a hotel, but at the last hour, Michael let us cheaply rent one of his luxury homes conveniently located right behind ours. Off we went again, packing up the green suitcases, emptying the fridge, collecting books, markers, and small toys—stuffing them into the children's backpacks. I was getting good at this and could complete the packing up in a matter of hours, but I was tiring of it.

As we settled into Casa Verde, I finally forced myself to accept that things were not going well. I was experiencing a deep sense of homelessness, as if we were a soaring kite flying unconnected to a string—floating from place to place. I gazed at Nick and Em, at their unsettling lack of reaction to moving around. Casa Verde was a stunning house with vaulted ceilings, wild furniture, a game room, two pools, and a million other cool details, but I noticed as we moved in that the kids were unfazed. They didn't ask how long we would be there or where they would sleep. They just plunked themselves down and hunted for paper to do coloring. Thankfully our sense of being together as a family provided some comfort, but I was starting to question whether it was enough to sustain us.

I picked up the phone and attempted to call England to reach my sister. Deep relief swept over me as she picked up right away—the sound of her voice was enough to send me into a sobbing mess. Gripping the phone and dragging it to a bedroom where I could hide my sorry state from the children, I sat on the floor with my back to the door and began to admit to her all that was happening. "It is all too much,

Helene. I am tired of moving around, tired of making new friends, tired of not knowing what the future will look like or where we will be from one month to the next," I sobbed. I admitted it was becoming eternally frustrating to not have a home because our homes had become rental businesses and not homes. I spared her the details of Manuel Antonio, the dengue, mudslides, crocodiles, and drug abuse. Sharing that would mean confessing that my beloved freedom was now becoming maddening, my worst enemy. Taking a breath, I waited for her words of wisdom, her sage advice that I could always count on. Feeling the lump in my throat tighten, I readied myself to fess up to her, to admit that the worst part of it all was that I had created this—we had chosen it. There was nobody to blame but ourselves. Then the phone line suddenly went dead—the power had gone out.

Things spiraled from there. I started to lose sleep, worrying about everything. *Where are we going to live while our house is rented for the tourist season? How can I get myself organized enough to homeschool? Why are all these people, friends of ours, numbing themselves day in and day out with their self-destructive habits? Will the boat business work? Should I be worrying about dengue fever? Will the kids be attacked by the croc at the beach or swept away by the deathly undertow? How will I manage when John is in Australia? How can a house simply slip down the hill overnight?*

Control over our lives was slowly slipping through my fingers. I needed to get myself together, and fast. I tried to find solace in yoga, drowning myself in the music and incense, the sweat dripping from our bodies and the tick-ticking of the old ceiling fan. I was finding my own way to numb myself. Our experiences in Costa Rica were becoming an endless series of dichotomies, good and evil sitting side by side: tremendous success and haunting failure, beautiful nature and rampant addiction—the enormity of the dripping, growing, crawling expanse of the jungle and the destruction and greed of development. We had all come in awe of the land, but so many just couldn't stop themselves there. They had to have it, to own it, to squeeze it so hard there was nothing left of it or themselves in the end. It was becoming too hard to stand witness between the forces. To be a part of this. This wasn't at all what I had been searching for. *Wrong road, Lydia. Wrong fucking road.*

One night I sat in the bath staring at a flickering candle, hoping to ease the weight of my anxiety. I found my mind wandering to when we lived in Orlando, to our clean house with polished wood floors and a white picket fence. Everything I had wanted to escape then I now dreamed to have back, if only for one minute, long enough to savor the comforts of normality, predictability. That horrible word I had loathed—*security*—rang in my ears. It was everything that life was not right now. Nothing was sure anymore. Our safety, health, house, education, and finances were all at risk. Everything could unravel at any moment. But as I stared at the wax dripping down the side of the candle, pooling on the natural stone that surrounded the bath, my thoughts wandered back to the temples in Cambodia. Breathing in the moist bath air, I remembered the deep sense of peace—the profound, spiritually grounding comfort I had felt. I remembered how it had pulsated from the earth, into my feet, up my body, and through my head. So powerful, so endless, so beyond anything that I ever found in a place or thing, and there was no need to worry if it had a beginning or an end. Opening my eyes, I knew that it was not my life in Orlando that I needed back. Neither a house on the hill nor a business of any sort was going to give me the sense of comfort, the sense of purpose, I was searching for. It was time to listen to the messages, to trust that within me I had access to all that I needed on my journey.

One morning after yoga, I asked John if he would consider the unthinkable: throwing in the towel, accepting defeat in a game where the stakes were too high. "John... what are your thoughts about going home?" I said, bracing myself for his reaction. And the funny thing was, I didn't even know where I was referring to as *home*. I was deathly afraid of what his reaction would be. All of the months of planning, not to mention the months of actually being here, had added up to an enormous effort on his part. I couldn't imagine him feeling OK about leaving it all.

"I would consider it," he said rather easily, as if he was just waiting for me to come out with it. I could feel that, somewhere deep down in him, he wanted to quit the game too. It was a challenge we did not have to overcome, a game we did not have to win, a game we didn't even need to play. We could walk away.

The whole thing had become unsavory, like a party gone bad—one where everyone has had too much to drink, has said too much. The kind where you wake up and wish you had stayed home curled up by the fire with a book. And while perhaps you hadn't done anything too wrong, you had been a part of it and had made no effort to leave when you should have.

Over dinner at our favorite restaurant, nestled under a canopy of jungle growth, we made it final to leave Costa Rica. The following morning we told the kids. Within minutes, the spark that made Nick whole returned, and a grin spread wide between his sweet flushed cheeks. The rest was a blur and flurry of making plans, changing flights, and packing. We told all of our friends, and none were too surprised. I thought back to all of the comments that were made when we first arrived, all the doubts expressed that we would be able to make it there. How I had thought it crazy that there would be something we couldn't muscle through.

It was strange that we never considered moving back to the States. I don't remember it ever being a consideration. France fell into place as if we had never left, like Costa Rica had all been a long, consuming dream. Not long after our return to France, we sold the house in Manuel Antonio, and I spent days crying over the loss of something I couldn't quite put my finger on. For years it had represented my escape from reality, yet the previous months had only been a brutal reminder of the pointlessness of such an escape. I had wanted freedom, and that was just what I had found— but there were limits to this personal liberty I so sought and cherished. I cannot say truthfully that leaving Costa Rica did not feel like a failure, because it did, and we had never truly failed at anything. But I also knew that, with my little ones at my side, this was not the time to test fate.

We boarded the plane from Costa Rica realizing the profound value of finding a place to call home and knowing there were infinite merits to predictability in one's life and in that of a family. Life was not to be played with. There were more important things to do. These were the small but important lessons we took home with us. Despite this mix of emotions, I was incredibly thankful for the opportunity to have experienced what we did during our time in Costa Rica, to have made our mistakes. It reinforced that if you have the courage to venture out, life will greet you at the doorstep, and if you have the faith to trust it, it would safely guide you to the next place.

9

Old Stones

When it is quiet, the mind returns to its cause.
Patrick Levy

Vernègues, France
Fall 2003

I woke up surrounded by the serenity of the cool stone walls tucked into the breast of Provence. A chilly autumn wind pushed itself against the windowpanes. I had dreamed that we had lost everything we had, our house, possessions, savings—no doubt born out of lingering fears from our experience in Costa Rica. In my dream, the material loss was both liberating and frightening. Liberating in the sense that the houses we had owned had given us a false sense of security—had anchored and burdened us—yet I was frightened and unsure of what was there if we took it all away.

Later that morning, Nick stated loudly from the adjoining room, "Mom, there is more life than money."

"What...?" I said. I considered my dream, still unleashed from my private world. I remained quiet for a moment, wondering to myself whether I had actually heard what he had said correctly—what an uncanny coincidence. Then I wondered whether perhaps he meant to say, "There is more *to* life than money." But he repeated himself again, several times, as if struggling with the words himself. He kept saying it over and over and over.

"There is more life than money. There is more life than money."

I slowly walked into the room where he was and found him lying on the floor gazing up at the ceiling, the faint morning light flickering on his pink cheek, a Zorro figurine dangling from his hand.

"What do you mean exactly?" I asked as I stood dumbfounded.

"You see, Mom, there are three things. The first is that there is more life than money. The second thing is that money is just to play. The third," he said, pausing a moment, "is that life is better than money. And by the way...you don't use any money in heaven. Only your sweet manners."

I stood motionless, paralyzed. How could a seven-year-old come by such thoughts? Had he heard this on TV? Was he repeating something he had heard from an adult? But over the course of the day, even the weeks that followed, I realized it didn't matter. I was going to be better about heeding the messages I was getting from the universe. His statements had the weight of revelation at that moment in time, even though I struggled to understand the exact truth in his words.

Returning to France represented another major shift for us as a family. For once, we had a genuine desire to settle, take root somewhere. We actually felt the urge to have a normal life, whatever that meant, and to become part of a community. Given this was everything I had run from a few years back, I figured I had either lost my mind or found my center. Since leaving Orlando, we had mused over where home was going to be, and committing ourselves to Provence simply felt right. The kids returned to school, tucking themselves into the cozy stone building of the École Maternelle at the foot of the ancient village in Vernègues, alongside a hundred other children from the surrounding hills and valley. I desperately needed to nest after close to three years of moving about, and as precious as Gancel was to me, it was still our livelihood, one that meant renting and moving out of for months at a time. So with the money we had in hand from the sale of the Costa Rica house, we began the search for a new place to live, one that would be just ours that we could settle into when we had to be out of Gancel.

We looked at real estate through the dreary winter months, at everything from rundown barns to dark, lifeless village houses. Real estate in Provence had skyrocketed, as it had in the United States, and even abandoned *cabanons* were now selling for a fortune. Then there was the issue of our natural opposing forces, John being drawn to larger renovation projects and me wanting a small, simple place to unpack the green suitcases we had been living out of for what seemed like an eternity. We settled somewhere in the middle, finding a reasonably sized and priced *maison de village* tucked into the heart of Alleins, a quiet village at the base of the hill adjacent to Vernègues, only five minutes from Gancel.

The house sat on the main street that ran through the heart of the old village. It faced the post office and stood directly next to the *alimentation/tabac* store where everyone came for their daily packs of cigarettes and general grocery items. It was two doors down from the hairdresser and around the corner from three bread shops, a butcher, and a café/bar that got very rowdy on Friday nights. I was thrilled because it seemed manageable both financially and in terms of its size. John's pleasure came from the fact that it was four hundred years old and in a complete state of ruin. Essentially, it was a heap with potential. Everyone thought we were crazy to buy this pile of stones—it had been uninhabited for over forty years. It sat in a row of houses along a street with no outdoor space for the children, no pool or terrace during the hot summer months. After the death of the boat business, it was just what John needed to fill the void that Costa Rica had left, so we welcomed another challenge. This one, I hoped, had a home attached.

For the next eight months, John pulled on his grubby clothes and worked day by day alongside Denis, the mason we had hired, learning the ropes—what would be an intense *apprentissage* in everything from plastering to plumbing and electrics. Atypical for a mason in Provence, Denis worked almost constantly, seven days a week, only stopping for cigarettes, the odd pastis, or whole dark chocolate bars, which he ate by the pound. Rail thin from days of physical work with little food, his body appeared worn, but his eyes always revealed a man with an unwavering zest for life. Through the cold, wet, overcast winter months with the treacherous mistral winds blowing, John and Denis spent almost every waking hour together in the damp *chantier*, or work site, surrounded by dust and crumbling house.

While they worked, Denis taught John the intricacies of French grammar, something John had failed to digest during our first years in France. I often thought of what an odd combination they made. John, a born-and-bred American with a fire in his belly, an oftentimes impatient man who salivated at the thought of business opportunity, working alongside a patient and tranquil mason who delighted in the slow cut and build. But they were both *bons vivants*, men who lived life to the fullest, loving laughter and apéritifs, and thriving on hard work and precision. At noon they would walk side by side down the brick streets to the Café du Commerce for pizzas, *sandwichs poulet mayo,* or the plat du jour and a cold *pression* or two, covered head to toe in dust that puffed out from various places as they moved. They would chat away like two old women, chuckling about this and that, discussing politics and their progress on the *chantier*.

As we labored away restoring this village house on the Rue de La République in Alleins, across from the post office and a trickling fountain, we let ourselves sink deep into our Provençal life. The long days of renovations were peppered with visits with our friends Louise and Gilles, Gary and Fiona, Charlotte, Eric, Yael, Frank, and all of their children, who mucked in with our kids, playing tag in between the rows of vines until midnight as all of the parents shared the week's happenings.

In the process of renovating, we managed to enrage neighbors on every side of us. The dust from our project lined the shelves of the store next door, and the poor lady who ran the shop suffered with terrible allergies that were exacerbated by our dust-making work—dust covered all of her inventory. The two old ladies to our other side sent a letter to the *mairie*, the town hall, requesting all work to be stopped because we had installed windows that overlooked their rooftop—impinging on their privacy, they protested. What if our children decided to climb out and wander on their roof? And it was no small detail that the dust from our project nearly killed all of the plants that they so carefully tended to in the pots outside their front door.

As we chiseled and banged away inside our house, walls cracked and crumbled on the other sides, in the homes of all our adjacent neighbors. Seeing how hard John worked, the neighboring *provencaux* forgave the missteps. When he made the rounds with armfuls of wine and chocolate, and a very expensive bottle of Scotch for the ladies with dead plants, and after he promised to clean up dust and redo walls in their homes, all was forgiven over an apéritif.

Some days I would join John and Denis, and they would set me up with what seemed like easier, more manageable projects. "The whole section of stone needs to be scraped clean of years of plaster, Lydia, then regrouted," John stated one day. With a mason's pick, I began to chip off plaster along a wall hundreds of years old. Sometimes the ancient plaster crumbled off easily, making neat little mountains around my feet on the cracked terra cotta tile. Other areas of the wall took several minutes to chip through a mere square inch. Beneath the plaster lay stones we wanted to expose, *pierres apparentes*—beautiful, rugged, everyday Provençal stones that were as common as baguettes and wine.

For several weeks, I worked on my wall, carefully scraping out all of the hard earth and old grout in between the stones. At times I couldn't tell what was stone and what was just ancient mud or concrete. So I would chip more, scrape more, feel with my hands where it crumbled, where it didn't. The ticking clock became irrelevant through the chipping, scraping, brushing, and breathing. Then slowly, as if out of darkness, the shape of a stone would emerge, protruding proudly and firmly, and I would feel like a mother who had just birthed a baby. With a tiny hand brush and archeologist's conscience, I would brush away the remaining dust and dirt all around the stones, its deep pores now free of mud and glowing a mixture of soft yellows with traces of rich ochre. During those moments, there would be nothing more important than these stones, their texture on my fingers, the freshness they exuded, their faint, cool odor of earth. At the end of the day, I would stand back with dust in my ears, nose, and hair and admire my treasured *pierres,* wondering what they had withstood over their lifetime. Then I headed to the elementary school to pick up the children looking quite a sight.

We lost ourselves in the dusty monotony of the tedious stonework before us while the kids were at school. But my

work on the stone walls paled in comparison to the efforts
John and Denis made during the Alleins renovation. Day
after day for months on end, John single-handedly lugged
thirty-five metric tons of sand and cement up and down
the four flights of stairs in buckets by hand, and equally
as many tons of old rubble out. It was a backbreaking job.
Looking back, I see that it made the renovation of Gancel
seem like a walk in the park. He spent unfathomable hours
on his back on rickety scaffolding, sanding the traditional
wooden-plank ceilings and beams. He ended his days with
a thick layer of muck on his clothes and skin, sometimes
with only the whites of his eyes showing. But there was
an unmistakable contentedness underneath all that dust,
one that I hadn't seen since his days of mowing lawns or
redoing Gancel. It seemed as though the house was literally
drawing us in, tempting us to lose ourselves in the process
of doing something instead of just getting something done.
I was now beginning to see Provence as a wise and mature
old woman, bent on teaching us sacred secrets if we were
willing to stop and listen.

Occasionally we noticed the Alleins townsfolk slowing down as they walked by the house to get a peek at the
transformation. With baguettes tucked tightly under their
arms, they marveled at the sight of a young foreigner dirty
in work clothes, oozing the energy they once had. The
house that had stood uninhabited for nearly half a decade,
with its cracked and faded brown shutters hanging precariously from old hinges, now began a new phase of its life. We
threw the windows open despite the cold; through clouds
of billowing construction dust and the sounds of screeching power tools, the villagers peered up from the street to

admire our *pierres* standing proudly with new grout. From the road, they could see the golden-colored wood in the traditional Provençal ceilings emitting the cozy warmth that only ancient things can exude.

"*Qu'il travaille comme un fou* (crazy man), *cet Americain.*" Word had it that villagers were shocked by the intensity with which John and Denis worked. We knew from having redone Gancel that foreigners weren't known to get themselves so dirty—they didn't normally mix and shovel their own grout. Americans renovated in the South of France but rarely themselves. For us there was something hidden in the muck of mixing this concrete, a cryptic lesson in the time it took to do it. This work involved something you just couldn't contract out.

Everyone on the street had to comment on our choice of colors for the shutters. "*C'est trop clair* (too light)*!*" they cried.

"*Oo la la, trop foncé* (too dark)."

"*Un peu sombre n'est-ce pas* (a little somber), *no?*"

After four tries and several hundred euros in wrong colors of paint, we settled on one that everyone in the village seemed to be happy with.

And while the villagers enjoyed stopping to ask what it was that brought us to renovate in this relatively unknown village in Provence, what they really loved to do was share their own life stories. A old man who walked almost folded over with age and had no more than two teeth remaining always lingered to recount magnificent stories of his days herding sheep from the ports of Marseille to the peaks of the Alps. And there was Madame Chaix, proud and always magnificently put together despite her age, who extended her shaky pointed finger and nostalgically recounted her days living in what was now our house. She was a shameless gossip and a hoot to chat with, giving us all of the village dirt.

In between renovating the Alleins house, we managed the day-to-day of the villa business, checking guests, who were mainly from the United States, into Gancel. Greeting the renters provided a connection to our own culture that I have to admit we missed and found comfort in at times. Heads would take wild spins from left to right as renters tumbled from their cars, exhausted from their travels across the ocean. We could sense their amazement and heightened curiosity as they absorbed their new surroundings—the house, the lavender, the vineyard—what would be their home base for a week or two as they explored the area.

I was often still winded from helping the maids clean the bathrooms between the groups, and while I welcomed the newest batch of visitors, my mind would whirl, wondering whether I had remembered to put the last load of towels in the dryer. Noting how young we were at the time, most probed, some discreetly and others not so discreetly, as to how we came to renovate a farmhouse in France. Somewhere along the line, moving to Provence had been packaged as something you did after you had finished your professional life, when you had retired and were ready to sit back with a nice glass of wine and enjoy the beauty in things. You didn't do it in your youth as we had, with young children and schools to consider and 401(k) retirement accounts to think about.

When the days got shorter and the fall weather brought a nip to the air, the American tourists would go home—and so would we, back to Gancel. Slowly, we reconnected with another way of life, one that was a little more tranquil and private than life in the village. The house that was, for summer months, filled with strangers on holiday once again became our intimate hideaway. Emma wandered in the vineyard picking wildflowers, and Nick took off on his bike or played with makeshift swords in his make-believe world.

We made the rounds around the house, fixing things that had been broken during the season and enjoying the last warm days on the terrace. Friends and neighbors came over, and together we would handpick the grapes in the vineyard and then shuttle them to the cooperative, crossing fingers for a good production. When the leaves on the vines turned golden and dropped, we closed and padlocked the pool and put the garden chairs away, marking the end of our season.

As the renovation in Alleins came to a close, I thought back on John's first year in France, spent virtually in silence due to the language barrier. And now, only four years after leaving a busy professional life in America, he was completely immersed in Provence life, satisfied by friendships and projects in the vineyard, in the house, in the community. Completely at ease with the language, the culture, and a career switch from business to masonry, he was a walking example of the goodness you can gain by chipping away at old stones, by stepping out of your life and opening yourself up to another.

Life was strangely beginning to feel settled—a word I had run from for so long. I was perhaps finally making amends with the concept, feeling very fortunate for the richness in our daily lives. Out of the blue I felt a familiar grain of guilt return, my old friend from Lancaster Drive. But thankfully this time it didn't last—there was too much goodness in helping others enjoy, explore and soak in Provence. Life was showing me in its own strange way that there was so much more joy, so much more satisfaction in sharing whatever it was that made us happy, what we found genuine passion and beauty in, than in keeping those things for ourselves. At the time, I didn't know that these were the seeds for the next major stage in our lives. There was still a year between that moment and the day the fevered girl at Reaching Stars Orphanage would slip herself onto my lap, and two years before life would bring a new blessing into our family. For the time being, the universe was leaving me the crumb path that I would just have to follow.

10

A Plane Ride Away

It is remarkably easy to do things, and much more
frightening to contemplate them.
Ted Simon

"Lydia—have you ever read *City of Joy* by Dominique Lapierre?" Louise said to me one day as we panted up the steep rocky path at Caire Val.

"City of what?" I responded.

"I cannot believe you have not read it," she said. "You must. Just get it."

Louise knew all too well that my visions of India were like old friends. They had been around since my schooldays, and, like John, she was probably wondering when on earth I was just going to act on what was already deep in my soul. Over the course of the following weeks, I read *City of Joy*, its oftentimes sickening, unfathomable accounts of daily life in the slums of Calcutta, and in turning each page, I could feel my heart beat faster. Alongside the putrid smells of open sewers and leper villages was something nobody quite imagined would be there—joy. By the end of the book, the pages in the middle were falling out like leaves on an autumn tree. I would desperately pick them up, knowing they held some of the deep truths that I longed to understand more.

Funny that it was John who managed to take that first step. I was sitting on the big couch at Gancel, huddled in a blanket next to the fire, watching *BBC News*, when I saw an ad for Incredible India tourism. Flowing saris and images of the Taj Mahal flashed across the screen. "John, we have been to so many places around the world, and yet I have never been to the one place I have been dreaming about my whole life. How is this possible?"

He turned his back to me and walked over the bookshelf that housed all of my precious books. Returning to the couch, he got down on one knee, just as he had done on the day he asked me to marry him, and he handed me three guidebooks on India. "Happy anniversary," he said, grinning ear to ear.

"What?" I said, dumbfounded, unable to catch my breath.

"Well, first of all, I wanted to allow ourselves the honeymoon we had never had. And secondly, it was time you realized that India is only a plane ride away. I have watched you help plan some amazing experiences for us as a family, some that have required some pretty decent risks. We have moved across the ocean two times, but I often wonder why you have never booked that one trip that holds a key to something important for you," he said.

He had a point. It was strange that I had avoided going directly to India, a place that I knew already was somehow fundamental in my life learning. Later I would be able to see it in other people—that reluctance, that downright avoidance, that fear of taking a step they knew they needed to take. They would fight, sometimes until the very end, to not give in to it.

John had planned everything, from arranging for my sister Helene to come from London to watch the children, to organizing every step of our journey through India's Golden Triangle—New Delhi, Agra, and Jaipur—silently and lovingly organizing a ten-day journey. We arrived at the Marseille airport, holding hands and feeling giddy like we were fifteen again. When the lady at the check-in counter asked for a copy of our Indian tourist visas, I watched as the blood rushed out of John's face. In all of his arranging, he had forgotten one thing—the visas required to enter the country. I didn't even have the words to complain; I was shocked. In a crazy panic to get control over his mistake, John decided to get us at least to Frankfurt, where he was sure we could secure a quick visa at the embassy. The airline attendant looked at us with a doubtful grin and checked our bags. We spent the following two days at the embassy in Germany begging, pleading, and making endless phone calls to the Indian embassy in New York to secure last-minute visas. Some unknown blessed person, whom I am still thankful for today, made it happen. At the end of day two in Germany, we were handed our visas, and off we went.

For the remaining seven days, we meandered through the vivid, living streets of a place I had spent the better part of my life envisioning. We gazed at temples from the backs of intricately painted elephants and sipped Darjeeling tea at the Imperial Hotel. We sauntered through the intricately marbled Taj at sunset, stunned at its beauty.

But as much as the trip was surreal and exotic, the images I had held of India had been of a different kind. I knew that to know only the aesthetically beautiful parts of India was to not know her at all. In my heart, I knew I needed to learn of her pungent and bitter profile, her extremes, her poverty. And somewhere deep down, I had a gut feeling that I had to work within it.

India was now calling me from the very depths of who I was. All of my searching for freedom and all of my need to travel, to get away, had to do with this. A short six months after returning from our anniversary trip, I found myself in the whirlwind of India's breast again, this time teaching English to my sweet fourth and fifth grade students and sipping tea from make-believe cups with the girls at Reaching Stars Orphanage. From there, the ground underneath me would shift, and the following chapters of my life would unfold.

11

Falling for Isabelle

We are the mountains we must cross.
Marty Rubin

At the time, I didn't see the India trip as the precursor to adopting Isabelle, but now, looking back, I see that the two are so inextricably linked. Chennai opened doors in my heart I never knew existed. It was as though the little girl with the fever who had fallen asleep in my lap had brought me a silent message. I tried as best as I could after the trip to pick up my life where it had left off, but I felt something wasn't complete; a piece was missing that I simply couldn't put my finger on.

One day while on a run, I was admiring the tidy rows of vineyards—and the next minute, I was imagining adopting a child. It was as though the choice had already been made. Over baguette sandwiches one afternoon, I informed John that I felt it was time to adopt a child. Smiling, he said, "I thought you would never ask."

I will forever have this image of the four of us huddled around the computer on the kitchen table in the village house, each of us intently looking at pictures of children, mostly babies and toddlers from China. The mood was serious as we advanced through the files. Some of the children had gaping cleft-palate holes in their faces, while others had club feet and hands, Hepatitis B, epilepsy, heart problems—the list went on. But they all had important things in common—a need to be loved, a wish to wake up to a mother and a father, and a right to a future that was safe and bright.

The idea to adopt was somehow collective. It was true that I had been carrying a burning desire for another child. I was one of those women who secretly coveted the babies at the grocery store. Nick and Emma fed the fury—they wanted a little one too and urged me on, baited me, tempted me however they could. "Oh, Mom, look at these sweet little socks. Mom, come look at this baby," Emma would say.

They would constantly remind me that they would be old enough to babysit—I would have so much help, and it would be a cinch, they insisted. And if I allowed myself to forget about the idea, they forced it to resurface at every turn. It went on like this for a couple of years: me pushing away the thought of getting pregnant with another baby, yet somehow the idea returning with greater force. As I came back from India, the concept of a third child transformed and broadened, and I found myself wondering about adoption. It somehow finally felt right to me, and the other members of the family were as willing to go this route as I was. Whatever had been blocking me seemed to have been removed.

Questions then tumbled into my world rapid-fire. Where should we begin, which country should we consider, would we choose a boy or a girl? We were an American family living in France. Would this pose problems in the process—would it be more difficult? Slowly, after we combed Internet sites for long hours, the details became clearer. Many Americans, especially military families living abroad, successfully adopted every year with little extra hassle. There were international adoption lawyers to help with the legalities and English-speaking social workers in different countries to conduct the home studies. Then I searched hundreds of sites managing adoption services in order to find the most reputable. I made calls to several, and at least two raised concerns over our living abroad. Then I contacted Children's House International (CHI), an agency used to dealing with expatriate families. I spoke with several women who headed up different programs, and all of them seemed full of information and knowledge. I would later learn that they had their own special stories to tell—many had adopted children themselves over the years and knew firsthand the trials and frustrations of the process. In wanting to guide other families through the grueling process, they had individually founds jobs at the agency. Comfortable with having found the right organization, we next needed to choose a program, in essence choosing a country from which to adopt. Many programs had had problems due to governmental concern over evidence of baby trafficking. At the time, Cambodia, Vietnam, and Guatemala were under great scrutiny. Russia and other eastern European countries had well-established programs but had higher risks than other countries when it came to fetal alcohol syndrome.

I kept returning to China, as it appeared to represent a stable, predictable, well-established process. Unfathomable numbers of baby girls were being left abandoned due to China's one-child rule, implemented in 1979 to curb population growth. Boys were preferred over girls, as they could carry on the family name and provide a better means of supporting their parents. I started looking at photos of the Chinese children who had been adopted by other families and began having visions of my own sweet bundle. Soon after, we took the plunge and entered into what was referred to as the "Traditional Program for Healthy Babies." The agency told us to expect an eight- to ten-month period of "paper chasing." Then, on one special unknown day, we would be matched with a baby, most likely somewhere around twelve months old.

During our wait process, CHI encouraged us to have a look at the files of waiting children, those who fell outside the category of "healthy." I don't remember when it was or how far into the process we were before we looked at that file, but I can tell you it wasn't immediate—the image in my mind of my sweet bundle was perfectly healthy. But one day, I threw the question out to John, if anything maybe looking for reassurance that we would be wise not to take the risk. "What do you think about the idea of considering a child with special needs?"

But without a second's thought, he responded, "Oh, you know me. I would take any of them. They all need to be loved. I don't care what they have wrong with them."

It was so clear and simple for him. I was stunned and silent.

Quietly I started to peek at the files of waiting children, and eventually the faces of these sweet children, who had for some universal reason been asked to face incredibly tough challenges, crept their way into my dreams at night and sat on my shoulders during the day. All it had taken was for John to spurt out these simple and courageous words for the door in my heart to creak open just a bit farther. It was then that my perfectly formed image of my bundle started to transform. It now took the form a three-year-old child without a hand, or a two-year-old girl born with an eye closed shut, or an eleven-month-old with a malformed leg. I approached the matter delicately with Nick and Emma, who were not even eight and ten years old. While they were open to the idea of a child with medical needs, I don't think they knew what exactly that entailed, and I am sure that the photos they looked at were not what they had initially imagined for a brother or sister. But they were very brave, and together we walked through each file, painfully admitting to one another what we could and couldn't manage.

I was intrigued from the minute I set my eyes on Zhuang Luzi. There was an agelessness about this mysterious child who stood so stout and proud in her pictures, as if to let everyone know the strength of her spirit and the hope in her heart. At eight months old, she showed barely a hint of a smile, was bundled in a worn sweater and had a clearly deformed leg. But something about her images revealed a child who was ready to live life to the fullest. We all agreed to request more information on her medical file. Born on February 6, 2005, she was abandoned on the steps of the YiFeng Orphanage in Jiangxi, China, on March 9, only a few weeks after her birth, with only the clothes on her back and a note in her pocket with her birth date. She was born with fibular hemimelia, a congenital disease causing a missing fibula in her right leg. The missing bone causes a shortening of the leg and stunts the growth of the foot and toes. Zhuang Luzi was described as having a small limb difference and missing two toes on the right foot.

In general, the details we received from her file were vague and few. There were no X-rays, exact measurements on the difference between her limbs, or information on her mobility. I dove headfirst into researching hemimelia and limb differences. The net sum of my findings was that the method of treatment depended on the exact length of the difference. If it was slight, she could wear a shoe lift and function normally. If it was significant, attempts could be made to lengthen the limb, sometimes a long and painful process. The alternative to limb lengthening would be amputation. The word shot through me like a bullet. I wasn't quite sure I was prepared for that.

As I dove further into the medical findings, I discovered a rather heated and ongoing controversy over which method of treatment was best. While amputation seemed extreme, a child could be up and fully functioning with the use of a prosthesis from an early age. From eighteen months, she could begin a normal, active childhood. The benefit of limb lengthening, on the other hand, was that the child could keep her leg and foot and, over the course of several operations, regain the difference in length. The downsides to this approach were that it involved many painful procedures throughout childhood, resulted in a leg that would be severely scarred, and that it promised only uncertain final results at the end of all the effort.

This was all so much to digest at the outset. Within a short period of time, I had gone from perusing adoption sites and dreaming of babies to researching infant amputations. But I kept returning to her photos—over and over. Something in her eyes spoke to me, and I just had to proceed. Whatever she needed to go through, we would go through with her. The agency informed us that when we felt sure, we could petition to adopt her. If there were no other families petitioning, then, barring any complications with our dossier, she could be ours. *Ours,* I thought—somewhere deep down, I questioned the meaning of this term and whether it would be that simple.

It was all happening so quickly, as if out of my control— yet I knew it was completely within our control to proceed or not to proceed. But strangely without any further thought, we sent off the petition, and within hours I had a return e-mail from the agency:

Mrs. Dean,
I am pleased you have reached the point that you understand the risks and long-term possibilities of having her as your daughter. We have changed her status to "My

family has found me." Congratulations, she now has a family, and it is YOU!

I jumped for joy, screeched, and cried. Plaster dropped in clumps from the ceiling below us in our ancient village house in Alleins. Zhuang Luzi had found her home. The enormity of it—what this meant for her, and what this meant for us—was baffling. The kids and John were at choir practice in Aix and wouldn't be home for hours. Not knowing what to do with my energy, I rushed to the store and bought the makings for a party, along with a photo frame and a precious pink dress that would hang on my bedroom doorknob for almost a whole year until she came home. In the middle of the table, I placed her photo and a single blooming red bromeliad that would take the place of our growing flower in China, one that we would tend to each day as we waited. When John and the kids returned, I shared the news. Together we named our sweet girl Isabelle Luzi, and from that evening on our family had grown. We were no longer a family of four. Somewhere thousands of miles away in an orphanage in Jiangxi, China, was a child who had already found her way into our hearts.

Then we waited and we waited. For months on end. Nobody can prepare you for that horrible, grueling wait. It's like giving birth to a baby that you aren't allowed to see. I wanted to crawl out of my skin—I wanted to scream and pull my hair out. It was all completely out of our control, and there was only one thing to do. Wait. All I could think of was Zhuang Luzi living in Lord-only-knew what conditions. Was she being properly cared for, held, loved? I read horror stories on the psychological effects of early childhood institutionalization and the resulting attachment disorders. We had been told that special-needs children took a fast track through the acceptance process, but for some unknown reason, there were serious slowdowns within the China Center for Adoption Affairs in China. Acceptances were only trickling out.

But one morning at the end of the summer, that long-awaited e-mail arrived, giving us formal travel approval from the Chinese government to go and pick up Isabelle. I flew to New York and met my mother, and together we flew to Beijing, then on to Nanchang, where we joined John. Three weeks after receiving that e-mail and only twenty-four hours after landing in China, we heard a knock at our door, and we knew that finally our wait was over.

Nanchang, China
Fall 2006

When you give birth to your own children, you have memories of a particular moment when your child arrives. It's a private, treasured moment that marks the beginning of that child's life and yours being inexplicably entwined from then on. As I would learn, adoptions are a very different experience. Never would we be able to compare biological birth with adoption. They are separate experiences with separate journeys altogether. With Isabelle, that special moment came as I opened the door after hearing the knock. A wave of emotions swept over me all at once—relief, joy, and pain for what I knew was going to be an extremely difficult day for her. The head caretaker from the orphanage carried her in her arms and sat on the edge of the bed. Isabelle looked stunned and listless, her eyes slightly crossed. At nine-teen months, she looked nothing like the strong child in the pictures. She was small, weak, and pale, and I wanted more than anything to take her in my arms, to let her know everything was going to be fine. But we weren't allowed to just yet. More waiting was required. We had been told only to observe, to use the initial time while she was calm with the caretaker and the translator to ask questions about her. It might, they said, be our only opportunity to learn about what she liked, what she ate, what her routine had been, whether she had been sick. Considering that we knew noth-ing about her past whatsoever and that we were not allowed to visit the orphanage where she spent the first year and a half of her life, these few minutes of information gathering were more than important.

I pulled out my carefully put-together list of questions and, with shaking hands, tried my best to focus on them, but my eyes kept returning to Isabelle. She looked as though she had shut down entirely, her slight little body slumped and still. We asked about her foot and whether she was mobile.

"Oh, yes," they said emphatically. "She goes all over very, very fast."

John and I looked at each other with some relief. Her condition couldn't be that bad.

When they finally left, I took her in my arms while she sobbed fearfully. It wasn't a violent scream or cry. It was more like a moan from deep inside her, a primal, haunt-ing moan. Then she did just as I was told she would do.

Overcome by shock, she cried herself to sleep. I sat in that dark, humid hotel room with my sleeping baby in my arms and felt time nearly stop. The long, grueling wait was over, she had found a home, and I was never letting go. I breathed in the smell of her milky skin, still wet from crying. That sweet scent was uniquely different and foreign to me, and I couldn't get enough of it. I wanted to drink in that smell. Somewhere in my body, my mother instinct was registering it into my very being. I stroked her forehead and prayed that I would have the strength to give her all that she needed, to fill whatever holes she might have. I pledged to give her every ounce of love I had in me.

After she woke up, she remained calm yet was still clearly scared. She looked around the room with little reaction. I sat her on the bed and peeled off all of her clothes, her little blue socks, and her tattered shoes. Pulling off the turtleneck she was wearing in the middle of the hot summer, we were startled to find a large, quarter-sized birthmark on her neck. Further inspection revealed a truly beautiful child, and I couldn't tear my hands from her tender body. We then looked at her three toes and her deformed lower leg, and upon first glance, we were shocked by the difference in length. I put her on the ground to see her move, but she only sat and soon cried. Over the course of the next few days, we realized she had no mobility at all. At nineteen months, she wasn't even crawling. How much of this had to do with being institutionalized and how much had to do with the hemimelia remained a mystery. But my gut told me right away that we needed to prepare ourselves for the most difficult of options.

The following couple of weeks in China were a blur of walks in the park, bureaucratic offices, and hotel rooms. John went home to look after Nick and Emma while my mother stayed on to finish up what seemed like endless paperwork. Quietly, Isabelle and I got to know one another—we learned that she liked eggs, fruit, and noodles and that she slept hard. Our remaining time in China was all rather dreamy and unreal. While other adoptive families dealt with rejection from their children or other assorted behavioral challenges, Isabelle snuggled in comfortably, laughing and joking often and playing nicely. I thought that we had truly bonded and that all my attachment fears had been alleviated. I don't think either one of was ready for the shock of real life at home in France.

It started at the airport in Beijing—the whining that progressed into crying, then later screaming. Interestingly, for years she would react similarly within minutes of entering airports. Worry set in as we boarded the seventeen-hour flight to New York City, and she still wasn't settling. I immediately felt bad for the Chinese businessman that was seated next to me, my mother, and my screaming baby. Four hours into the flight, she was still screaming—not a whine or a moan, but one of those full-out deafening screams. Her nose was running, and she was running a slight fever but nothing that seemed out of the ordinary. Calm Isabelle had been replaced by someone overcome with fear.

Chinese woman of all ages squirmed in their seats, wanting to sweep this child into their arms and do what they each thought would get her to stop. One woman couldn't stand it any longer and asked me kindly if she could take Isabelle to try and calm her down. I was relieved at the offer and flagged the hostess within minutes to bring my mother and me glasses of wine—we were shattered, frustrated, and helpless.

The woman took Isabelle into the bathroom and returned a few minutes later—the screaming continued. "I tried to breastfeed her," she admitted. "I thought it might calm her." *I'm not sure she would know what to do with a breast,* I thought to myself—I don't know if she ever had the opportunity. She handed Isabelle back to me, feeling as helpless as I did. Here we were, two mothers, one Chinese and one American, with a child in our arms that neither of us could soothe.

The trip went from bad to worse. Midflight the captain informed us that the plane was returning to Beijing for mechanical problems. The screaming continued. Seventeen hours after taking off, we were back in the same place as we had started. We deplaned and were given sandwiches in a waiting area. I took the opportunity to call John on my cell phone and sobbed uncontrollably at the sound of his voice. "I don't know what to do with her—I don't know what she needs..." I said, unaware at the time that I would cry these same words many times over—for years to come.

Eventually we made it home, after a brief stint in New York City to get Isabelle a passport signifying her American citizenship. She fell in love with John, Nick, Emma, and the dog but reacted immediately to the competition for my time.

She screeched, cried, hit. She panicked over food. I couldn't leave the room without a major fuss. For months we battled with the transition together, everybody in the family feeling somewhat destabilized. Thankfully, there were many joyful moments when we simply watched Isabelle explore and experience basic pleasures for the first time—gazing into the roaring fire at night, scooting herself on the tricycle on the terrace, tasting *pain au chocolat*.

But we lived these moments alongside so many difficult periods as well—tantrums, screaming, and incessant moaning. She must have been eternally frustrated and scared, having been ripped out of her predictable, hypercontrolled environment at the orphanage and dropped into the fold of a busy family speaking two languages. She couldn't crawl, walk, or talk during a time of tremendous change. I am convinced that she was fighting to protect herself with her behaviors because they were all she had. I knew that we wouldn't get to know the real Isabelle until she felt safe and relaxed. It became clear that love was not something that she had been able to predict in her past; she treated it like an awkward object in her hand. She didn't know what to do with it—to grab hold of it for dear life or to fight with it in fear. And I had my own struggles. Mothering her as I had Nick and Emma, I expected our relationship to take the same route, yet it felt awkward for me as well.

I sought advice from other adoptive families, who reassured me that time was the key. "Lydia, you are just going to need to put expectations aside—I mean completely aside. Just let the time do the work. She has a life to put together, and she is going to have to do this for herself, with the strength of your love by her side," advised one adoptive mother.

Some months later, we were seeing grains of hope that things could be normal. We would lie together, and she would take my face in her hands and kiss me so gently and so slowly on the lips. She would do it over and over, savoring some sort of primal intimacy that she had missed in her early days. I could feel the depth of her need in her kiss. I felt how much she had to give, how much goodness was inside of her just waiting to be received. In turn, I poured every bit of goodness, strength, and love into my kiss back, and prayed she felt every ounce of it and more. Despite the ups and downs of that first year, her true spirit and strength continued to reveal itself every day. I caught glimpses of it as she toddled off, as best as she could on her not-so-sturdy foot, into the garden with the wind in her hair and a smile on her face. On these rare occasions, I noticed she wasn't looking over her shoulder to make sure I was there. Little by little, she was learning she could let go and trust us and the world around her, knowing that she was no longer the only one fighting for her well-being.

Anxious to get medical advice on her hemimelia, I sought feedback from doctors both in France and in the United States. We flew home to the United States to consult with American doctors, whose consensus was that amputation would be the best route. If we went through with the operation soon, she would adapt very quickly. The doctors in France, however, vehemently disagreed, favoring the painful but increasingly successful limb-lengthening procedures.

Ultimately, the agonizing decision would be ours. Her well-being and the shape of her future were squarely in our hands. I struggled to sleep through the night, feeling as if it was a tremendous choice to make for someone else. We dug as far down into ourselves as we could possibly dig and looked high up toward the sky for the answers. At some point, we made a decision that she needed to be offered a new life firmly grounded on even legs. She deserved a leg and foot that functioned as well as anyone else's, just as she had the right to a loving family. We made the painful choice to have her foot removed to make way for a prosthesis. In the next year, she would learn to run, hop, and play like the rest of the children her age. Just as we had hoped, a bright and happy future awaited her. Hopefully she would embody the courageous soul we had seen in her picture and hold her head proudly as she had in that dossier photograph.

I'm often asked to describe what it was like to adopt a child, and nearly every time I hesitate, stumbling over my words. There is no easy way to explain the magnitude of those early days. It was simply enormous: enormously important to watch a flower open up and radiate, enormously frustrating to feel ill equipped to fill the hole she had inside. There would have been no way to predict the roller coaster of this experience—the waiting, the joy of finally holding her, the stress of not being able to understand what she needed, the hardship over making a medical decision for her. It was and continues to be an unpredictable happening requiring difficult ingredients—a giving up of control, a willingness to let life take its course, to let love take its course.

12

Time to Go Home

To love a place is to feel for it, to let it wound you so it leaves a
scar, a permanent keepsake that helps you identify yourself.
Eleni N.Gage

I laced my shoes, pulled shut the wobbly door we were forever complaining about at Gancel, and walked into the early-
morning misty dampness that autumn brings in Provence.
I considered my running route options—across the fields
to the vineyards of Château Bas and up around the winding footpaths leading to Pélissanne or straight up the hill to
Vieux Vernègues and its cluster of Gallo-Roman stone ruins
overlooking the Luberon.

It had been on these trails that I had made all of my
most important decisions. These rocky, herb-studded paths
had been home to all my personal epiphanies. Lost in some
sort of private freedom, I would sort through issues in my
head and connect with the part of me that makes sound and
clear decisions. But that day my pace was sluggish; my legs

felt heavier with every step. Every scent of fresh rosemary and pine stabbed at my heart, and every sight of sleeping lavender was a brutal reminder of an end to come. We had come to a very big decision recently, and my mind struggled to come to terms with it. In a few months, we would sell the cars and the Alleins village house and bid farewell to our life in Provence, where the crazy world had been left at bay. We would return to the United States to upstate New York—we were going home. I wondered for a moment what that word even meant. Where was home? What was home? I couldn't begin to answer that question at that moment. For the time being, it meant where our little family was together. The backdrops could change, but that remained constant.

I stumbled on a rock in the path and landed on a mossy mound. Big heaving sobs came tumbling out, and I felt like a schoolgirl who had lost her best friend. Wiping away my tears, I looked up and was greeted by an entire field of grazing sheep. The whole herd suddenly stopped eating to stare at me. I found strange comfort in their wet, earthy scent while they looked with baffled curiosity at my sorry state.

The moves we had made in the past had all been born out of some wild flight of fancy, some sort of "Hell, why not—you only live once" attitude. This time it was different, and logic had ruled the hand—the children needed English-speaking schools, Isabelle needed her operation and a prosthetic leg, and the administration in France had squelched any decent prospects for a secure financial future.

Our children had now spent more of their lives in France than they had in the United States. They were as comfortable speaking French as they were English, and luckily this happened without much effort at all. They had learned their French on the playground. While I am sure they must have had their moments of frustration, as we did, they had made it appear rather painless. When they had walked out of the house each day, they had entered their French world; anything English had ceased to exist until they had come home. Their closest friends, their activities, and their education had all been French.

Being raised in Provence had forced them to lead duocultural lives, requiring them to switch from one culture to the other as the context required. Spending any time with them would reveal the patchwork of cultures at work, with huge gaps missing from what they knew of an American life. When we visited the United States, they were oddly out of sync with things, unaware of the latest fads. Their sentences were oftentimes constructed in strangely translated ways. They stuttered a lot, something we later learned was common among children who spoke two languages.

Gazing at those smelly sheep, I thought of all that had transpired during our years away.

It had been hard to start a life in another country, in another language. There had been sacrifices of all kinds. We had missed big events at home, the births of babies, the death of our friend's mother, the illnesses of family members, and the sharing of an unforgettable American tragedy in 2001. My heart had ached as Nick curled up in my arms and cried about feeling different at school. "I don't like being called the American kid at school," he had said on so many occasions.

But looking back, I felt that since that first summer trip to Costa Rica, since my mini life crisis seven years before, we had finally found the strength to live in a way that was closer to both who we were and to the earth around us. We had learned more during these years than in any other period in our lives so far, from the most mundane of lessons to larger shifts in priorities. All four of us had become totally fluent in French. I could spot herbs from a mile away. I knew a good foie gras from a bad one and could even make a decent one myself. I perfected a *sanglier daube* (wild boar stew) along with a million other regional recipes. Emma and John could pluck a pheasant fresh after it had been shot. We picked grapes and olives in the fall and cherries in the spring and foraged for wild asparagus and mushrooms on Sunday afternoon walks. John could tend a vineyard and trim a cypress tree. Nature had taken center stage in our family theater. John and I had both reconnected with our childhood dreams—his working with his hands, bringing new life to ancient stones through renovation. I had found mine in finally venturing to the varied corners of the world and connecting with people who had shared some of life's treasured truths.

Our priorities had changed, and living had become more important than succeeding. The importance of image and where we *ought* to be in life no longer affected our decisions. Provence and the time away had helped us put this into perspective. Our moving abroad had us examining just how we were living before and what might have been missing. I knew now that, for us, it had been time that had been absent—to think, to breathe, to appreciate—time to get to know ourselves and one another and to develop a foundation for our family. We had finally afforded ourselves these beautiful and fundamental luxuries. I often wondered whether I could have forged the next path without having done so. In the time away, I had discovered an inner strength and an inner voice that I didn't know existed. During those treasured years, I had learned to not only listen to that voice, but to trust it.

Leaving Provence was like finishing a deeply moving book where you find yourself terribly choked up as you close the last ragged, dog-eared page, as if you have been transported on your own silent journey that has shifted the pieces inside your soul. Our time in Provence, and in all the other great places we visited during our years away, had been that book for me. I had visited all of the places I had dreamed of and read about on my porch in Orlando.

Days before, I had broken down and cried to Louise. Wrapping an arm around me she said, "*Je comprends* (I understand), Lydia. It's a big decision moving home...it must be difficult."

But I then surprised myself by saying, "No, Louise, that's not it. I am crying because I feel I am being prepared for something much more important, and yet I don't know what it is, and I am so tired of being in the dark. I'm so tired of feeling like I'm not the one in control. There is something out there we are supposed to do, and our time in Provence is up."

I was scared. Scared of the unknown future and scared that I was going to be asked to do more than I was capable of doing, give more than I was capable of giving. Somewhere hidden among all these reasonable and logical reasons we had to go back to the United States lay something greater at work. There was a deep pull toward something I couldn't explain.

There have been a few times in my life where I have gotten the briefest and clearest look into the future. Sitting in a heap of tears with Louise was one of them. I was speaking to her from the bottom of my gut, speaking things that I had not even admitted to or thought of myself. Tumbling from my mouth were words that surprised me as much as her. "Provence has been our respite, our time to give to ourselves and appreciate all things that everyone deserves in life." For once I no longer felt guilty about all the goodness and beauty around me. I had allowed it to seep into my being, so much so that it was overflowing. It was time to give some of this back.

"So now what?" I asked the sheep. "Tell me, what I am supposed to do now?"

13

The Idea Is Born

What we think, we become.
Buddha

One of the most difficult challenges facing our pending return to the United States had to do with what we were going to do with ourselves. What would we do for work? Provence had allowed us to have ambiguous job titles—villa managers, renovators, vine trimmers, goat-cheese tasters, and wild-asparagus pickers. It was all beautifully vague, but we knew we couldn't continue like this in the United States.

We considered going back to executive search—for about two split seconds.

"I could continue in renovation and real estate," John said one day, "but the economic news coming from the real-estate market is just abysmal. The villa business has a lot of potential, and we could certainly grow it more, but I'm not sure that's a career path...a life path."

Truth was, the villa business had begun to grow all on its own. We were now managing bookings and reservations for five other houses in the region because our house was always rented. We agreed it was a shame to put the brakes on a business that was already organically blossoming, silly not to do more of what was coming naturally. It had some clear potential, and it logically interested John more than me, as it incorporated a blend of several things he loved. We decided at the very least that he would continue with what we both knew, but there was a seat at the table for something more.

The wet, cold weeks drew on, and my mind emptied of ideas as to what we could focus our energies on at home. *Our years away have been such a beautiful gift—what can we do in return? What can we build that really makes use of the skills we have? What have we learned by being away? Whatever that is, that's what I want to do*, I thought.

Then my mind went virtually blank.

Sometimes it's good to have a clean slate. Like taking all your clothes off—you can't hide from yourself. What you are left with is simply you, and that's how it felt. I started thinking about the love of freedom, travel, foreign sights and sounds, nature, the wind in my face, building things, connecting with people. My mind wandered to all the thoughts I had had as a child and young adult, of traipsing around the world with little more than a duffel bag and a desire to contribute to something in a worthwhile way. The Hope Volunteers Abroad program in India had changed me—and so had our travels. We couldn't just go home and pretend to be the people we had been before living all of this. Our journeys had been a search for personal freedom, yet had more importantly allowed us the opportunity to listen to and learn from others, to share time with people from all walks of life and backgrounds.

If we had learned anything, it had been that, at the end of the day, we are all so much the same. Mothers all want the best for their children, children are all hungry to learn, community members all want to help each other, and people all feel good about the things they build for themselves. Travel had challenged our beliefs and our thinking, had given us a richer, more profound view of the world. It had lit that flame and cast a light on what was really important—feeling a part of something greater than ourselves and having genuine concern for one another within that something greater.

Then on one blue-skied day in Provence, an idea floated onto our radar like a soft white feather that silently falls at your feet. I was sitting at the table in Alleins while John painted a hallway, getting the house ready for resale. I was at the computer and had been communicating with a contact in India with respect to a girls' school in the slums of Calcutta. For days, my mind had churned with images of the girls and the challenges they faced daily. The woman I was in touch with was trying to find a way to get the girls sponsored so they could attend private schools outside of the slums. The cost per child was about five hundred dollars a year, and that would include everything from tuition to books and transportation. It was a ticket to a new life. I sat and gazed at John and the hundred-euro pot of paint he was dipping into.

Then I started imagining what we could accomplish if, instead of spending all of our time and money restoring old homes, we helped build opportunities for people who really needed them. *How can we shift our energies to supporting others?* I wondered. I shared the feelings with John. Of course, none of it was a surprise to him—I had been harping on the same desires since we were fifteen. At some point, though, he stopped painting, looked at me, and said, "What are you waiting for?" And I couldn't for the life of me find an answer.

Then John did what he does best—he took some key thoughts we had had over the years and mobilized them. In a matter of minutes, he spat out a half dozen ideas relating to combining travel with giving back. "Just think of all the guests that come here to Provence. They are all looking for something meaningful when they leave home, something that makes them stretch as individuals. People are ready to go beyond and do more in their travels, and so many talk about what a deep desire they have to give back to life. We could pave the way for that, help open doors for them to do just that. We could build a travel company that involved exploring the world and making it a better place. Maybe it's time, Lydia. Maybe it's time to do something that really matters. We know how to build a business, and we have our whole lives ahead of us to learn about the rest. We could call it something like *Travel with Conscience or GoPhilanthropic*... or something like that."

Slowly, out of the darkness, ideas started pouring in until the light was so strong it felt like a big, bright, flashing neon sign beaming into my brain. All of the stages of our lives had linked together into this one idea that was just simply right. Suddenly there was no time to feel the loss of leaving life in France. There was an unimaginably big and complex job ahead, and while I still had no clear picture of exactly what that was, at least there was a vague impression of what it could be. I knew from the bottom of my heart that we had to do it.

For the next few weeks we scratched out our ideas on the backs of the kids' coloring pages or on napkins at restaurants, brainstorming how we were going to build GoPhilanthropic. We didn't know a thing about philanthropy in its formal sense, other than knowing it meant contributing to humanity. The word had such a lofty, inaccessible feeling to it, as if reserved for individuals or foundations with millions. *We can all be philanthropists,* I thought. It was time to get that word off the high shelf and dust it off.

14

Difficult Days

*She stood in the storm, and when the wind did not
blow her way, she adjusted her sails.*
Elizabeth Edwards

Rochester, New York
Summer 2007

The summer we moved back to the States was probably the
single most painful, challenging, and emotional of all our
moves put together. You couldn't pay me a million dollars to
relive it again. While I knew that we were going home to the
comforts of something known, deep down I was scared as
hell that our previous lives would somehow seep back into
our beings and wipe away all that we had gained while being away. The future felt so unknown to me—so full of possibilities but so very unclear.

We also had Isabelle's amputation date looming, planned
only a few short weeks after arriving, before the onset of

the school year. I could get my head around the concept of going through with the operation, but digesting the reality was another matter altogether. I decided that not thinking about it was easier, and so I created a lovely, compact little box in my brain to conveniently store the fear and pain of actually going through with it. Trying my very best to collect myself emotionally, I wanted to show Isabelle I could truly be there for her. Back in the hotel room in Nanchang, I had promised her that, but balancing this with denial as a coping mechanism was becoming more and more of a challenge.

In all other life situations we had endured together, John had been the sturdy pillar to count on, but I was noticing that he could barely manage talking about the operation himself. It had taken such immense energy and strength to come to the decision to actually have the foot taken off that, once it had been made, we couldn't let ourselves waver, couldn't risk letting uncertainty allow us to go backward. While we knew deep down that we wanted her to have a fresh start with a prosthesis, there was this lingering wisp of knowledge, the disquieting but growing fear that she would someday blame us for the decision. She had gone through so much already, had lost so much already, it felt so unfair that she had to give up yet more.

Coupling all of this with leaving Provence seemed too much to bear. Sitting at the airport in Marseille on that last day in France, I tried my best to push all of the sad thoughts away—we were cutting the cord to a life we had so carefully built for ourselves, a foundation that we had desperately needed. Strangely, life was going to continue on without us.

Mas de Gancel would run as usual with dear Louise as the manager and guest meeter-greeter. As we were leaving, it was the beginning of the high tourist season at the Gancel, as well as for all of the other rental houses, and tourists were streaming in with their overstuffed suitcases and questions about markets and wine. I knew that when it was over at the end of the summer, a big machine would run through our vineyard to collect the grapes instead of us doing it by hand. When the last rental group left at the end of October, we wouldn't sit on the terrace and gaze at the leaves on the vines turning their golden red and orange, rejoicing at being home and happy to stock the woodpile for the months of crisp nights ahead. All of this would have to go on without us.

To add to my deepening discomfort, Nick stayed behind in Europe to tour with the boys' choir he had been singing with—Les Petits Chanteurs d'Aix. At age ten, he had become a very talented classical soloist, singing Mozart with the purest, most angelic clarity, and we did not want to deny him the experience of a big tour. In all, Nick was to be separated from us for five weeks, a big step at age ten during a massive transition. It felt horribly uncomfortable to be apart as a family during such a big change for all of us—we had endured everything together. Five weeks would feel like eternity for me. The whole nightmare was made a thousand times worse when, at some point on the way home connecting through an airport, I got a call from him, sobbing.

"Mom, I'm scared. I'm all by myself in this French family's home I have been assigned to. I feel weird—they seem nice, but I don't know them," he cried. "I want to come home."

Home, I thought. Where on earth is that? As Nick cried into the phone I mustered all the strength I had in my body to respond with what he needed to hear.

"Nick—things are going to be fine," I said, swallowing the growing lump in my throat and taking the deepest breath possible to reassure him, though at that moment I was scared and unsure myself. I hung up wanting to melt into the floor as we waited in a lengthy airport security line with Isabelle in the midst of her thrice-daily tantrums. People stared. I didn't care.

One thing was for sure in all of this. I had been in that place many times before, and I knew not to give the emotions any credence or to let the fear get even the slightest hold on me. I knew the moment would pass; it would shift with the wind for me as it would for Nick. And it did. Two days later when I called to check on him, he was having the time of his life. "Huh?...Am I OK?...Oh, sure, those guys were fine. And this new family I am staying with is great! They live in this great château and have three pretty daughters, and we are lying out in the sun on their trampoline," he said.

Our house in Alleins hadn't sold by the time we moved home, so to play it safe we held off buying a home in the United States, instead settling ourselves into a small blue rental with a peaked roof on an unpretentious street in an unpretentious neighborhood in Rochester. A few months prior, I had made a trip over from France to find a suitable place to land, and the real-estate agent had asked what I wanted. Filled with a heavy heart for what lay ahead with

Isabelle, all I remember saying was, "It needs to have light, lots of light. It needs to be a happy place." Where we landed couldn't have been more Main Street America, and it was probably the farthest thing from how we had lived for the past bunch of years. Yet it represented a safe and cozy nest from which to ease into a life that had become a strange but old friend.

In coming home, I felt as though John and I had come full circle. Rochester, New York, was where we had met and fallen in love as teenagers. It was where I had been lost at the breakup of my family, where I had, at the foot of my father's carpeted footsteps, experienced both my frailty and my force as a young woman. It was where our dreams had all started. The rental house was only two streets over from the apartment that John and his best friend, Alex, had shared right after college. And it was on these same streets that I had said to myself at the age of twenty-one, "I'm going to get out of this place and NEVER come back!"

Not long after the boxes were unpacked, we waited out the last couple of days before Izzy's operation. We enjoyed the time alone with her—picnicking, going to the library, enjoying the public swimming pool, and having dinners with friends we hadn't seen in years. It reminded me of the silent, slow pregnant days before Nick and Emma had been born, when there had been nothing to do but wait, stare at the packed bag for the hospital by the front door, and wonder about just how bad the pain was going to be. I knew life was going to change forever for the better, but there would be hardship in the process.

The day finally came, and we packed the car and drove the two hours along I-90 to Shriner's Hospital in Erie, Pennsylvania. We checked in, and Isabelle was briefly distracted and happy playing in their gigantic playroom filled with every imaginable toy. But having been there for two previous appointments in the weeks leading up to the operation, she knew exactly where she was, and she was clearly not at ease. After a solemn dinner, I bathed her, and we slept together in the family hospital room with the preop routine planned for the crack of dawn.

Early in the morning in the fall of 2007, the doctor drew a line with a black Sharpie pen around Isabelle's shin where they would take her foot off. I kissed her forehead, and together she, John, and I walked through the door we knew would lead her to the childhood she deserved.

John and I sat in the waiting room and endured the three agonizing hours during her surgery. I was suddenly startled as my cell phone rang. Thinking it was family checking in on Isabelle, I answered it only to hear the owner of a villa in France complaining about a renter who was not happy. She chattered away about the situation while my mind slipped somewhere else. Life was going on as usual in the real world, yet it had virtually stopped for us. When the surgeon finally came out of the operating room, he reassured us that all had gone as hoped, and we could join her in a little while. Later that night, we settled in the recovery room. Sometime around 2:00 a.m., she stirred and moaned, a moan that brought me back to her early days in my arms after having been united with us. I knew enough already to know it was a moan I couldn't provide a solution to. Not knowing what else to do, I crawled into her bed, curling up next to her, the faint small of anesthesia on her warm breath.

In the morning, Isabelle opened her eyes, and a faint smile spread across her face as she took in the sunshine steaming through her room. Then I watched as her eyes followed the top of her leg down to her bent cast, too short to have encompassed a full-length leg. Just at that moment, a nurse came in, handing to Isabelle the little bear that we had sent to China while she was still in the orphanage. It had been given a matching purple cast. She took the bear and tucked it safely under her arm, patting its arm gently.

The first few nights and days were as one might imagine—consumed with pain management and gut-wrenching emotion. I just put myself on auto-mom-pilot and waited for better days to come. Thankfully the worst of it appeared to be over. We would have six long weeks of healing in the cast before beginning the process of fitting her for her "new leg." There was nothing left to do but to wait for the day that she would be running next to us.

Nick and Emma were brave souls through the whole ordeal and remained amazingly positive, helpful, and spirited during a time when John, Izzy, and I felt weak and wounded. Luckily they had lived through many changes and challenges in their little lives and were both set on just getting on with things. They were enjoying a honeymoon of experiences they had dreamed of having—school taught in English and kids to play with on the same street. We rode on the back of their positive wave, trusting that easier days would come.

15

Our New Normal

In all chaos there is a cosmos, in all disorder a secret order.
Carl Jung

Work became our anchor during the transition home. Had we not been busy with something new, there would have been too much time and space to feel the ocean's distance between Provence and our new home in the United States. John knew that GoPhilanthropic was going to take time and money to get off the ground and that a steady income was needed to take the edge off of this initial launch period. He was motivated to build again to create a steadier flow of income, so he immediately set out to double the number of villas we rented through our villa website we had named Only Provence. Luckily people now flocked to our website and felt safe renting from us, knowing we had lived there and knew its corners personally.

Meanwhile, my mind went wild with thoughts on the mission behind GoPhilanthropic. The connection between travel and philanthropy was powerful and the potential limitless. I dreamed of dismantling the fences of fear people create that keep us from touching life outside of what we know. Travel would provide people the opportunity to break down those superficial barriers—the picket fences that separate us as cultures and people. From even the earliest days in creating the GoPhilanthropic concept, we saw the travel part of the business as the car, a vehicle that could take people to the doorsteps of villages, schools, and organizations. From there the journey would be personal. Our job would be to provide a safe car, one that had large windows to see out of, one that stopped where good people were quietly doing great things.

Essentially I had to build both a travel-logistics company and an organization that identified and evaluated good and honest nonprofits. I knew very little about either one. Clueless and passionate, I set to building the business as I learned myself. Needing to start somewhere, I dove into researching everything I could find in the travel market that had to do with philanthropic travel, volunteer vacations, altruistic trips, giving-back vacations, and do-good holidays. It was not as though we were doing something novel by combining travel and giving back. The volunteer vacation market was booming, almost overloaded with companies attempting to meet the ever-growing demands of people who wanted to do more than put their feet up and sip margaritas. There was a handful of reputable companies doing what seemed to be a good job, but I had also experienced the negative side of voluntourism and felt it had limitations, particularly with respect to transparency. How much of the funds from those journeys went to the programs themselves? How exactly did the programs benefit?

I wanted to create a different experience, a different journey altogether. I envisioned our travelers having a chance to meet the lesser-known humanitarians of the world, sip tea with them, learn from them, and share with them. The key would be finding these special people doing special things—individuals, small groups, or community programs that weren't waiting around for a handout but instead were courageously filling in the gaps where the rest of the world turned a blind eye—people who fought for those who were handed less in life. I wanted to find them. From there I hoped to build a simple and direct way to support them in their efforts.

But each day that passed by, I would ask myself, *What on earth do you know about philanthropy, Lydia? Who are you to launch a business with that word in it?* People who are involved in philanthropy serve on boards of foundations, have millions of dollars, wear tailored suits. I had a solid set of business skills and had learned to navigate the world, but this was an undertaking that completely intimidated me. Somewhere deep down, though, I knew that I had to find a way through these questions. Packing my bags and running away was no longer an option. I had been given a tremendous opportunity to see the world, and there was work to do in return, in helping others do the same.

I turned, as I always had, to books to guide me—to those who knew best on the matters of economic development, global public health, and poverty alleviation. I read and researched in all of my free time, early in the mornings before the family was up and in the afternoons as I sat on the front steps waiting for the school bus to come. I devoured books by everyone from Jeffrey Sachs, an economist; to Muhammed Yunus and Jacqueline Novogratz, who offered microfinance for the poor; to Paul Farmer, who had devoted his life to providing health care where there was none. The evidence was plainly clear that traditional aid and charity handouts were not the way forward. GoPhilanthropic would follow in this good wake of thinking. In my gut, I knew the focus would be on working with people who didn't need to be told what to do—they themselves knew what they needed. They just might need help with their tool kits. Our mission would be to help them do more of what they were already doing. I envisioned working with programs devoted to caring for vulnerable women and children, programs that challenged and encouraged them and provided them with opportunities to learn, programs that were run by people who had time to listen to their dreams.

If we knew little about the grand and powerful domain of philanthropy, we knew even less about building a travel company—working with ground operators, local guides, or the booking procedure for flights and hotels. We had experience assisting people with booking their villas and arranging chefs, but it was quite another world dealing with a broad and endless distribution system involving custom-built philanthropic tours in faraway places such as Indochina and India. I didn't know a thing about arranging all of this, and I wondered how I was going to personally make sure that every detail on every trip was taken care of from my home office in Rochester, New York. The website had to be created, a system for data management and billing needed to be designed, and an affordable way to advertise what we were doing needed to be put in place.

I woke up in the wee hours of the morning and chewed on how I was going accomplish it all. When I would stress, John would ask, "What's the hurry? Just put one foot in front of the other, stay true to your ideas, and look up every once in a while to make sure you are heading where you want to go."

The previous decade had been about living, traveling, and learning—this first year at home was about thinking and reading, wondering and worrying about how I was going to go about putting it all together. If I was comparing GoPhilanthropic to a vehicle, then it was currently in a heap of pieces on a garage floor. My saving grace during these early days was the images I had stored in my memory, etched so deeply I knew they would never leave me. Visions of being crammed in that dark orphanage room surrounded by bright and deserving yet direfully poor children in southern India would flash through my brain. I thought of the young girl in Cambodia selling her bracelets at five in the morning outside the temples of Angkor Wat who should have been getting ready for school. I couldn't forget about them. It was as if some angel was lighting the way through a dark and misty tunnel that emerged at the foot of a mountain where there was nowhere else to go but up.

While I dove into my new project, the kids had full-time jobs adjusting to and navigating their new lives in the United States. Their days were made up of all that we had come home for—school, neighborhood friends, after-school activities, and cartoons instead of school on Saturday mornings, as they had had in Provence. Both Nick and Emma had created glamorous pictures in their heads about what life would be like in the States, thinking for sure it would be like what they had seen in movies and on the Disney Channel. "Things are just going to be cooler in the States, Mom," Nick had said before we had left. "France is great, but I am sick of being stuck out in the countryside."

I guess in some ways their new US life did live up to what they had imagined, namely access to junk food, trendy clothes, and pop culture. Emma finally put a face to Hannah Montana as did Nick to the Jonas Brothers. But underneath the initial buzz, I sensed their slight discomfort. There was an ocean to cross socially in order for them to truly feel a part of things. They didn't quite fit in as easily as they had thought they would, and I knew I couldn't help them. In France, Nick had always been slightly on the fringe, known as the American boy, and now he was known as the kid from France. He was in his first year of middle school, and suddenly he was in a world and at an age where looks and clothes mattered, yet he was clueless as to what was in. And I was no help. He was also confused by all the different groups kids formed in his school. There were the jocks, the nerds, the artists. In Provence there had been one class of thirty for his grade, and they had always been together in the same class since age five. Either there weren't enough of them to form cliques, or there was more acceptance of differences. This new concept of groups and cliques was totally foreign to him. Alongside these social challenges, he was dreadfully behind in English reading and writing. We thought we had been diligent about reading in English, but the French academic system had them weighted down with heavy loads of homework, and apparently the time we had carved out for English had not been enough. During the first year home, he resorted to his lifelong companion of music, pouring his heart out into his guitar and songwriting. While the jocks didn't initially accept him, the girls eventually swooned after he won the talent show. Life would slowly come together for him but not without painful steps.

Emma experienced similar stresses. She had entered fourth grade and was struggling to feel comfort in a school of eight hundred, coming from her village school and her class of twenty-five that had been together since age three. There were no fields of poppies or vineyards for her to lose herself in at the end of the day. Emma had always been an earthy, fun girl, spending hours picking wildflowers, wild green onions, and fruit, and riding horses. Alongside her deep connection to the earth, she somehow had always managed to maintain a large and diverse group of girlfriends. Now in the States, it was as though her world had been thrown upside down, and she didn't know where to seek comfort.

Both kids thought that school in English would be a breeze, but they were immediately tested and tagged as needing extra help in anything related to reading or writing. Like Nick's, Emma's written English was not up to par and, because she had never taken a multiple-choice test before, her standardized testing skills were nowhere near where they should have been (though interestingly she won the town poetry contest the same year). Eventually she was put in a class for children who had English as a second language, along with kids whose primary language was Chinese. Embarrassed and marginalized, she slowly became quiet and unmotivated at school. Her teacher sent notes home describing her as "checked out," something Emma had never been in her lifetime. During vacations, we traveled back to Provence, where she would quickly become herself again, at times admitting that she didn't want to go home.

While I worried and tried to help by assuring them it would pass, I knew this was something they had to live and sort out on their own. I was confident that they would find the strength to simply be themselves in the States, but it was an awful process to see them so insecure. We were asking them to make a huge shift socially and academically.

And then there was Isabelle. Besides the challenges relating to her foot operation, she had developed some behaviors that were not easy to manage—rarely playing on her own and moaning or screaming when she didn't get what she wanted. We had her evaluated, and the results revealed pretty serious language delays, which we had been told were rather normal in internationally adopted children. The months in France had only confused her. She would need significant speech therapy along with physical therapy.

Attempting to find solutions, John and I felt she needed to be in an environment with some other children with whom to play, so I reluctantly signed her up at a preschool run out of the basement of the local Episcopal Church. It was nowhere near as polished as the handful of other flashy preschools adorned with intricate playgrounds and computer rooms, but it was filled with loving caretakers and a lack of pretense. Their focus on simplicity reminded us of Provence life, where children are happy to be in a room with each other to play. We soon learned that the small program was also filled with other little adopted Chinese beauties, several of whom had orthopedic leg challenges. One family had adopted an older child from China who had a birth defect similar to Isabelle's. They were living the gut-wrenching phase of research needed to make the decision to lengthen the limb or amputate.

While the children were at school during the day, John and I would sit across from each other at our combined dining room and kitchen table working on our respective business projects. Living and running two businesses in a tiny house presented a challenge from the start. We could hear each other clicking away on our computers. If a phone call came in, we had to hide in the bathroom or in our bedroom to hold a quiet conversation, and if the kids were home, in the car. The dog barked when we were on business calls. At the end of the day, it would take half an hour to clear off our "desks," so we would have room to lay the dinner table. Adjusting to the new cramped quarters added yet another layer of stress to an already difficult transition time.

Discussions about buying a house encouraged the typical John and Lydia banter, with me wanting something reasonable and John leaning toward large colonials. But as we began this cycle we had come to know so well, we caught ourselves. "Aren't you sick of the energy it takes to make these decisions that ultimately don't mean a thing?" I said one day. "Aren't you tired of houses and things? Does any of it matter? I don't know about you, but I am ready to think beyond all of this. We have moved in and out of so many places over the years that I am wondering if it matters at all where we are. I just don't have the mental energy to think about a house. There is so much other stuff to get to."

The decision we had made together over that hundred-euro pot of paint in Alleins crept its way into reality. On that day, we had decided to focus on a different set of priorities, and this meant a certain letting go of things, of houses, of status. Now home and immersed in a time and place we knew placed an emphasis on the size of one's foyer, we had to test our commitment to that decision. Just as the kids were feeling their own level of social disconnection, we both were too. What we had experienced in the years being gone had changed our priorities—time, strength, and determination were what we were all focused on at that moment. I felt friends quietly wondering if we had run into financial troubles, as the jumps from our lifestyles in Orlando to France to here didn't quite add up. There had to be a reason why, and it was logical to assume that it had to do with money or success, one or the other perhaps slipping through our fingers. Renting a house, instead of buying, made it easy for us to not make a decision about settling in at home. It allowed us to keep propped open that window of opportunity to, at any point, resume a more linear, logical life—or to continue to set fear aside and ride the raft life was providing us.

"I will always love old houses, but no...I guess none of that does really make a difference. You are right—there is so much to do right now, so much to learn; it would probably just be a distraction."

The transition had been a difficult and challenging one for all of us, Isabelle's loss being top of the list. Our comforts were coming in different forms now, in knowing that we had each other to count on. John and I would light candles at the end of the day and share details from our respective days as packs of neighborhood kids would traipse happily through the house. We asked Nick and Emma if they cared that we were living in a tiny rented house, with its one bathroom with peeling grout and a kitchen the size of my bedroom closet in Lancaster or France. "Nope, we don't really care," they said. "It's just nice to be able to hang posters!"

And so the matter was put to bed. We decided to just live and work and build in the small blue house in Rochester.

16

Ten and Two

When you get to the end of your rope, tie a knot and hang on.
Franklin D. Roosevelt

Luckily for us all, Isabelle's six-week postamputation period turned out to be somewhat of a breeze. She had found a way to scoot around on the ground, and over time we noticed her hobbling on the end of the stump. The purple cast had been a blessing as it allowed the leg to heal without needing to be tended to. But our upcoming visit to Shriner's Hospital in Erie to remove the cast was quickly approaching, and we were all aware, except maybe for Isabelle, that this meant a return to reality—her having to accept living without a foot and the family needing to come to terms with it as well. I had created a nice image in my mind of what her stump would look like as the cast came off—beautifully smooth new skin, perfectly rounded and ready for her prosthetic. Bike rides and strolls in the park were at arm's length. The worst, I was sure, was behind us. It wasn't until I parked the car at the hospital that it dawned on me there might be some unrealistic elements to the packaged picture in my mind.

Adrienne, my dear friend from Costa Rica and Isabelle's godmother, was thankfully with me as the doctors fired up the minisaw that cut into Isabelle's purple protective cast. I held Isabelle, and she held me. I think we both buried our faces in each other's arms while Adrienne stayed keenly focused on the leg. As pieces of the cast were removed, we took careful glances at what was there, my stomach a bed of nerves. Isabelle's face turned white, then a shade of gray. The time had come for us both to face the future together. Tentative and scared, we took our first long looks at her leg together.

"Now look at that!" bellowed Adrienne with her die-hard positive attitude. "That looks great!"

The doctors echoed similar remarks as they peeled away remnants of the wraps. "Lookin' good, my friends!" the doctor said proudly.

And there it was, not at all how I had pictured it would be, and somewhat of a shock to both Izzy and me. "Good Lord," I muttered to myself. Thick black stitches poked out harshly around an ugly line of a scab. There was nothing pretty about it, yet everyone besides Izzy and me was celebrating the success of her procedure.

Before I could even come to grips with the sight before my eyes, the doctors launched into the litany of specific instructions we needed to follow when bathing and treating the wound. It would be weeks before it would heal entirely, they said. Then, rather abruptly, we were ushered out of the hospital. "Come back in six weeks," they said, "and we can begin to talk about the new leg."

Stunned, scared, and in a semitrance, I carried Isabelle to the car and began the two and a half hour ride back to Rochester. Izzy went silent as she stared at her leg minus her cast, minus her foot. I stared ahead on the road in front of me, hoping she would fall asleep, so I could let out the tears that were welling up in my throat. *I know it will be fine; I know in my heart this child is going to thrive; I am so thankful that she will have a chance to do all the things that kids do.* But I also felt her loss. Yes, *loss* was the word—and I hated it more than anything else at that moment. It was a stupid, awful, unfair, four-letter, motherfucking word that I felt hovered over her like a dark cloud. She had had to deal with just so much of it in her short three years of life, and I felt helpless, useless, in making her pain go away. Waves of emotion rushed through my body—all of the tears that I had held back and hidden in that protective box in my brain for months were now aching to be released, and all I wanted to do was pull the car over and cry for a million years. Cry for her having been abandoned, cry for her not knowing her mother, and cry now for her foot that was gone.

As we approached the Buffalo tollbooth, Izzy began to moan—that moan I had come to know so well in China and that we had lived with since. I thought of the promise I had made to her in Nanchang. I had vowed I would have the strength to give her all that she needed, to fill whatever holes she might have. It was true that she had landed in a loving family who would attempt to provide her with everything she would need to set off in life and live her dreams, including a solid foot, but I knew what that moan meant. I knew that ultimately she was mourning what we couldn't give back to her. I wanted to scream and yell and cry because I felt I was failing her. What I had to offer wasn't enough.

Adrienne tried to keep my mind on concrete things. She could tell I was being sucked into a vortex of pain, Izzy's pain, and she wasn't going to let me go there. "Let's review the wound healing dos and don'ts," she said positively.

But Izzy's moan slowly transformed into a whine, a non-stop whine that she had become accustomed to using when she wanted something but didn't have the words. I knew when it started that it wouldn't end. Another reminder of how much we didn't understand. My sadness now shifted to frustration. Then it hit me like a ton of bricks—"Shit!" I said. "We leave for Cambodia in six days...how on earth can I leave her at a time like this? How on earth can I expect a sitter to deal with this...and the kids? I need to cancel. I can't leave now, Ade. I can't *leave* her!"

The timing for this particular trip couldn't have been worse, coupled with the fact that John and I were scheduled to go together. We had interviewed a grounded and focused University of Rochester student named Heather to stay in the house with the children and make sure that their lives stayed constant. Isabelle had hated her from the start—well, not *her* really, but the concept of her or anyone else in my place. It had only been about a year and a half since bringing her home from China, and me disappearing was understandably difficult for her.

"Ade, I can't go away now," I stated emphatically.

The intensity of Isabelle's whine increased. We offered her everything we could, snacks, drinks, toys. Nothing would calm her.

Turning to back to look at Isabelle, then looking directly at me, Adrienne then yelled, "Ten and two!" jolting me out of my desperate state.

"What?" I said confused. "What on earth does that mean?"

"Didn't you ever learn ten and two in driver's ed?" she said. "Just put your left hand at ten p.m. and your right at two, look ahead, and keep your eyes on the road, Lydia. That is what you need to do right now. That's what she needs from you. Just keep moving."

"OK, OK!" I belted back.

With our eyes glued to the road, paralyzed with emotion, the strangest thing happened. Out of the blue, we both burst into laughter—I don't know who started it first, but it quickly became gut-holding, tear-jerking laughter that felt so good, so much better than the pain. We laughed for miles and miles, until our stomachs hurt, until our faces were wet from tears, until the world felt a little brighter. Izzy was so entirely baffled that she forgot about her sadness, turning instead to the little board book in her lap, later drifting off into a peaceful sleep. When we finally collected ourselves, the sun was setting golden on the fall leaves, and I thought about the deeper meaning in Ade's words. Maybe that was what Izzy needed from me—to stay strong, look ahead, and keep the hands on the wheel, the foot on the gas. I may not have had been able to fix all she had lost, but I could stay focused on the road ahead.

"Lydia, there is nothing complicated about caring for her stump, and there is nothing complicated about you going away for ten days. Life must go on," Adrienne stated matter-of-factly. "She needs to become accustomed to who you are, and that means trusting that you will always return home, perhaps a little jet-lagged, but always there." Good, sound logic and a bit of laughter were exactly what we had all needed at that moment.

Pulling into the driveway, I wondered for a split second about how Nick and Emma might react toward the cast being gone. I had done a crappy job in preparing myself, so I could not have done a stellar one in preparing them. But they were brave, the first to peel off her sock and bathe her, full of smiles and giggles just as they had been before. "Mom... it's fine," they reassured me individually, patting my back. Isabelle picked up on their light-hearted acceptance and caught their positive energy. I was humbled and amazed at their collective strength and enjoyed, even if just for a brief period, the weight of the world lifting just a little bit.

17

A Return to Cambodia

It's opener, out there, in the wide, open air.
Dr. Seuss

Heather listened carefully to all the instructions, nodding that she was confident all would be fine. "Go, go...we'll be fine."

As John and I crept out of the house at 4:00 a.m. for a 6:00 a.m. flight across the world, I couldn't help feeling like someone was literally pulling me in half. There was a job out there in the world to do, but there was also an incredibly important one right at home. Over the years, I would learn to manage well, capably weaving in and out of the two, but these were still early days. We had been such a tight little unit for so long, had experienced everything together up until this point. I was unaware that I was entering into a stage in my life that would require more than a fair share of self-reliance. For as much as the following years would involve the building of a business, and later a nonprofit, much of it represented a spiritual journey—a pilgrimage that at times I would have to walk alone.

During the twenty-seven hour trek to Cambodia, I continued to contemplate what exactly it was I wanted to accomplish in the pilot stage of GoPhilanthropic. I needed regions where there was an established tourist market alongside significant community needs. I could then start connecting the dots. Cambodia and India were obvious places for me to start. I knew them both, and there were steady streams of travelers going to both, yet they also suffered from tremendous social, health, economic, and education problems. The most significant task during our scout visits would involve connecting with the right types of projects. There were countless organizations, charities, and small NGOs (nongovernmental organizations) fighting to meet the staggering needs, from massive multimillion-dollar-budgeted organizations to tiny projects run singlehandedly. Endless questions had to be answered. What types of projects would we identify? Which ones were applying the most effective and creative solutions? How would we know they were run well and were honest with donations? In what way would we facilitate the contributions?

As we described to various people what we were launching, some would immediately wrinkle their noses and ask, "What are your vetting procedures? What are your measures for examining a program's sustainability and long-term outcomes? How will you measure impact?" So green was I to the charity world that I had to look up the word *vet* in the dictionary.

Yes, these questions were important, and no, we did not have the academic credentials to show we were qualified to *vet,* but I knew one thing. I trusted my gut implicitly, and I didn't think it would take a Harvard graduate to identify great people doing great things around the world. Forging ahead, I put my blinders on to the doubters, taking one step careful step at a time, learning whatever I could and making mistakes along the way. Heading to Cambodia, we were hopeful that we could find a way to channel some of the tourists' flow of resources to community projects by at least making travelers more aware of the need for them, by encouraging visits to them.

But aside from all of the logical reasons to begin in Cambodia and India, there were also less tangible explanations. Like Provence, these places had spoken to me in other ways, in whispers and soft dialogues that hinted at things to do, people to meet, lessons to learn. Landing at the small airport in Siem Reap, I felt it all come rushing back— the intensity of the immense, almost unbelievable spiritual grandeur of the temples of Angkor Wat. Dropping my bags at the foot of the bed in the hotel room, dizzy from the hours of travel, I soaked in the smokiness of the air, the hum of the motorcycles, and the lingering scent of lemongrass.

With the wind in our faces on our tuk-tuk rides, we were reminded of a shocking statistic of Cambodia: one in five children die before the age of five due to unclean drinking water. More than 80 percent of the population lives in rural areas with limited access to quality health, education, or public services. We were sure that the educated, intellectual crowd of people from all over the world visiting the temples would seek more than their pictures at the temples. They would also want to see the whole picture. If they were made aware that a child could attend school for the cost of one night's hotel room, they would act—I was confident they would.

In the following days, we met with several humanitarian organizations, from the most basic orphanages made up of a lean-to tin roof, to one providing prosthetics and physical therapy to land-mine amputees. One of our most inspiring visits was with Journeys Within Our Community, run by an American couple, Brandon and Andrea Ross, who had moved to Cambodia years prior to build a bed-and-breakfast and tour company. In launching their business, they were exposed to the needs of the squatter village behind them, specifically its need for clean water. Villagers were depending on ditch runoff as their primary source of water, and as a result they lived with chronic illnesses. But Brandon and Andrea went beyond helping the village themselves. They shared their efforts with those who were visiting the area and staying at their bed-and-breakfast. Travelers were soon funding water wells left and right, and the beginning of the Journeys Within nonprofit was formed. Over a five-year period, it would blossom into a beautiful example of travel philanthropy—one where visitors were educated first, then offered the chance to support financially. Eventually travelers, including ours, were funding not only water wells but scholarships students, classrooms, computer projects, and a microfinance program. We agreed that in joining forces with Journeys Within, GoPhilanthropic could provide further exposure to the efforts of Journeys Within and broaden the wake of those wanting to do more than see the sights on their vacations.

As we headed back to the hotel on one of our last days in Siem Reap, Saloth, a sweet and deeply compassionate woman who had been acting as our guide, motioned our tuk-tuk driver to pull off to the side of the road.

"This place isn't really a very established NGO, but you might be interested just the same," she said, as she started to pile out of the vehicle. Peering up we saw a grass hut, a lean-to, and a small, hand-painted sign that said OPPORTUNITIES OF DEVELOPMENT THROUGH ART (ODA). A few children were milling around, an older boy cooking dinner over an open fire. Approaching the grass hut, we were surprised to find it full of the most incredible paintings—some illustrated majestic temples with their classic tree trunks wrapping around crumbling temple rock, while others depicted everyday Cambodian life. We stood in awe, taking in the incredible artwork, a warm breeze ruffling through the leaf roof. Then a smiling man in his late thirties approached us, introducing himself as Leng. For the next half hour, he told us how he came to be running this tiny shelter for twenty children—all with different, largely traumatic backgrounds, but all with no one able to care and provide for them.

Leng had witnessed the brutal killing of his father by the Khmer Rouge during the Pol Pot regime. Fortunately, his uncle had taken him in and provided him with food and shelter. Years later, and after obtaining his fine arts degree, he vowed that a part of his life's mission would be to help other severely needy Cambodian children. Amazingly, out of his own harrowing personal experience, he formed the ODA shelter.

Leng and his wife, Sry On, were hired to work on the restoration in the temple complex. Using their meager income, they helped feed and care for the abandoned children they encountered living in the complex. Leng and Sry On took them in one by one and spent hours teaching them the art of painting. In doing so, Leng wasn't just teaching a skill but also sharing and transmitting their heritage. Together they painted away the horrors of the previous decades and the harsh realities of their current situations—some having been abandoned outright and others having illnesses their parents could not manage to take on. The paintings were sold to tourists and the income used to support their livelihoods and school expenses.

John and I listened to Leng's painful and courageous story as the rest of the tourist world whizzed by. Through his words, I could sense the depths of both his gratitude for what he had and his compassion for the children he cared for. But it was clear that Leng was determined to help these children help themselves—they were being taught the value of an education alongside a skill that could offer an income. He didn't want them to be holding their hands out as so many other children did in town. He wanted them to feel and grow their own abilities and strengths—after such difficult histories, their dignities would need to be built on this.

The setting sun forced us to peel ourselves away. We shook hands with Leng. "I'll be back. I promise we won't forget what you are doing here, Leng," I said, struck by my own words. We were not at a stage to be making any promises to any organizations, and certainly not to one we had only spent a half an hour with. We were in a research stage—I wasn't even sure he had an established NGO. But in leaving Leng, touching his hand, and looking into his eyes, I was overcome with that strange feeling inside that something important had just happened. I knew that I had found a quiet angel, one I would join, hell or high water, in his fight to give back to a world that had been both brutal and inspirational to him. Waving goodbye to Leng and the children, I had to trust that the little flame that had been lit in Siem Reap years and years before was lighting the way forward.

Back at the hotel, I rushed to call Heather and the kids, to check in on how things were going with Isabelle, to tap into my other world that at that moment felt far, far away. "I am managing well," said Heather, "but I am challenged with a small health issue. I have this strange spot on my back that isn't healing. I don't feel altogether well; it could be a staph infection, so I am checking it out."

My body literally went numb as I heard the words *staph infection*. All I could think about was Isabelle's healing leg wound and Heather tending to it. The risk that she was carrying a recent and lethal drug-resistant staph infection was too much to bear so far away. She said she would find out for sure and call me back. In the meantime, we agreed that Nick and Emma would do all the tending with respect to Isabelle—washing her, getting her dressed, etc. I sat in a crumpled nervous heap thousands of miles away in a hotel in Siem Reap, Cambodia, wondering what on earth I was doing so far away from my nest.

Later in the day we got word that Heather was indeed infected with that horrible strain of staph. She had acted quickly and arranged for her mother to fly in from New York to take care of both her and the kids. John and I made our way home praying that Heather would be fine and that Isabelle's leg had not been exposed to the infection. We returned exhausted and frazzled yet relieved to find all was completely under control. The sight of our children and their three glowing faces was such a relief to me. The looks on their faces said, "Where on earth have you been? I am so glad you are home."

18

Where Have You Been?

Great things never came from comfort zones.
Unknown

"Where *are* you?" and "Where have you *been*?" were common messages from my friends and family. They rang in my ears, becoming part of the fabric of my new life. My mother had to get out the atlas to track the places I'd ventured to during that two- to three-year period of building GoPhilanthropic. Those few years were a blur of trips, a whirlwind of amazing encounters and haunting environments. Once home from a trip, mentally inspired and physically exhausted, I would set the alarm to get up to make lunches, throwing myself back into the routine of daily life—groceries, walking the dog, homework, and sleepovers. Reentry into normal daily life sometimes proved particularly difficult. The divide between the filth, warmth, and beauty of the people and places I was visiting and the easy, clean, and uncomplicated life in the United States was just too large a jump to make. For a few days, I could be caught mentally lost somewhere over the ocean.

At times, John and I went out with friends on the weekends. I would straighten my hair and put on a pair of trendy pumps in an attempt to feel normal, but I was far from being really present. When the invariable "Where have you been?" surfaced, I found myself unable to get beyond the basics of the city and country I had traveled to. Where would I begin? How would I start to give justice to what we were seeing? It would take more than an evening, more than a few drinks. It would take a lifetime, and maybe deep down I didn't know if I was ready for that yet. Scared and intimidated by the scope and magnitude of the problems I was seeing in the world, yet humbled by the strength of the human spirit, I found it easier, for the moment, to keep it all inside.

Before any given trip, I would spend weeks researching on the Internet, sourcing programs in a particular region, reading articles and books written by those who knew the areas intimately. A little nugget of information would then lead to a link, a blog, at times a small website if they had one, describing a tiny educational program. Sometimes I was given recommendations to organizations through our local ground operators or guides, those who would manage the travel logistics of our journeys—they knew and cared about their own communities and were as eager as we were to create these new channels for assistance. Most of the organizations I sourced were virtually invisible to international funding groups yet served some of the neediest in the communities. Almost all were run on a shoestring, or rather a thread, and normally depended on the tenacious hopes of one determined and selfless individual.

Motivated to meet them in person, I would then set off on these journeys, armed with a small carry-on filled with only the essentials—Cipro for the nasty can-kill-a-trip sicknesses, a journal, a few pieces of clothing, a handful of toiletries, a camera, and a computer. Then slowly, little by little, I traveled through Central America, Southeast Asia, India, and Tanzania, being led to dozens of humanitarians who would change my perspective on life.

It was my guide in Guatemala who led me to the town of San Juan La Laguna on the volcanic banks of Lake Atitlan, where I visited a small school that provided support to children suffering from disabilities. As I approached a modest set of concrete buildings set into the verdant hillside and surrounded by coffee plants, I heard cheers and screams of laughter as a small group of children with various disabilities, from birth deformities to Down syndrome, played games under a shade tree in the school's makeshift courtyard. Leticia, the school's director, greeted me with open arms. Out of breath yet wide-eyed, she explained that they were celebrating a birthday. "It is a special day for them— but please no pictures or videos of the children," she said with the air of a protective mother as she ushered us into a bare classroom.

Taking a deep breath, Leticia launched into a passionate, heartfelt dialogue describing the mission of the school and its need for resources. She spoke in fast Spanish that I struggled to keep up with, gathering at best 50 percent of what she said. It was evident that what she was relaying meant the world to her.

"This is the only place for a child with Down syndrome to come," she said. "And then there are those with muscular problems and other syndromes—there are those with hearing problems and retardation. This small school takes one hundred and fifty of these students in all, and somehow we must provide therapy—speech and physical—plus education to all of them at their individual levels. We have little to no help from the government. It is near impossible, but we are their only hope. We have one vehicle that we use to make the rounds and pick them up. This vehicle is so important because most families are ashamed to have a child with disabilities, and they are hidden away in a back corner of the family hut, deprived of attention and their basic right to learn." Sitting in a quiet corner of her humble shelter, she explained to me in her broken English, "There are many who never get here, many we aren't reaching."

I was quickly transplanted back to Rochester where Izzy went for her weekly sessions of physical therapy, a huge brick school with polished floors, state-of-the-art equipment, monthly evaluations, and progress reports. And it didn't stop there—she had triweekly speech sessions with a therapist who would drive to see her in her play-school setting so as not to disrupt her routine. The children in Guatemala were lucky if their parents were open and brave enough to put the stigma and humiliation aside and let them leave the house, let alone brave enough to find the one school that would meet their needs, though it was miles away and teetering on the edge of closing due to lack of funds and materials.

In the northern jungle area of El Peten near the ancient Mayan ruins of Tikal in Guatemala, another guide, Eric Garcia, slowed down the car after I explained to him why I was in the country. Finally bringing the car to a full stop, he looked at me in the eyes like we were old friends. "Lydia," he said in a serious tone, "lots of my clients want to pull money out from their pockets and give it to these poor people. This is not the way," he said, waving his finger. He then pulled out a black folder from the front seat of the van. "I want to show you something. I have a little *projecto*...it's a baby *projecto* but I think an example of the way that we can help poor people in a good way.

"I love orchids, Lydia, and all plants," he said laughing. "We have many, many wonderful plants here in Guatemala, Lydia—you would be amazed. I have bought a little piece of land not far from here, and I have this idea to make a small orchid trail. But I would have more than orchids, Lydia. I would have all plants that are indigenous to this area, and medicinal ones too! And I love art—I am not just a botanist, but I am a lover of Mayan art, you see..." he went on, turning the pages of his black book excitedly. "You see, this is an example of the beautiful Mayan pots that we will paint and have on the trail—with symbols of Mayan life and ancestry. The trail will represent much of Mayan culture and the way that we can live off of the land. We have so much here on the land that we can make use of—we have more food than we need if we can relearn how to make use of the land.

"The thing, though, that makes my *projecto* really special is this...the land is surrounded by very, very poor villages. My vision is to have the village children work on my orchid trail, and during our work together, they will learn about the wonderful value of what they have at their fingertips—their plants, land, and culture. Eventually they will learn to be as proud of it as I am, and it will give them hope for their future," he said. "There remains much here, Lydia. There is so much to make us happy; we don't need handouts."

I traveled to Vietnam several times, meeting with programs ranging from large concrete institutions housing children battling with the aftereffects of Agent Orange used in the Vietnam War, to simple community-run programs focused on small-business development for women. Le Ly Hayslip, a Vietnamese war survivor, and I spent endless hours together both in the United States and near her home village of Ky La in central Vietnam discussing her harrowing adolescent memories of living on the front lines during the war. After her autobiography, *When Heaven and Earth Changed Places*, received significant recognition, she spent the next twenty years building two foundations fighting to bring health and education services to her country. When Oliver Stone, a Vietnam veteran himself, made a movie about her life, she became the poster child for turning pain into positive action in her war-torn country—her foundation funding new clinics and schools through Vietnam. Her latest project involved bringing small wooden mobile libraries to government schools that still lacked basic teaching tools.

Most of the time I traveled alone, with John staying home to watch the kids and focus on getting Only Provence on its feet. A few times, though, we mixed it up, one or the other of us taking Nick or Emma along for the ride. It was important not only that they understood theoretically what we were attempting to do and build, but also that they live it with us. We valued their thoughts, ideas, and input and had always learned from their fresh perspectives. The decision to include them on our scout trips would later become a key value for GoPhilanthropic: *Get your children out of their comfort zones, and connect them to the world.* But of course there were those all-too-familiar questions and doubts from those around us. "You are going to bring them where?" they asked. "But what about missed school?"

Blinders, blinders, put up the walls and blinders, I told myself. *Don't listen.* I would become deaf to these questions and doubts. There was a voice so strong in my head screaming at me—continue, roll on, put fear aside, and get on with it. There was a road to walk, a road that needed to be walked.

One cold January morning, John traveled to India with Nick, then nearing age twelve, while I stayed on the home front. Nick was chuffed at the chance to be with his dad solo, and he was also sporting a new video camera. He had been a wild-eyed artist in every sense, moving between singing, acting, writing, and now filming as passions. We had offered to buy the new camera under the condition that he get some footage we could use from India. He obliged happily.

There was no delay in being thrown into the whirlwind of India's special blend of sweet and sour, and within a few hours of landing, the two set off to visit Life Tree, a shelter that assisted abandoned and homeless children. After crossing open sewers and weaving in and out of sleeping cows, they arrived at the crumbling building in a particularly rough part of New Delhi and were greeted warmly by Pascal, a tall and lanky thirty-eight-year-old Frenchmen who had found his calling in caring for boys whose families could no longer provide for them. The children had extremely rough histories of abandonment and abuse, both physical and sexual.

"Many of them are pulled from the railway station. When they arrive, they are so crushed and lost," Pascal said as he guided them through a labyrinth of narrow hallways, dorm rooms, and makeshift classrooms shockingly void of chalkboards and supplies. Children seemed to be everywhere.

"Some have been so abused that they have lost their sense of identity completely," he explained. He showed Nick and John a row of photographs, each depicting one of the boys with his name clearly written underneath. "These boys are healing from an ugly, nasty place in life, yet they unite together as a family and are now learning about who they might be inside. Slowly, they are looking toward some sort of future," Pascal said. "It's becoming dangerous here, though. The building is managed by the local slum mafia—they are bad people, and the children are not safe. My dream is actually to start my own shelter somewhere safer and independent."

Bright, energetic, and spirited kids floated everywhere, yet in some sort of organized chaos. There was an unmistakable glow to the place despite the crumbling walls, exposed wires, and peeling paint, and a warmth only found in a family-like setting permeated the shelter. It was clear that Pascal was the nexus of this newfound stability and security. The boys were excited to meet Nick, a newcomer who was about their same age and who seemed at ease and pleased to be meeting them as well. After playing soccer in the decaying courtyard, the boys proudly showed him their stark bunks with tattered sheets. Later, as it was nearing time to leave, one boy carefully pulled out a small tin box, in which, he explained, he stored all of his precious items.

"Mom, it was wild to learn about how these kids lived on the streets, how they used to steal—they were real thieves... then they moved into the shelters, and they stopped doing that, starting new lives. It's like they found themselves."

Found themselves, I thought. *What might a twelve-year-old know or mean by that?*

"Some of the children are dirty, and they are so skinny. But they are not miserable though, Mom, like you would think. That's the thing that's weird. They aren't miserable. They are hopeful."

While John and I had been looking at where these children had come from, the quality of their surroundings, and what they might need in the future, Nick had picked up on the small nuggets of truth that were perhaps more important—*they aren't miserable. They are hopeful.*

Chiang Mai, Thailand
Spring 2008

One evening, Emma and I stared out over the tops of the ornate city rooftops in northern Thailand. Inhaling the incense sneaking in from the nearby temple, we soaked in a hot tub, and I thought of the sea of faces we had witnessed that day at a home that cared for abandoned children with HIV. The institution was now beginning to heave—its numbers nearing a thousand children. I thought about how we were searching for a way to make a difference for all of these programs, but seeing the enormity of the institutions, packed as they were with hundreds of children who were lucky to have a roof over their heads and even a slim chance at being educated, made me question the value in even trying.

As I sank farther into the warm water, sharp and nagging questions swept through my consciousness—was I giving false hope to those who perhaps saw some glint of optimism in my visits? Looking into Emma's deep-blue eyes, I asked, "OK, now what? What do I do next?" I continuously felt as though I was standing at the foot of a huge mountain I needed to climb, but as I slept at night that mountain stretched farther toward the sky.

"Mom. Don't worry. You'll figure it out," she said with such relaxed certainty, as if she knew that, over time, it would all unfold as it was meant to. For a minute, it was just she and I back in the playroom in Orlando when I could barely put one foot in front of the other. I thought about whether I had been handed a prescribed text of next steps back then—and surely no, I hadn't. Life had simply provided the next stepping stones. Life had led me to Costa Rica and to France, closer to my older children and to Isabelle. It had now led me to the doorsteps of so many important human beings—I just had to trust that it wasn't all for naught.

Listening to the stories of these quiet angels and attempting to understand what sort of special, magical strength had been woven into their souls, I wasn't going to stop until I knew what I was going to do next, having found them. While the plan was to build trips around the work of their organizations, somewhere deep down I had a suspicion there was more at work than that.

Meeting people like Pascal, Leticia, Eric, and Le Ly forced me to think deeply about the kind of giving we would facilitate. It was becoming clear to me that education and empowerment would be the needed underpinnings of the programs we chose to assist. But I was unsure of exactly how we would offer our support without falling into traditional cycles of dependency. I trusted, though, that the way forward would become clearer as I went. So I did the only thing I knew how to do—I gathered all of the painful, fearless, and heroic stories from these beautiful people, their aspirations, dreams, and hopes for the future—and I put them in a sack. Making silent promises from my heart to theirs, I then slung that sack on my back and continued to walk.

19

Tea with Gandhi

It is better to light a candle than curse the darkness.
Eleanor Roosevelt

Alok, the guide who had assisted John and Nick during their trip to India, happened to ask John where he was from. When he learned that we lived in Rochester, he was immediately overjoyed.

"That's where Arun Gandhi lives—Rochester! He's the grandson of Mohandas Gandhi. Do you know him? I assist Arun when he is in India every year. He is a dear old friend. What you are trying to do with your travel project might interest him. He speaks all over the world, spreading his grandfather's message of nonviolence, and he is also working on a wonderful school project south of Mumbai in the rural areas around Kolhapur. He is trying to help children who are exploited by the brick kiln industry. His dream is to build a school for them," Alok explained excitedly.

I had heard about Arun Gandhi living in town during our first house-hunting trip to Rochester the year prior. I distinctly remember a flutter in my stomach with the simple realization that a member of the Gandhi family could be within arm's reach.

A few weeks after John and Nick returned from India, we received a message from Arun. He had learned of our efforts with GoPhilanthropic, no doubt through Alok, and was interested in meeting. It turned out Arun lived only a few miles from our house, so we agreed to meet for coffee at Panera Bread, which for me seemed like a terribly unceremonious place to have a one-on-one with the grandson of the great Mahatma Gandhi. I was so excited I had to pinch myself.

We sat in Panera that day, and I nervously awaited his arrival, wondering how similar or different he might be from his grandfather. Arun had been born and raised in South Africa and had found it very difficult to live under its apartheid. He often referred to himself as not being white enough for the Europeans or black enough for the Africans. As a result, the young Arun was subjected to racial violence from all sides. Luckily, his parents could see he needed some time with his grandfather. From 1946 until Mahatma Gandhi's assassination in 1948, Arun lived with him in India, learning firsthand the importance of his teachings on nonviolence. For the rest of his life, Arun would continue to share with the world the valuable lessons he learned during those precious years.

When he arrived, he embraced John and me warmly and smiled softly, sporting a light twinkle in his eye—a look that I would come to know well. We sat and chatted that day for what felt like hours about life and our common interests—India, his background, the need for development within rural villages, our desire to bring awareness to grassroots programs through travel. He had been guiding a Gandhi Legacy Tour through India for many years through Global Exchange that focused on spending time with small yet effective programs in rural communities. But while people hurried to sign up every year for the trip, it was not successful in generating funds for the programs it visited. He hoped maybe we could help.

After that initial meeting, I invited him over for dinner, and I recollect still being nervous around him, not knowing what to prepare. I don't remember what I finally decided on as a menu, but I distinctly remember fussing for hours. He was so appreciative, but he said, "Lydia, you needn't have gone to such an effort." And he meant it. It was clear from our earliest visits that he was a man of great humility and calm who carried tremendous passion for his grandfather's principles, rooted in a return to simplicity. There was no need to fuss over impressions when there was so much work to be done in the world.

Over the course of the years in Rochester, I would meet with Arun many times—most often for tea, which we would enjoy in either of our small kitchens. The walls of his simple apartment were adorned with aging photos of his family; his late wife, Sunanda; himself with the Dalai Lama; and his grandfather, M. K. Gandhi, one hand holding a walking stick and the other draped around the young Arun. I learned a lifetime of lessons sipping tea with Arun. He was so easy to talk to, and so I shared everything with him, the ups and downs of daily life, some days pouring my heart out over my concerns with Isabelle—her sense of loss and my seeming inability to compensate for it. As I continued my scout trips to find programs, I shared the weight of responsibility I was beginning to feel and my deepening concern for how I could possibly contribute to them from my little house on Seminole Way.

There was one story that Arun shared that would stay with me forever. He described the tremendous emotional pain he had felt after his grandfather had been assassinated. "Alongside feeling the loss for such a great man, I felt an almost crippling responsibility to live up to him, to walk in his shoes, to be like him," Arun explained. Arun's mother had seen that he was struggling and offered some sound advice that would help ease the pain. Who would have known these words would put him on a path that would guide his life's work.

"You have a choice, Arun," she had said. "You can bear the weight of responsibility of being a Gandhi, carry it on your back like a ton of bricks—or you can carry the flame of his message before you like a candle, casting a light as you go."

Carry it on your back like a ton of bricks. The words struck me, and I all but stopped breathing. I thought of the sack on my shoulder. The sack that held Izzy's pain and the collective stories from all of the people I had met over the past few years—the sack that was starting to become too heavy to carry.

Arun chose to carry the flame through his life, continuing to share his grandfather's teachings wherever he could. For thirty years he wrote for the *Times of India*, he built an Institute of Peace, and he spoke on university campuses all over the world.

As I drove home that day, rain pelting the windshield, Arun's words spun over and over in my head. It would be pointless to carry the weight and responsibility of everything I was experiencing—I couldn't go on like this, I admitted to myself. Arun was right. There was another way. I needed to see things from a completely different perspective. *Maybe I could focus on shedding light on what these wonderful people are doing, carrying the flame of their strength and courage, instead of carrying the weight of the problems,* I thought as I pulled into our driveway.

In 2009, Arun and I developed a GoPhilanthropic journey that would consider philanthropy in light of Gandhian principles. We would travel through India together, guiding a group, taking a personal look at various projects in the slums with some of his grandfather's teachings in mind.

Before the trip, I had shared a concern I had been chewing on for a while, one that I hadn't been able to get clarity on. "It's sensitive, Arun, the giving part of our trips. I want to make sure that the support is handled right—that it doesn't represent a handout or charity. All of the clients who travel through GoPhilanthropic have different reasons and purposes for wanting to travel and give back to the communities they visit. Some might do it out of guilt, because it makes them feel better. Others genuinely want to support those who are working toward building better lives. Should I worry at all about the intentions of those who are giving, or should I simply focus on making sure the funds go to the right place?" I had asked.

After a long moment of silence and a few bites of cookie, Arun had responded.

"Yes, Lydia—I think the intentions of the giver are very important. My grandfather always said that giving must come from compassion and not pity or guilt. If you have compassion, you have a deep awareness of someone's suffering and a genuine desire to help relieve it. If you give out of pity, you are not seeing the other as an equal; you simply feel bad for them. If you don't see them as an equal, what you have to offer will be of less value, and the receiver will feel less worthy in the process. Grandfather spoke of trusteeship as opposed to ownership—that in life we don't really own all that we have the way we think we do. We are more like trustees, and we must manage what we have, wisely, for the benefit of others as well as for ourselves."

Months later, Arun and I were sitting in a bus driving through the clogged and congested streets of Mumbai, past high-rise development projects on one side of the road and the famous Dharavi slums, the backdrop to the movie *Slumdog Millionnaire,* on the other. Arun shared with our group what he had explained to me earlier that year about trusteeship. The meaning took on a more profound significance now that we were in India, where the need to share what we each had could be seen on every street corner.

"Grandfather's message about trusteeship goes beyond sharing our financial resources. We need to be willing to share the natural talents and skills that each of us has been given. We have to be willing to share *who we are*."

Share who we are. I was instantly reminded of my guide, Eric Garcia, in Guatemala. Like Arun, Eric had been a teacher on so many levels. As he had guided me through the enchanting complex of Mayan ruins, he had often referred back to snippets of wisdom taught him by his grandfather, a man of pure Mayan descent who believed very strongly in its ancient wisdom. We had talked about happiness and simplicity and the joy of life not being found in the material world.

"Lydia—my grandfather taught me important lessons that our culture believes are at the heart of our purpose as people. He told me that each one of us has a special talent and gift. When we are doing that very thing, we no longer have to worry because we will find life's happiness as we are doing this. I may not be rich, but I love what I am doing. I get to share these beautiful ruins, meet people, and work with my orchids. I am a very happy man," Eric had said.

Arun took us through the tiny back alleyways of Mumbai to a variety of women's empowerment organizations developed out of grassroots efforts and based on education, opportunity, and most importantly, self-sufficiency. We saw schools being run on train platforms and in two-foot-wide shacks by the side of the tracks. Despite the conditions, the children were engaged and teachers spirited. Finally, Arun guided us to a place he had been telling me about for such a long time, to the city Kolhapur two hundred miles south of Mumbai. It was there that he and his wife, Sunanda, had been supporting a small group of children who had been rescued from child labor. The determined, driven woman behind their rescue was Anuradha Bhosale, who had devoted her life to empowering the poorest, those sometimes referred to as being below even the untouchable caste in India.

As we sat in a hot, small room, Anuradha explained how she had been forced into domestic servitude at the age of six, but even at this early age she had known that the path out of a life of poverty would be through education. She had saved every penny and later put herself through school, earning a master's degree in social work. But she had never forgotten her humble beginnings, and from the start, she had used her knowledge to encourage others to do the same for themselves. After graduating, she had been sent to Kolhapur and immediately exposed to the needs of migrant children who crushed the rocks used in paving roads. She would later learn that more than thirty-five thousand children were involved in daily labor for local industries. While her initial response had been anger and outrage, she had known she had to start with empowering those who were being exploited. For the next twenty years, she had held meetings under trees, on platforms, in the brickyards, educating people, particularly women and children, with respect to their rights. Day in and day out, she had fought for the prevention of child exploitation, labor, and trafficking, and female infanticide. She had introduced these families to the principles of microfinance and assisted in setting up self-help groups for women.

Anuradha was now the director of AVANI, an organization that facilitated the rescue of child laborers and provided migrant children the right to health care and education. It organized the construction of schools inside the brickyards and ran a residential home for migrant children. "Child labor is a cyclical phenomenon oftentimes beginning with women in vulnerable positions. Empowering, educating, and uniting disadvantaged women to build sustainable futures in a male-dominated society is the backbone of our work," she said with deep conviction as she pushed flies away from her forehead with the back of her hand.

As we walked through the smoking brick kilns, I paused, marveling at the strength that came from deep within her. On the long trip back home to the United States, I thought about how Arun had helped me see things from a new perspective. It had taken some time—months of drinking tea and yet another trip to India, this time by his side—but I could sense the beginnings of a fresh look at how I was going to make my way forward. Illuminating what these wonderful people were doing, listening to them, telling their stories, would create a cornerstone for what we did. And the support wouldn't just come from our pocketbooks; it would come from our hearts—from *who we are*. I didn't exactly know what that meant, but I knew one thing for sure—when we gave like this, it would be enough.

Slowly, I could feel a soft but uncontrollable smile start to spread across my face—my body and heart began to feel a little bit lighter, a little bit freer. Closing my eyes and breathing more deeply than I had in all our years since returning to the United States, I was lulled into a thick sleep by the hum of the airplane.

20

Mystery Calls from the Canaima Canyons

We thought that we had the answers, it was the questions we had wrong.

Bono

I felt my mother sitting on my shoulder, cringing at my irresponsibility as I crammed myself into the back of the single-prop plane headed into the lost world of the Gran Sabana in Venezuela, an area known for the archeological and mystical wonders of the *tepuis*, tabletop mountains, the spiritual homeland of the Pemón Indians. There was a collective hunching over of cell phones as each of us sent the last text messages and e-mails. We would be totally cut off for several days as we explored this magnificent wonderland of cascading waterfalls, jungles, winding rivers, savannahs, and Pemón culture. The plane's propeller lunged into motion; the pilot flung open the window letting in gusts of air. "I hope he plans on closing that," muffled Val as we were whisked from the ground.

Valentina was our first hire for GoPhilanthropic, and I was thrilled to finally have some regular company on such a mind-boggling project. Together we were now making great strides in uncovering worthy programs and arranging itineraries, but some trips raised more questions than answers— leading us to figure out more of what we wouldn't do with GoPhilanthropic than what we would. I was quickly learning the complex ways growth, development, and aid could upset a delicate ecosystem of ancient cultures. Val had come on board to manage travel to Central and South America for GoPhilanthropic. She had a profound passion for ecotourism and responsible travel and had been longtime friends with Paul Stanley, the founder of Angel Conservation, dedicated to conserving the cultures of indigenous peoples of Venezuela. In developing GoPhilanthropic's tours, she believed there might be opportunities to assist with Angel Conservation's community projects.

Our group of five was led by Paul and consisted of Anthony, an Italian journalist; Martha, a Venezuelan anthropologist; Valentina; and myself. The plane plunged steeply around the sandstone cliffs of the *tepuis* as we entered Canaima National Park, named a UNESCO World Heritage site in 1994 and home to the tallest waterfall in the world, Angel Falls. The immense watershed of the Orinoco Delta lay to the north, and Brazil and the Amazon to the south. I gasped at the incredible topography around us yet also feared death in this little plane. Out of the corner of my eye, I noticed Martha nervously trying to reaffix a piece of metal that had fallen off the inside of the plane.

Nervous too, I forced myself to take a few deep breaths and sink into the comfortable state of bliss that I seemed to find in traveling to new places. An hour later, I was jolted back into reality with the sudden impact of landing and squeaking wheels. I released Val's knee that I had unknowingly been gripping for the entire flight.

We crawled out of the plane onto the great savannah. I was immediately stunned by vastness all around me. Massive expanses of golden, flat plains gave way to jutting table mountains.

For the Pemón, the *tepuis* are sacred mountains, "guardians of the savannah," where the spirits are said to steal the souls of the living. The word *Canaima*, from which the national park gets its name, signifies the spirit of evil. The Pemón believe that the spirits make their home in the *tepuis*, which therefore should not be ascended. Of the nearly hundred mountains in the area, only about half are known to have been explored.

But in recent years, with the increase in tourism, some Pemón had begun to disregard these traditional beliefs, collecting a guide fee for taking groups of hikers to the tops of these sacred mountains.

Strangely there were no other sounds besides the faint howl of a forceful wind coming off of the mountains. Clemente, our Pemón guide, greeted us warmly, and with steady barefooted steps, led us to the encampment at Uruyen, a cluster of small, simple thatched huts. The group spent the next hour chatting with Clemente about our plan for the following days, an expedition that would entail a combination of hiking to the area's famous canyons and caves, and creating the outline for a cultural-identity program recently set forth by Angel Conservation. Over the course of the last decades, the traditions, heritage, and language of the Pemón had been steadily dwindling. With the tourist industry quickly developing, conservation groups were worried about what the future held. Questions were being raised about whether the Pemón were prepared to deal with the impact and implications of tourism—if they understood the consequences of what streams of tourists would do to their traditional way of life. Yes, there would be more potential for income, but they would be shifting from a system whereby they depended upon themselves to one where they needed tourists to survive for economic growth. This would be a delicate and dangerous road to take.

Paul and I were interested in exploring whether GoPhilanthropic could help support the Pemón in various ways. "They really need a lot," he said. "They are forever coming to me with lists of things they could use...computers, money to repair their buildings, etcetera." Paul also ran a tour company and had invested in various projects, such as helping the Pemón with Internet access so that they could better manage incoming tourists. Several Pemón had launched minitour operations or managed accommodations and meals for travelers through their connections to Paul. To them, Paul was somewhat all powerful, bringing business and income they hadn't previously had a need for. They had lived without interaction with the outside world for so long, and it would be a tricky road to navigate just how to balance preservation of past with the present.

A dusty ancient Toyota pickup truck with wooden benches lining the flatbed waited to take us to a trailhead leading to a hidden waterfall tucked into the walls of a nearby *tepui*. Cars needed to be shipped in by plane or helicopter in pieces and assembled on the ground due to the remoteness of the area. As a consequence, only a few were seen bumping down the handful of grassy roads leading to tiny villages in the area. This truck looked as if it had been creatively assembled. I sat next to a ten-gallon jug filled with some liquid and fitted with tubes going through the driver's side window. The driver, I noticed, couldn't have been a day older than twelve.

Setting off with the sun beating down on us, the group was silent as we took in the enormity of the plains surrounding us. Once on the trail, Clemente led the way, pointing out various plants and trees until the route got rocky and barren. Martha, not so nimble on her feet, clutched Clemente's hand—they would be joined like this for the days to come. "Careful where you grab for support," he said. "There are prickly spikes and possibly spiders and snakes resting on the branches." Glances were exchanged between the women. I briefly considered what we would do out here for medical help, then quickly brushed the thought away.

At some point, we were told to strip down and dump our clothes on the rocks but keep our river shoes on. When I had read *bathing suit* on our gear list, I had pictured sitting by the odd pool or splashing in a river at day's end. I hadn't pictured trekking through the jungle in it with a group of young Pemón. I was now scrambling to keep my bikini straight as I trudged and tramped through the brush, up and down the thin steep path that bordered a virgin stream. "What does *L-O-S-T* mean?" asked Martha in Spanish, reading the letters printed on the ass of my bikini bottoms. Some stupid attempt at branding now took on a different meaning as we trudged deeper into the canyons of a lost world. I was momentarily embarrassed and self-conscious to be half naked, but something about the energy of the earth around us, the grandness of the tabletops, put things in their right place. Only having been there a few hours, I felt it was clear that there were different elements at work—an intensity and power that I had only encountered in the jungle surrounding the temples in Cambodia. It was if the earth itself spoke, if we listened. Our bodies, hanging out of the edges of our various suits as we scrambled on all fours, couldn't have been more insignificant in the presence of what was around us.

Eventually our path became a stream, and we continued hiking through the water. After what seemed like hours since setting out, we swam a final turn in the river and were greeted with a vision out of a fairy-tale book. A waterfall, cascades of pounding water landing in a greenish-blue pool with shimmering rocks lined with bromeliads and vines, appeared seemingly out of nowhere. Sunlight streamed through forest growth, and the spray of the falls created a hazy mist as though we had entered another plane of reality. We dispersed; some dove off the rocks to the foot of the cascade, others waded at the water's edge. I climbed on a rock smooth from endless years of water erosion and basked in the warmth of the sunlight. Time slipped away into an unknown sphere. Few words were spoken, some photos were taken, and then at some point we stood to make the trip back.

The sun set a golden rose over the savannah as we bumped back to Uruyen. After a dinner I scarcely remember, sleep came deep and dense as the wind hurled through our hut, along with the strange, ever-present silence.

In the morning we were greeted with the smells of eggs and pancakes alongside sliced white bread, like we were at Denny's.

"What do the Pemón eat for breakfast, Clemente?" I asked, trying to mask my disappointment in the authenticity of the food before us.

"Oh, we have soup with hot peppers, manioc bread, and fish," he said. "Same as we have for lunch and dinner. Always the same."

After some probing, it became clear that those involved in these early stages of tourism were encouraged by an old-school mentality, government driven, that the tourists would want what they had at home. Paul explained, "It's an awful battle trying to convince the Pemón that travelers are interested in learning about and experiencing their authentic way of life. In this sense, travel could be a powerful resource in encouraging the preservation of their culture."

We ate our pancakes as Clemente pointed to a hand-drawn map, which was to be our route for the day. The flatbed would bring us first to the village of Kamarata. From there we would continue on by dugout boat to a more remote village, where we would attend a unique event—a soccer tournament that had been arranged between ten

Pemón villages. In the evening, the dugout boat would drop us on the banks of the river, where we would spend the night in hammocks under the stars.

Piling once again in the back of the dusty Toyota and heading into the expanse of the savannah, we each held on to whatever we could for support. Every so often, we came to rushing streams choked with small- to large-sized boulders. Instead of slowing down, the pickup gathered speed, hurling itself through the river and up the steep muddy embankment on the other side. *"Cuidado!"* someone yelled, and we all ducked as the pickup plowed through low-hanging branches.

And so it went until we reached Kamarata. Standing fortuitously on the edge of town was the mission school, oddly vacant as the school children were home for carnival. English Protestant missionaries started to Christianize the Pemón at the end of the nineteenth century. But despite this introduction to Christianity, the Pemón remained intimately connected to their spiritual and mystical beliefs, a fascinating blend of magical invocations, chants, and various secret rites. I suddenly wished I had another three months to spend learning more of this ancient culture.

We headed to the house of Hortensia, the village leader, for discussions about Angel Conservation's cultural identity program. Most of the Pemón folklore is passed on orally with little to no documentation. Their language, rooted in rare Carib linguistics, is a uniquely distinct dialect that has been watered down with Spanish over the past decades. Increased access to the outside world in the past forty years had also provided a natural pathway for younger Pemón to leave the region, further threatening the purity of their distinctive culture and language. Martha, the anthropologist, had spent years in Mexico facilitating similar cultural programs, and like the others she had managed, this project would entail a careful gathering and recording of data from the village elders regarding their music, ancient stories, and traditions. The success of the project would depend on Martha's ability to connect on a level with Hortensia, to gain her trust and confidence. While Martha was Venezuelan, she was not Pemón and was considered as much of an outsider as we were.

We sat around the table as hours slipped away, discussing the difficulty of Pemón life and the elements of their economy that now depended mainly upon fishing and agriculture. Out of a local population of about fifteen hundred, only forty or so had jobs that generated money. This seemed like a tiny figure, yet the Pemón life had always been one of subsistence. Soil degradation was now a major concern in the valley, and their recent efforts at keeping cows, something they had never done before, had failed miserably. "Help" from the outside had come for the cow project, yet the funders had neglected to teach the Pemón how to care for the animals and how to carefully process the milk. The cows were dying one by one.

I carefully studied Hortensia's facial expression and demeanor as Martha presented the reasoning and importance of the identification project. Over the course of the afternoon, Hortensia's body language changed from closed and stoic to relaxed and engaged. Some slight transformation had taken place, and Martha had achieved step one with Hortensia in the process—trust that we were not there to sell anything to, or take anything from, the Pemón. By the end of our session, cold beers and soda crackers were served, and warm embraces were exchanged.

Our next stop was a remote village for the soccer tournament. Our group was lucky to have been invited to the celebration, offering us a rare glimpse at what normally would have been a private Pemón affair. The dugout boat wound for two blistering hours down the river. I hid for most of the time under a towel, attempting to shield myself from the power of the sun and focusing on my feet burning a rich red with every passing minute. The boat was manned by two men—one in the back steering and another young Pemón dangling his legs over the bow, using hand signals to the driver to indicate logs, rocks, and shallow ground. The water level was terribly low. It was painfully slow going, the driver often needing to quickly jerk the motor out of the water to avoid rocks and sticks in our way. We stopped several times, so the men could get out and push. Roasting like a pig on a stick, I attempted to shift my weight to ease my discomfort from sitting on the hard wooden benches. I was told off twice for leaning too much to one side or the other.

It had been a long day already, nearing three o'clock, and we hadn't eaten since breakfast. The monotony was broken by the sudden chatter of children, and as we rounded a bend, I spotted several other dugout boats parked at the river's edge. A couple of other boats were loaded with excited Pemón children who had come from miles away for the much-anticipated match, some in soccer T-shirts and others dressed in traditional grass skirts, headbands, and loin cloths. Catching the excited buzz from the children, we disembarked and joined the procession trekking through the open valley, passing clusters of girls giggling under trees as they strung together traditional skirts made from palm. The children smiled and turned shyly away from our foreign presence and attempts to greet them, the odd brave boy running up to us, then taking off grinning from ear to ear.

We were ushered into the communal hut for formal introductions, but the children were visibly eager to get started with the match. A feast had been laid out of local specialties, potatoes, manioc bread, bananas, two different spicy soups with fish and whole chili peppers, and a homemade tribal alcoholic drink made from sweet potatoes. I immediately spotted the plate of rich reddish-brown sauce served alongside the main dishes. We had seen and tasted this unique sauce made of ants, and sometimes termites, a few nights earlier. It had been served as an appetizer alongside roasted grubs! While at first we had been hesitant to try it, we now proudly dipped our bread and spuds into the sauce, marveling at the taste. Ravenous from the day's activities, we dug into the communal bowls.

I broke off a piece of the hard manioc bread and dipped it into the soup as I was shown to do—it was wonderful, perfectly spiced. On the next bite, I got a little more daring and scooped a whole green pepper into my mouth. Surprisingly, it wasn't as hot as I thought it would be. Spying a single red pepper in the bowl and being the hot-food freak that I am, I mounded the whole thing on a hunk of potato and popped it into my mouth, downing it with a swig of the local alcohol. The effect of this simple action took only about five seconds to hit me. *Fuck*, I thought. *I think I am seriously in trouble.*

I knew right away that something was terribly, terribly wrong. Searing, scorching, burning flames engulfed my throat. Eyes watering, I fumbled for anything to wash it down with, shoving bits of sweet banana in my mouth and gulping more of the alcohol. "What's wrong?" asked Val.

"I ate that red pepper in the soup," I sputtered. "And something tells me I shouldn't have." By this time I was nearly doubled over in pain. Clemente came over and asked what had happened. I told him I had eaten a pepper, and he immediately asked me what color pepper it was.

"It was red," I sheepishly admitted. He grabbed me by the elbow.

"You did what? You ate a red pepper? You are not supposed to. They are not for eating! These peppers are grown especially here in our valleys—they are fiercely hot and potent and not to be ingested," he yelled.

I briefly stopped to think of our conversation over the pancakes that morning and shuddered to think of what he now must think of our request to "go local." My head spun, and I was overcome with nausea. The pepper was now making its way down to my stomach. I felt every move it made with a resulting searing as if was literally burning holes in my intestines along the way. I made a quick scan of my surroundings for a place I might be able to throw up, and without making a scene, I made my way to some tall grasses, Clemente at my heels.

"We are finding a hammock for you, Lydia!" he reassured. More sweeping waves of nausea and I fell to my knees, fearing a total pass-out. One of the men who had been assisting Clemente with our group approached us, and Clemente filled him in. Shocked, he quickly went back to the hut returning with a cup of Coke. Instead of bringing it directly to me, he turned his back and hunched over it. "It is an ancient secret, what he is doing," Clemente said. "You mustn't worry...you will be fine, but you must drink it all, every drop." I wondered what on earth he was doing to this Coke and for a brief second got a flash of my family, my three children, and how far away I was.

I was handed the cup; shutting my eyes, I began to take sips. Valentina and Martha had arrived and everyone was staring at me, anxiously awaiting my reaction. Within seconds of draining the cup, I felt the nausea vanish completely. I don't mean a little; I mean entirely. Slowly, I got to my feet and took a breath. "What on earth did he do to it?" I asked Clemente, brushing the dirt from my knees.

"Ancient traditions," he said as he guided me back to the hut, where a hammock had been set up for me to rest.

The pain had now vanished, and only a faint soreness in my stomach remained as we enjoyed the tribal dancing the children had prepared. Suddenly all I could think about were the sounds of swishing grass skirts and rattling bamboo instruments that filled the valley. I looked around at the rest of the group, and all seemed equally sucked into the surreal and dreamlike ancient calls of the dance.

Later the sun set golden as we trekked across the open fields toward the river's edge. It was late, and by the time we got into the dugout to make our way to the camp, miles up the river, it was totally pitch-black dark. With a single flashlight, it was nearly impossible to see the boulders and trees in the water. I developed vivid visions of the boat hitting a branch and our various bodies being scattered in the river. Again, the men needed to get out from time to time, now in total darkness, to push and guide the boat through the shallow parts. We were told to get out at a certain point, and, grabbing our bags and food for the night, we made our way down a jungle path, dense and dark. One of Clemente's helpers carried a machete and a shotgun slung on his shoulder. I wondered what for.

We fumbled in the darkness in single file, Antonio staying close behind. I could tell from his breathing and the quickness in his step that he was as uncomfortable as I was. We had no idea where we were going or how long it would take to get to the camp. I felt a creeping angst settle into my stomach. I knew better than to let the fear take hold, and so I let it roll off into the blackness of jungle.

Finally, after what had felt like hours, we arrived at an extended hut lined with hammocks. Martha rolled into one and didn't appear until morning. Clemente brought Valentina and me a bucket of river water to wash in, then returned with two cold beers and soda crackers. I realized just how relative things were. These few simple details—water, a cold beer, and a handful of crackers—out here in the Venezuelan bush were as luxurious as a bubble bath, champagne, and caviar would have been at home. Huddling around a candlelit rickety wooden table, we tucked into fried fish and plantains that melted in our mouths. Soon after, I fell into my hammock and silently prayed the hot pepper in my belly didn't seek exit in the middle of the night. I was lulled to sleep by Martha's snoring, drowning out the jungle noises.

In the morning, we braved another river trek, bringing us deep into the canyons of Kavak. Val had visited the canyons before. "There is an intense level of energy in these canyon walls," she stated as we inched our way over river boulders. I wondered what that could mean exactly, what energy she could be referring to, yet I had been pondering an unexplainable, mysterious sense I'd had since being here. In listening to the stories and mythology associated with the Pemón beliefs, I had come to respect and appreciate the profound connection they had to the earth and to their ancestry. It was as though the elements—the land, the *tepuis*, the savannahs—had been intricately linked with the spirit and energy of Pémon ancestry. My mind struggled to make sense of it all.

As we entered the steep canyon walls, Clemente stopped, telling us to line up and hold hands. He yelled out words in Pemón that we were to then repeat out loud. These words represented a request to the ancient spirits to let us enter the depths of the canyon. Like kids in a preschool classroom, we obediently yelled out the words before diving into a pool that led us into a canyon. Submerged up to our heads, we then traveled the canyon walls holding on and advancing by a single rope. Looking over my shoulder, I suddenly felt as though I was being watched. I stopped moving along the rope and looked up at the walls around me. They revealed the most spectacular facial outlines.

"Valentina!" I yelled. "Do you see it? Do you see all the faces?" I shivered with goose bumps as I floated in the water completely stunned at the sight.

"Yes, it's beautiful—they are so beautiful!" she yelled back, ecstatic. "Look it this one, and over there...look at her face."

We were surrounded by a sea of faces etched naturally by years of erosion into the rock and unlike anything I had imagined. I thought of the spirits and could only wonder if they were represented here on the faces of the canyon walls. Almost paralyzed with astonishment and wonder, we inched toward another pool.

Suddenly the force and power of a waterfall descended upon us, the sound almost deafening. Water dropped from what seemed like the sky itself. A beautiful Pemón woman had joined our journey, and we all watched as she dove in the pool toward the base of the falls. Antonio followed, with Martha and Valentina close behind. I advanced tentatively, feeling intimidated by the power of it all. The force of the water and the strength of something unseen were almost palpable. *Energy*, I thought. Is this what it was?

I swam toward Val, and we held on to each other. Then a tremendous feeling came over me, as though all of the earth's energy was cascading off those falls and onto our bodies. Strangely, I noticed that we were all laughing and half crying like bewildered children. It felt like a combination of fear and cleansing—like I was entering a car wash that I knew would hurt but that would cleanse my deepest workings. I hung on as long as I could under the falls and then got a distinct and defined internal message to get out of the water.

"I have to get out!" I yelled to Val. I was now in a panic state to flee the falls. I swam to the side, climbed over several boulders, and lay exhausted in a patch of sun. I sobbed; I don't know why, but I simply sobbed.

What on earth just happened? I asked myself. I was drained, unnerved, and euphoric all at the same time. Val came over at some point, gasping as she climbed onto the rock I was lying on. "The strangest thing happened to me in there," she panted. "I was being pushed by something, and it wasn't the water…"

Back in Kavak, we packed our belongings, first carefully emptying them out entirely to check for roaches. The night before, I had gotten up to use the bathroom and noticed several roaches running around the toilet. Shuddering, I screeched softly—then loudly as I noticed a sea of roaches covering the sink, soaps, and toothbrushes. Disgusted, I ran to my bed and hid under the mosquito netting. Val got up next, and I immediately heard a guttural cry as she experienced the sight of the roaches. "Oh, my God!" she yelled. "Lydia, they are everywhere!"

That's when we noticed hundreds of roaches crawling in and out of our suitcases, purses, clothes on the floor. The ground and the shelves that held our things were in fluid movement with roaches, hundreds and thousands of them. We broke into tremendous, unstoppable laughter, probably some creative female coping mechanism. We collected ourselves and amazingly rolled over and went to sleep.

Finished with my packing, I wandered around the grass huts. Our time in Canaima was closing in on us. I stared at the lump swinging in the hammock—a closer look revealing it to be our pilot, our ticket back into the civilization I questioned wanting to return.

I found Antonio wandering around, kicking aimlessly at the rocks around his feet. "I don't want to go," he said flatly.

I understood. I took a good look at him and noticed a new Pemón necklace around his neck. "That really suits you," I said. And it did. Antonio looked different to me overall—as if he were smiling from the inside and out. Actually, he was beaming. Over the course of our days here, he had somehow transformed. Before me stood a totally different man, who I could feel was firmly planted within himself, like some great battle had been fought and the best part of him had won. He looked beautiful.

The pilot woke up from his nap and loaded us into the plane. Taking off, we saw the grass huts of Kavak slowly disappear behind us. That same sudden feeling of crying swept through me again, as it had in the canyon. I turned my face to the window to hide the tears, feeling a terrible, primal loss, like I was being torn away from my mother as a child. I took a glimpse at Val, and she admitted, "It's so weird, Lydia...I just felt this overwhelming need to cry." Then Martha leaned her hand back to clutch us both—I held on to this dear person with whom I had lived something private. I hadn't understood most of what she had said to me during the trip as it had all been in Spanish, but we had experienced something miraculous together, something we would all have difficulty explaining to others. The plane circled, and we did a flyby of Angel Falls, which had only a trickle of water jutting over its 979-meter free fall, fifteen times higher than Niagara Falls. In the walls of those canyons and on the plains of the savannahs, something magical had happened, and it had gone way beyond stripping ourselves free of our daily lives, the trappings of our bodies, and the bulleted goals we so diligently set out for ourselves. Reduced, yet connected to the wind and the water, out there we just *were*.

Leaving Venezuela, I became aware of just how delicate and light our footprints ought to be as we were invited into villages and communities around the world, how easy it might be to walk in with bags of solutions. Nobody on the outside of Pemón life had any right to come in with any solutions for the Pemón. We simply weren't equipped, nor had we the right to make any judgments over what was best for them. Genuinely unsure about the effects that travel could have if tourism wasn't handled with great care, I worried about the negative, exploitative effects on such a preciously untouched culture. Ultimately, we decided we would wait rather than risk making a mistake by running trips there. If

I had learned anything, it had been that the Pemón are the ones who have something to teach us.

In the end, though, what I had thought I was coming to do had been minimized by something greater. Whatever that was, it refined my belief that there are powerful forces at work out there in the world. It was on this journey that I was reminded just how much we can't see or begin to understand, how important it is to listen to the unspoken, less obvious language of the world. It made me think of all the other silent messages the earth had sent over the years—through the cool empty air in the Orlando library, in the searing buzz of the jungle in Costa Rica, in scraping old stones in Provence, in a packed and sweaty room of children in Chennai.

21

The Power of Partnership

When someone makes a decision, he is really diving into a
strong current that will carry him to places he had never
dreamed of when he first made the decision.
Paolo Cuelho

Things really started to come together in Rochester on
several fronts—beginning with the kids each developing groups of friends and continuing to thrive in their individual pursuits. It had felt like it was taking an eternity
to settle in from the move from Provence, but we were finally getting there. Nick was becoming a serious singer/
songwriter, waking up early on the weekends and lugging
his guitar and a small red rug to lay out at the Rochester
Public Market. Generous and encouraging Rochesterians at
the market would fill Nick's guitar case with one- and five-
dollar bills. Saving every single bit he earned at the market,
he paid for a studio recording of an original song, one that
would put him on Simon Cowell's *The X Factor* a year later.
Emma rode horses, played piano, and dove into her middle
school social world, while Isabelle began to run and play

with school and neighborhood friends as we had dreamed she would. We bought a little yellow kayak and on Sundays would plunk it into the water at Mendon Ponds Park. Our trips back to Provence allowed us to keep one foot over the pond and gave us the respite we needed to forge on. We might not have been leading a typical life, but we had found a comfortable rhythm.

The original plan was for John to get the Only Provence villa business stable enough to kick out a reasonable income, and then he would join me in working on GoPhilanthropic. When we had returned to the United States in 2007, we had been renting five other houses apart from Mas de Gancel on our Only Provence website. In 2008, there were fifteen, and by 2009, he was managing the bookings for more than thirty. No longer able to handle all of the inquiries and contracts on his own, he sought help from my stepfather, Magnus, who rolled up his sleeves and, with his Swiss hyperorganization, began to put some much-needed structure to the administrative side of the operation. By 2012, with help from Gilles, Louise's husband, Only Provence would be one of the largest suppliers of luxury villa rentals in the South of France, offering a selection of over 150 villas and châteaux. John was seeing the results from his long days working at the dining room table and was beginning to get a clear vision for the potential of the business overall. Most of all, though, it was evident that he was really having fun. He had found a genuine joy and purpose in what he was doing. It combined two things he loved, business and old houses, and took place in a region that had taught him to slow down and appreciate all of life's little beauties. The downside, though, if there was one, was that it was becoming increasingly clear that he wouldn't be joining me at GoPhilanthropic anytime soon.

While we may have been stuffed in a small house with one and a half bathrooms, we occupied our own mental spaces that spanned the globe with our separate businesses, allowing us both a creative environment in which to grow independently. While I would be on Skype calls to India or Vietnam, I could hear him chatting in French to villa homeowners. Thinking back to our discussions and dreams as fifteen-year-olds, we were driven by very different passions, but we had now arrived at a point where we needed to not be threatened by our separate goals. It meant that we no longer had to do the same thing and that neither of us had to give something up entirely for the other.

We were finally making some strides within the small but growing world of travel philanthropy. Collaborating with a handful of diligent ground operators, Val and I booked a steady stream of philanthropic tours for couples, families, and groups. The idea was working—people enjoyed their privately guided vacations together with visits to fantastic little organizations devoted to education, clean water, and empowerment. Creatively weaving visits with those organizations into our tours, we offered our partner programs a connection to broader international exposure and allowed for some funds to flow directly into their work. Our travelers were donating water wells and sponsoring students at Journeys Within Our Communities in Cambodia. They delivered tens of portable mobile libraries in Vietnam through Le Ly Hayslip's Global Village Foundation. Families brought supplies and funded daily needs at worthy shelters in need, like Leng's program, ODA, in Siem Reap. Pascal had successfully launched his own home for children in Delhi, TARA Homes for Children, and our travelers began helping out with his expenses.

When travelers wanted to support a program they visited on a trip, we would arrange for the donation to go directly to the program, allowing us to maintain complete transparency. GoPhilanthropic then carved out a percentage of its own profits from booking the travel and made a contribution to the program. It was a win-win. Most importantly, though, and as we had hoped, people came home from the trips admitting to having experienced something deeply profound. The visits had made them think more about the fragility of life and about how joy could be found in so much of what we took for granted on a daily basis— education, access to health services, opportunity. So many acknowledged that they had received more than they had given—a strange twist of fate.

About a year after hiring Val, I received an e-mail from Mary Jo, a mother of three living in Minnesota with twenty years of experience running global events and trips for corporate clients. Skimming the résumé she had attached to her e-mail, I saw that she had traveled to what seemed like every country on the globe yet had a particular love for Africa. Mary Jo loved her job—it was clear she had the right blend of work ethic and drive to be successful at it, but she wanted to use all that she had gathered in her professional experience in a more meaningful way. In the small amount of free time she had between her family and a job that had her on the road much of the month, she would volunteer her time raising funds at her children's school or within her community. "Would you consider running GoPhil trips to Africa?" she asked eagerly. "I would love to help you expand there."

Over the course of the next year, Mary Jo did just that. We didn't have very much logistical experience and were thrilled to benefit from the experience she brought to the table. Combining her love of guiding with a meaningful cause in a region that tugged at her heart was all the encouragement she needed to join our growing, spirited team. I had very little to offer in compensation, though; the business was still fledgling and the profits slim after our marketing expenses, but she was happy enough with a pay-as-you-go arrangement, agreeing to making a commission off of any trips she arranged.

Our work expanded into what was referred to as donor travel, developing tours for other nonprofits that wanted to connect their donors to their programs on the ground. We partnered with Discovering Deaf Worlds and developed some of their first journeys for deaf and hard-of-hearing persons. The trips involved a connection with grassroots deaf organizations in developing countries. Busy with wearing all other hats within the business, we hired another avid and hard-working travel bug, Ingrid. Soft-spoken but deeply principled, she dove into developing these unique journeys, which required a complex network of guides trained in both ASL and the local regional sign language. We were all honored to work with Discovering Deaf Worlds, a young, like-minded, and passionate organization that lived by a similar mission to ours—finding small nonprofits supporting deaf communities in Cambodia, Thailand, and Costa Rica and exposing them to valuable resources and tools outside of their countries.

Several magazines and local TV stations ran stories on GoPhilanthropic's fresh approach to philanthropy, an approach that encouraged people to not only donate but also to engage in person, to allow the people behind the programs to speak for themselves. *BBC Travel* in the United Kingdom caught wind and traveled with us to India to broadcast our idea, the one that had been created over a pot of paint in Provence. The *New York Times* ran an article in their prized Thanksgiving addition. People seemed to appreciate at the time that there was no requirement to give, no obligation to support the programs they visited, yet all of our travelers did give. If we had done a good job in finding worthy programs, and we believed we had, the founders of these small organizations would be able to inspire our travelers to take the next step. In the early days of GoPhilanthropic, we stuck to incredibly simple objectives—find great programs, link the travelers to them, and let the rest unfold organically.

While I was undoubtedly pleased at the results we had achieved so far, there had been a sizable investment in getting the business on its feet. Slowly we were starting to see some returns, but I felt continuously clobbered by heavy marketing bills. If we were going to be present online, we had to play ball with the bigger tour companies. My workday, which included evenings and weekends, didn't leave enough time to dig into to what my heart was drawn to—figuring out how to help these programs do more of what they do. The more time we spent communicating and visiting these programs, the more we learned about the skills they desperately sought, the knowledge they craved to run more efficient organizations. This is what I wanted to spend my time doing.

There was another more fundamental concern—one that had me increasingly tossing and turning at night. I realized that if I added up all that we had spent to start the business, we could have built three schools in a developing country. Suddenly I felt sick, as though I had gone down the wrong road. Yes, we had partnered with some inspiring programs, but getting support to them was dependent on selling trips and tours, and the money we needed for marketing those trips and tours was an uphill, expensive battle.

Sometime during 2010, we booked a trip for a family in Rochester who wanted a philanthropic journey to Southeast Asia with their three young children. I customized a three-week journey that would have them exploring Cambodia, Vietnam, and Laos. Inspired by their experience, the mother, Tracey, contacted me within ten days of their return. "What a fantastic trip," she raved. "Can we meet for coffee?"

A few days later, Tracey explained that, now that her children were a little older and settled in their school routines, she was ready to return to work. She didn't want to return to the high-profile telecom management job she had left shortly after becoming a mother; she was looking for a meaningful way to use her well-honed business experience. Besides being equipped with razor-sharp professional skills, Tracey also came with a long history of travel, and not just corporate. In her younger years, she had spent months traveling across most of the world's continents with little more than a backpack and a bike, staying at hostels along the way. I was intrigued at what she might have to say.

"I would love to explore how GoPhilanthropic can scale—do more than what it does. There is so much potential here," she said.

Tracey spent the next six months under the hood of the GoPhilanthropic business, analyzing everything from its core mission to the most effective market segments. Surely she would be able to tell me how we could shift things so that more focus could be spent on the organizations themselves. We met for lunch regularly at the Panera around the corner from my house to discuss her findings.

She took me by surprise one day. "Lydia, I've spent a lot of time evaluating what you are doing. I have an important question for you—and don't take this the wrong way. Why are you building a business when what you really want to do is run a nonprofit? You couldn't care less about turning a profit. Quit wasting your time selling tours and get on with it," she said in her British no-nonsense tone.

What she had realized was that the underlying purpose and passion behind the work was to genuinely assist the programs to become stronger and to broaden the work they were already doing. The programs could really use help with their internal organizations, budgeting, short- and long-term strategic planning. The foundation could help in this respect. GoPhilanthropic Travel, the for-profit side, would continue to take care of running the trips and bringing potential donors to the doorsteps of the programs, while the foundation concentrated 100 percent on the partnerships with and development of the programs themselves.

I had toyed with the idea of starting a nonprofit before, knowing we needed a solid legal entity for the fundraising, yet I was wearing so many hats within the business I couldn't fathom taking on any more. I worked closely enough with other small nonprofits to know that getting the paperwork done alone would be even more draining than running the business.

"Not to worry," said Tracey. "I'll do it."

And so the GoPhilanthropic team grew once again, with yet one more amazing and talented woman willing to jump aboard. Looking around our little table, I was filled with the most immense joy, gratitude, and relief. I knew that the pieces were coming together for a reason, and slowly, together, we were en route to building something really special, something that could ease the load that the quiet angels carried each day. It was in these early days that the concept and power of partnership really began to set in. It was becoming clear that when people came together, uniting in genuine passion and desire to make a difference, momentum became tangible. Much of what I had lived so far had been a relatively independent journey with my family. The fundamental lessons that Arun had shared with me over our tea sessions were now becoming alive and well before my eyes. GoPhilanthropic was becoming a place where people could share a piece of who they were, do what they loved to do, in an effort to help others. We were beginning to realize the special sort of magic that came from pooling collective experience and talents—we were beginning taste the power that came from partnership.

For the next several months, we carefully combed through the connections we had made around the world, knowing that we couldn't commit to helping all the worthy and devoted people we had encountered. By taking on a select group, we could focus more on their individual needs and make a more concerted effort to assist them in their work. As a team, we created the beginnings of a portfolio based on some key criteria. We decided to begin by partnering with the programs we had met that were helping to empower vulnerable women and children through education. Over the course of the next year, we would revisit these programs with different objectives in mind, digging deeper, asking different questions, and listening intently to their visions for growth. We would no longer just focus on what they needed in terms of donations, but instead attempt to better understand how they functioned and what tools and skills they might need to help them function even better.

Thankfully our team continued to grow. Linda, a retired health professional approached us with a desire to partner in our efforts. She was ecstatic at the chance to combine her lifetime of experience running a national health nonprofit with her profound concern for global issues. Linda's wise counsel, attention to detail, and uniquely spiritual groundedness came just at the right time for both the development of the foundation and for me personally. She would become an invaluable mentor over the years, gently offering me what we ultimately gave to our own partner programs—an honest sounding board offering encouragement to find personal answers and strength. Later, Linda would also add her passion for art and creativity to the mix of beautiful skills she offered to our work, running art workshops for children in the programs we had connected with as a means of self-exploration.

As we divided up our responsibilities, I happily obliged to return to India, jumping at the chance to revisit Pascal and Anuradha. Linda committed to nurturing our relationships across Southeast Asia, and Mary Jo didn't waste a second planning her journey to Africa to reconnect with a Maji Moto, a program rescuing girls from early marriage and female genital mutilation in the Maasai Mara, Kenya. She would also revisit M-Lisada, an inspirational music program and shelter for vulnerable children in the Katwe slums of Kampala, Uganda.

Launching the foundation reminded me of how at a certain point our identities in Provence had shifted from vacationers, foreigners looking from the outside in, to true residents involved in daily life. We had had to roll up our sleeves and learn how to trim the vines and rebuild crumbling walls, and our biggest lessons had been learned when we had really committed to becoming involved, when we had truly invested ourselves in what we were living. There was a vast difference between staying on the periphery of something and jumping in with both feet. Locating these wonderful programs was one thing; we had generated a steady stream of funding and donations for them, but we weren't really rolling up our sleeves and working alongside them. We weren't really investing in making them stronger, and we were all very motivated to get going on just that.

22

Digging Deeper

Lead me from death to life, from falsehood to truth.
Satish Kumar

"Ma'ammmm—sit here!" beckoned Amit, a spritely and sociable nine-year-old. The TARA Boys, barefoot and clad in various odd combinations of used clothing, ran around to get me plastic chair, a glass of water, and a metal plate. I was treated like an honored guest at TARA's family meal.

"Sit here," Amit repeated, patting the chair next to him for me to join him. There was no evidence that life before TARA took Amit to the very darkest corners of humanity. This intelligent, creative, and innocent child had been the village sex toy. His parents were aware but too hooked on drugs to care.

Beaming and excited, the boys fussed over the lunch preparations, switching from French to English, then back to Hindi. This was a far cry from where they had been two years ago, barely able to speak clearly in their own language. Ram, one of the eldest boys and one with whom I exchanged e-mails on a regular basis, plopped down next to me, grinning ear to ear.

"How old are you now, Ram?" I asked.

"I am not quite sure, ma'am," he said. "Maybe sixteen or eighteen."

Many of the boys hadn't a clue when their birthdays were, so their ages were sometimes given in a range.

"I think there will be too much spice for you, ma'am!" bellowed Sanjiv, a lanky, gentle-natured young man with scruffy hair, crooked teeth, and an unmistakable sparkle in his eyes. He pulled up his chair and began dishing out heaping platefuls of spiced cauliflower, yogurt, and chickpeas on top of mounds of fluffy rice. After serving the others, Sanjiv took his seat at the table and hungrily tucked into his food. I watched him discreetly as I dug into my lunch—despite Sanjiv's warmth and kindness, his demeanor revealed a deep vulnerability.

When the shelter first opened, Pascal had asked a partner NGO to refer a cook. They were happy to help, yet when the cook rang at the door, Pascal was shocked and horrified to find a scruffy and nervous Sanjiv at the steps. The cook that had been referred had been a child.

"Can you believe this? A charity that is supposed to be protecting children sends me a child to do the work of a cook for a children's shelter?" he shrieked. "What is wrong with this world?" He immediately picked up the phone. "Is this a child you sent as a referral for our shelter, or is he supposed to be the cook?"

"Well, yes, we did send him to cook," they responded sheepishly.

"But why? How is this possible?" demanded Pascal.

"Because I am sure there is not enough money in the budget for an adult-wage cook," they said honestly. This was the shocking reality of how many large NGOs and charities functioned. So many of them were far from being the safe havens we expected them to be.

"Well, I will take this Sanjiv," said Pascal indignantly. "But he will come and live here and go to school—like the rest of the children."

"What is the purpose of your trip?" Pascal asked as we sipped coffee and nibbled on toast and jam on his apartment terrace, surrounded by lush potted plants. Delhi's streets were beginning their daily morph into a maddening mess of blaring horns, whizzing rickshaws, teeming tea stalls, and wandering animals, the sweetness in the air slowly mingling with the city's more lively odors.

"Well, now that we have formed a foundation, we would like to know more, learn more, understand how we could help beyond simply funding," I said. Finishing my toast, I admitted a little more. "But the trip isn't entirely about work. Sometimes during the year, I like to wander out on my own to do the things that I want to do. To be perfectly honest, it's a selfish indulgence to visit TARA and the boys." I left it at that. What I didn't divulge was that my lifelong quest required a more genuine understanding of the courage it took for people like Pascal and Anuradha to do what they did. Deep down, I knew they had a vantage point that brought them closer to many of life's truths that I so desperately wanted to understand.

Munching on Indian snacks or riding in a dusty rickshaw toward TARA, Pascal shared a lot over the following days. After spending eight years as a social worker and psychologist in France for wayward adolescents who didn't seem to appreciate the assistance they were getting, he had sold his Paris flat and moved to India, carrying with him a single unshakeable desire to help children who had been left to fend for themselves.

But the commitment had meant a tremendous life change for Pascal, one he knew he could not turn back on.

"These children have already been abandoned once," he explained. "They had nobody to turn to—they were counting on me to never have that happen again. So I quickly went from a single man to a father of sixteen boys from families who could no longer care for them. Now that's a life change. The first thing I needed to do was to learn Hindi—and fast," said Pascal, chuckling.

And he did. For the next two years, he had worked around the clock, caring for the boys, exploring their varied backgrounds, feeding, clothing, and evaluating where they were educationally. Most had had little schooling. He had also had to consider the extent of the psychological problems the boys carried with them as a result of having lived through events no child should have to. Their rugged and raw histories of abandonment involved mixtures of poverty, parental drug addiction, or mothers involved in the commercial sex trade. Several of them had parents who had died or were living with HIV. Most of the children had been sexually abused. Somewhere along the way, they had each been turned over to either government-run institutions or the streets. It was a toss-up which place was better.

Academically there were huge mountains for the children to climb. When the boys first arrived at the home, they were so far behind, not even able to even keep up with the atrocious standards of local government schools, that Pascal had felt it was best to school them under TARA's roof, with lots of individual attention and the chance to fill in the vast educational holes the boys had acquired due to their lives on the street. Creating a well-rounded schedule consisting of yoga, healthy foods, chores, academic work, foreign language, as well as art and dance classes, the boys naturally began to thrive.

"Before when you asked them what they wanted to be when they grew up," Pascal said, "they did not know how to respond. The question in itself was odd to them, even to those who were older. The answers, if I got any at all, were odd. Ravi, for example, said he wanted to be a bird. That was about the extent of it. Now if you ask them, they all have dreams and aspirations—to be teachers, socials workers, scientists, astronauts," he said proudly.

After having been intensely schooled under TARA's roof with a caring and engaging staff of professionals and teachers, the boys had all been mainstreamed into varied city schools based on their abilities, two of them landing top spots in one of Delhi's most prestigious educational institution. They would later be admitted to university, an unheard-of path for a child raised in an NGO. Their pasts would no longer define their futures.

I spent the next couple of days just hanging around TARA, scooting cars on the floor with the younger ones, reading books, and organizing clothes on shelves. It was the weekend, and my time was spent not unlike it would have been at my own home. Kids floated on and off the Internet, sending e-mails to their sponsors, drawing pictures, and mucking around together. They were a joy to be around, and I was happy to just sit and chat and pass the time together.

Pascal had managed to recreate the security and love found in stable, devoted families, and a peacefulness radiated from inside this scrappy three-story boys' shelter in New Delhi. To take the poorest, most destitute children off of Delhi's streets and offer them a chance at an equal and dignified seat at life's table was in itself such a precious and wondrous thing.

At the beginning of every breakfast, the boys said a simple, one-sentence prayer: "Whatever happens, we are together." That's all it took, really, was for them to feel that they belonged and mattered to someone. They had mattered to Pascal, and now they mattered to each other, their caretakers, their teachers, and their fellow students. And they now mattered to me. I marveled at the concept that all of this had started with one person's decision to make a difference.

Pascal could finally take a breath now that the shelter was on its feet and the funds were trickling in, although unpredictably, from various sources beyond his own bank account. Hopefully though, with the help of more donors and sponsors, the dream of adding a second shelter for small children would come to fruition. I began to understand the statement Pascal had made to me back at his apartment when we had put our feet up after a full Delhi day at TARA. As Buddha lounge music had wafted through the air, he had said, "Now I could die and know I did what I was supposed to do."

I wondered for many days after how many people could so honestly assert the same.

I considered how I could get more exposure for Pascal's shelters as I boarded a flight to Mumbai, where I would climb a night train headed south to Kolhapur. My next stop was to check in on Anuradha and the little school for rescued child laborers that Arun Gandhi had dreams of expanding. I gasped as I mounted the train car, its handles thick with grime and its interior just as filthy. Train trips are infamous in India. Some say you haven't experienced the real India until you have taken a lengthy ride, or better yet, experienced an overnight trip like the one I was now on. I made sure that I used the bathroom before boarding and prayed I could hold it for the next eleven hours.

Restless and slightly uncomfortable in my berth alongside three large Indian businessmen, yet too tired to contemplate my safety, I settled into my top bunk. I arranged my bag containing my wallet and passport behind my body as my guide had instructed me. We had each been provided with sheets and a brown blanket. I inspected everything carefully for signs of bugs. The sheets were fine, but the blanket definitely looked suspect. I set it down by my feet. The overhead fan rattled loudly, and I stared at the filthy ripped curtain that hung loosely from a bent rod. The men I was bunking with seemed harmless enough as they dug into their packed dinners of chapati, rice, and dal and bantered in their native Marathi. Their food smelled good, and my stomach growled. I scrounged for the leftover half granola bar in my backpack. In addition to having being warned of the toilet conditions, I was told squarely to avoid all food served on the train—that the horrific conditions under which it was cooked would have you in the hospital for weeks. Closing my eyes and feeling comforted by the train's rickety motion, I took about two split seconds to fall into a deep sleep, my mind full of the TARA Boys, their hopes for the future, and Pascal's plans for the new shelter for tots.

Eleven hours later, I was greeted by Anuradha, who was wearing a stout and serious look and a slightly worn yet colorful sari, her hair pulled into a long twisted braid down her back. Despite the hardened look, she greeted me with a bear hug and a kiss and handed me a fresh-cut rose from her garden.

"Lydia," she said, "I am so thankful you have come again."

Scott, an American who had recently moved to India to assist Anuradha, stood by her side and also greeted me with hugs. Scott was a former architect and had traveled with Arun on a Gandhi Legacy Tour. Moved by Anuradha's mission and passion to help the region's rescued child laborers, Scott had accepted Arun's invitation to Kolhapur to assist in managing the architectural plans for a new school. After weeks of e-mail correspondence, it was a pleasure to meet Scott in person. He immediately relieved me of the suitcase I had lugged from the States packed with various items the school was in need of—lice shampoo, teaching tools, a laptop computer.

"Are you sure that you don't want to ride in something more comfortable?" Anuradha asked as I climbed into the used and battered rickshaw. I couldn't think of anything better than the wind on my face after the hours of being trapped in a train compartment. GoPhilanthropic had funded the rickshaw a year prior for three hundred dollars. With it, she could drive to distant villages to hold meetings with women, take a sick child to the hospital, or rescue another from a hazardous work site. Before having the rickshaw, she would spend hours and hours on buses getting from one place to another, and if there were no buses that went where she needed to go, she would walk. Despite being only forty years of age, her body was paying the price. She had been experiencing terrible pain in her feet and joints, but with her "new" three-wheeler, she could get around more easily.

While Scott headed outside of town back to the school with the supplies, Anuradha and I drove to the hotel, where I had a chance to clean up and have some breakfast. We were looking forward to catching up on all that had happened in the year since my last visit.

Tucked into a shaded corner of the hotel's outside patio, we sipped chai tea and enjoyed steamed rice cakes topped with a spicy coriander and coconut sauce. Years ago, Anuradha had given up a white-collar opportunity after having graduated from the Tata Institute of Social Sciences. Moving two hundred miles south of Mumbai, she had decided to educate children living in the slums of Kolhapur. What she discovered was that the children could not come to a school because they had to work during the day to supplement their parents' incomes. Determined not to give up on their education, she decided to go to them. So she began teaching them in the slums under lampposts and in makeshift schools set under tarps in the brick yards where the children worked. She could barely manage to keep their attention because they were exhausted after a whole day's work. Later, with the help of a friend, she was offered a small rental house with a yard to expand her efforts and create a permanent place to house rescued children.

As Anuradha had gathered more information about the families and histories of the children whom she helped, she had realized that she needed to do more than put them in school. She went into the factories and brickyards and stood up against the owners, reminding them of the laws prohibiting child labor. Then she fought the local authorities who were supposed to be enforcing the laws. Last but not least, she faced the families who were allowing their children to work, carefully examining the myriad of variables that forced these families into the darkest of places, where they could farm their children out to factory work, rag picking, or the sex trade. There she found combinations of things at work—extreme alcoholism, destitution, hunger, widows who were cast out of family networks and could no longer support themselves—all cornering them into situations where forced labor was the only way out.

After breakfast we continued to chat, yelling over the honking traffic, riding over the potholed roads through the outskirts of town and past a picturesque lake, cow-covered green hills, and harvest-ready sugarcane fields. Forty-five minutes later, we arrived at AVANI school, and I was greeted by swarming children holding handmade signs bearing my name.

"Hello, Lydia! Didi! Hello, Lydia!" they yelled.

I recognized many of their faces from my visit the previous December, the older ones looking more and more like men and women. Not having travelers to think about on this trip, I could become selfishly absorbed in what was in front of me—thirty-two beaming, barefoot, bright-eyed children.

I was ushered into the small, crowded school office, which bore two photos hanging from the wall in faded and worn frames—one of Gandhi, the other of Mother Teresa. I stopped to gaze at them, and a strange feeling washed over me. The craziness in the room, kids streaming in and out, colorful scarves whizzing across my line of sight, all started to move in slow motion, and a deep warmth seemed to fill the room. The clamor of motion around me fell away, and a silence crept into my head. I was suddenly confronted with one of those rare moments where the power of life's dots—events, people, experiences—all line up and lead you down a very certain road. A small voice from deep inside spoke to me—*Let down your guard, put down your walking stick, sit down. There is no need to search any farther.*

But in a flash, the moment was gone, and there was no time to contemplate further as staff, teachers, and volunteers all crowded into the room to say hello. My hands were grabbed and shaken, my body hugged and kissed, my hair patted. An elaborate lunch of local specialties had been prepared in the room where the girls normally slept—homemade breads, spicy lentil soup, fried mutton, and curried chickpeas, spinach, and onion, all prepared in the rich, local Kolhapuri spices. Every time I took a bite, someone refilled my plate. Tremendous effort had gone into the lunch, and I felt truly humbled yet a little uncomfortable with all of the attention. I was well aware of how limited their food was and what a gift they were offering in making such an elaborate meal.

After lunch, Anuradha took me by the arm to show me the progress they had made since last year. Our traveling group had pooled some funds and given it to her as we left. She had scratched out a handwritten note of all the items they desperately needed and would purchase with the money when we left.

"See the water tanks," she said as she guided me around the garden corner, pointing to massive black catchment tanks. "And here is the other one," she said excitedly. "Before your last group came, we had no way to keep the grains dry during the monsoon season. We had such little to begin with, and then there was waste. Now everything is dry." She smiled. I peeked into the bins holding rice, grains, dried lentils, and chickpeas, then snugly returned their lids.

Stepping over lines of children eating their lunches cross-legged on the floor, we continued into a small room no bigger than a closet where she showed me a wall lined with lockers. "Remember how we told you we needed a place for the kids to put their individual things? Well, look—now it is all organized, and each child has a private place to store things." To some, this addition might have seemed like a small thing, but to children who had only a few things to call their own, it was a big deal.

"And that's not it, Lydia. You must come," she said. Bringing me to the front of the house, she pointed to a small solar panel propped up on the roof with GoPhilanthropic hand-painted in white on the edge. "Now we have lights at night," she beamed, "and the children can study after dark."

I was floored at how a relatively small amount of money had gone so far. But I also felt the weight of how important these basics were and how we, in our world of have-everything, really had no clue, no idea, no inkling as to the profound value of these luxuries—electricity for reading at night, dry rice, a place to put our few precious things.

The issues surrounding the ugly sequence of child labor, I would learn over the coming days, were a complex mix of variables involving caste, tradition, a male-dominated culture, and women's lack of access to information regarding their rights. Simply put, it somehow boiled down to the vulnerability of women. If a woman was widowed, the government was supposed to offer a stipend, but it didn't because the widowed women didn't know they were entitled to the stipend. The migrant farm women who worked in fields were unfairly being paid twenty rupees (equivalent of fifty cents) for every six hours, drastically under the minimum wage. "The real work that needs to be done to drive change is out in the villages, in the homes of women who accept their miserable situations," explained Anuradha. She was dead set on getting these women up on their feet, empowering them to demand what was rightfully theirs, and encouraging them to build better lives for themselves and their children.

Sun and dust streamed through the car window as we barreled down a potholed road to a village meeting the following day.

"It sounds to me like the more progress you make in the villages educating the women, helping them access the services and resources that are already in place yet are not offered to them, the more chance there is that the children won't end up in labor," I said.

"That is exactly it," stated Anuradha emphatically, chomping on a banana. "This is the thing. While everyone spends all this time and money on ideas for the new schools, I am focused on a creating a world where the schools for the rescued won't be needed. I met a man the other day, a wonderful man who was running a school and orphanage. He was so proud that his school now had three hundred children. I found it strange that he was proud of his growing numbers and that people in general are working toward having more and more children in their shelters, like this is an accomplishment. I see things from a completely different perspective. I want to stop these numbers from growing," she said, looking me in the eyes.

Anuradha's activism based on prevention—nothing more than providing information to women and forcing government officials to actually deliver the economic assistance they are required by law to give—seemed a logical approach. What Anuradha needed to confront the issues at the source were a sturdy car, computer, and cell phone. And there was no doubt in my mind that she knew this to be the case.

I spent the following day in small, incense-filled community meeting houses packed with saried women organizing themselves for an upcoming march protesting government officials in Delhi. One village was still reeling from the death of a child bride who had been burned by her husband. Anuradha's movement had now gathered momentum, with some sixteen hundred followers willing to fight and stand up for their rights. She told me more than once that she no longer feared the police or jail. She had become a major threat to the status quo among lazy government officials as well as industry owners who had relied on cheap child labor.

Our afternoon meeting got very heated when a man entered and started yelling loudly. Several women stood up and yelled forcefully back. It was all in Marathi, so I didn't understand a thing, but I certainly got the gist of it. There was no doubt this man felt threatened by the undercurrent of change, and he told Anuradha on our way out that she would be beaten if she came back to the village.

"I am not concerned," she said. "Once these women feel as confident as I to stand up on their own, they won't need me. Their strength in numbers will be enough."

At each village in which she worked, she named twenty children as child-rights activists. They were the eyes and ears for any wrongful act toward children, including abuse, forced labor, or restriction from the normal food allowance in the government schools. These children were being taught at a young age to fight for decent education and opportunity. During the meetings, they sat quietly and listened intently. I could feel the energy in these rooms, see the intensity of their mission and movement.

I stuck out like a sore thumb during the course of the day on Anuradha's arm, but I was accepted and treated as a dear friend, brought into their tiny, mud-walled homes with impeccably swept floors and offered tea. Scoops of sugar were ceremoniously placed in my mouth, and endless red and yellow powders were dotted on my forehead signifying a blessing for good fortune. My hands were never let free—the warm grasp of another's hand was always there, be it that of a tiny old woman, small child, middle-aged woman. These women were the poorest of the poor; they were forgotten and forsaken, even by their fellow Indians, not to mention the rest of the world. Deep lines on their faces revealed lives of hardship. They had barely anything but the clothes on their backs, yet they radiated a kindness and dignity I rarely found in my world back home.

After a full day, Scott, Anuradha, and I retreated to my hotel room to discuss a plan for going forward. I was now fully convinced the focus had to be on her empowerment movement.

"Anuradha, I just need to know how I can help."

Then she pulled out of her pocket a small pink pad on which she has been scratching personal notes. Neither of us knew at the time, but these notes would be the beginnings of a massive women's empowerment movement called the Women's and Child Rights Campaign (WCRC), one that would receive national media recognition within three years of writing on that pink pad of paper, and one that GoPhilanthropic would provide the seed funding for, until it was strong enough to stand on its own.

"I stayed up all last night thinking how I can really spread the campaign. Eventually women will be doing it themselves, going from one village to another," she explained. "Just like Gandhi's message, it is about encouraging people to do things for themselves. It's the only way. I will need help to do this. I need an office as a central place where women can come for information. I will need a cell phone that I can get my e-mail on and maybe a motorbike," she said, as though she was asking for the sun and the moon.

Then she sighed and moved to my bed, sitting upright with her feet on the ground, clearly exhausted. She had been known to work herself so hard that she could go to bed and not get up for days. I crossed the room, fluffed the pillows behind her, and turned her body, lifting her feet so that she could lie horizontally on the bed. Closing her eyes, she said, "I am feeling so relieved for the first time in a long time. As if maybe I am not in this alone anymore." The setting sun cast long shadows through the room, and within minutes, she fell into a deep sleep.

23

Ants in My Pants—Again

Life is a challenge, meet it.
Mother Teresa

Rochester became a nest that we flew in and out of frequently. We never did buy a house there, continuing to live out of the tiny blue rental we had found four years prior. If homes represented suitcases, we were happy with a scrappy carry-on, filled with the few items we felt were important. Perhaps it was our way of hanging onto to some element of simplicity we had found in our life abroad, or perhaps it was a way to not really settle in at all. Either way, we enjoyed the freedom of a lack of ownership and consumed ourselves with raising the children and working on our respective projects.

I desperately wanted our children to be more involved in what I was seeing and doing. I also longed for the empty space to just be with them. Nick was nearing fourteen, Emma twelve, and Isabelle five. We knew we wouldn't have the joy of having them by our sides for too many more years. Over a simple candlelit dinner one night, John and I decided that a few months away wouldn't be too disruptive, that the children could use another strong dose of life beyond America. We hatched a plan that would involve returning to France that Christmas. We would then continue through northern Thailand, Cambodia, Vietnam, and Laos for three months, visiting existing GoPhilanthropic partners and finding new ones, but also taking the time to just be together as a family.

I proposed to John that we homeschool the kids while away, something that I had always quietly dreamed of experiencing. "I'll take English and social studies and you take math and science," I said to John. I longed to have the kids read some of the books that had affected me deeply—Paolo Cuelho's *The Alchemist* was on the top of my list. Le Ly's *When Heaven and Earth Changed Places* would be a must as we traveled through Vietnam. The thought of having liberty to choose what they read and wrote papers on brought me such joy, and to have the freedom to wrap these texts around what they would be seeing would be even more powerful. Overall, though, I thought it would be a wonderful chance to be able to connect with them individually.

Of course that all-too-familiar look of shock and horror came over the faces of school administrators as we described our idea to travel and manage their academics ourselves. Surely we couldn't manage to cover the needed material while traveling through such crazy, far-flung places. Nick's high school counselor's look of concern as he stated with an air of judgment, "You do realize, Mrs. Dean, that Nick will be losing a credit in physical education?"

"Do you believe the gall of that man?" I ranted to John that night. "God forbid he misses gym class while he visits rural development programs around the world." That was just the comment I needed to pull the trigger.

After a few months of planning, I found myself hanging off the side of a tuk-tuk, sitting on a makeshift seat the driver had made for me on top of a greasy motor battery as we sped through the mid-Sunday market traffic in Chiang Mai, Thailand. Emma, John, Isabelle, and Nick were crammed in the back, wind in their hair, Nick's guitar case squeezed under their feet. Now an accomplished singer/songwriter, he would be playing for various schools and orphanages throughout our trip. Emma had developed into a quite the singer herself, and the two performed amazing duets, their sibling voices blending delicately together. Tonight Nick had landed a spot playing at one of the local bars during the market hours. The owner was relieved at having found a cheap, namely free, replacement for another player that had stood him up.

Our tuk-tuk weaved through the mobs of tourists, mopeds, and stalls upon stalls of Chiang Mai vendors selling clothing from hill tribes, sliced strawberries sprinkled with salt and sugar, freshly made soups sold in clear bags, and grilled pork and chicken on sticks. We were finding the food sumptuously fresh and unbelievably cheap. One day we all ate lunch of steamed dumplings, pork wrapped in noodles, and fresh smoothies for three dollars total. Before making the decision to take the trip, John and I had done our due diligence in comparing the cost of being on the road in Southeast Asia versus living at home. We were quite surprised at how much we spent at home on groceries, kids' activities, and gas. Amazingly, we would find that the cost of a reasonable hotel, scooter rentals, and food from street vendors would equate to less than what we spent in Rochester.

From the moment we stepped off the plane in Bangkok, we noticed a slight bounce in Isabelle's step. Surrounded by other Asians, she definitely felt an immediate sense of pride. But we were also experiencing that a white family with a Chinese daughter was a spectacle.

"Where from?" a taxi driver might ask boldly.

"Not your baby!" they said.

"Where her parents?" others belted out.

In Asia there were no expected norms to follow regarding adoption-related questions, as there were in the United States. They were confused and interested and simply asked what they wanted to ask. They were commenting on her leg, gawking at her prosthesis, and sometimes even knocking on it. They pointed and stared at her, then chatted among themselves. It was very hard on her, and after the initial honeymoon of being in Asia had worn off, she was becoming visibly uncomfortable. She spent many of her days in a dark mood, I imagined logically caught between two worlds—her white adoptive family whom she knew loved her dearly and an Asian world she was not ready to accept she was from. The visits to orphanages understandably threw her into a whirlwind of emotional confusion. She would put her nose

in the air, keeping herself at arm's length from their sometimes dirty hands, as if to say, *I am not this.*

We spent almost a month in Chiang Mai, far from the
typical beach tourist spots Thailand was known for. Located
in the cool mountains of the North and surrounded by lush
national parks with indigenous hill tribes and cascading
waterfalls, Chiang Mai was a hub for trekking, bamboo raft-
ing, Thai boxing, cooking courses, massage therapy, and elephant riding. Golden Buddhist temples were found on every
street, spectacularly detailed and ornate, and robed monks
wandered in and out after their morning alms.

Our home took the form of earthy bungalows on the
banks of the Ping River, smelling of local woods and citro-
nella, with cozy beds covered in mosquito nets. We woke
to roosters and croaking frogs and showered outdoors surrounded by plants and a bamboo fence. Ponds separated the
bungalows, which were connected by wooden paths. John
routed the villa inquiry calls to his Skype account and had
a headset with a microphone. "Only Provence, John speaking," he would say as he answered at 1:00 a.m. on an enormous outdoor cushion with a chorus of frogs squawking in
the background.

In the mornings, we sat by the Ping River on a green
expanse of grass, surrounded by butterflies and birds, as
the kids did their schoolwork. Homeschooling became a
refreshing change in our routine, reaping all sorts of unfore-
seen benefits, the peaceful setting providing a perfect classroom. I wasn't sure the kids realized the hours were ticking
by as they read their texts, took online math quizzes, wrote

essays, and created short stories. There was this dead silence during their work time that surprised me, a most beautiful and unexpected observation that I could only describe as silence filled with thought—as if I could feel them thinking. It was an emptiness filled with everything. Distractions were reduced to an utter minimum, a buzzing mosquito, a flapping curtain.

Since our arrival, we had been flagging down cheap tuk-tuk rides as a means to get around. Wanting more freedom, we decided that renting scooters would be much more convenient—parking them at the hotel, we could come and go as we pleased. Leading up to the trip, Nick had been begging to drive one himself. We would promptly put an end to the discussions. "Nick, you are fourteen. It is illegal for starters. They have the same rules as in the United States, not to mention the insurance issue it would pose if you had an accident. Forget it—it's not going to happen!" we said on half a dozen occasions.

One afternoon in Chiang Mai, after having laid down six bucks a day for both scooters, I hopped on in the driver's position, motioning for Nick to climb on behind me. Izzy balanced her legs up near the handlebars on John's bike, while Emma held on to his waist on the back. Outdated helmets with broken buckles sat lopsided on our heads as we nosed out into the crazy madness of the city's streets. We got as far as one block before I became paralyzed with fear, entering into what only a mother knows to be a "mother moment," a unique combination of irrationality, fear, and inflexibility. I couldn't move another inch.

Was it that I had never driven one? *They are not complicated.* The traffic? *Yes, a bit crazy.* Izzy being perched precariously between John and the handlebars? *Undoubtedly not very safe.* Whatever the mixture of variables, panic took a hold, and there was no going farther. I pulled over, took off my helmet, and hung it on the handlebars. "Sorry. I am not going do this," I stated emphatically. I distinctly remember two shop ladies bursting out with laughter. My four family members just stared at me—as if thinking, *What on earth are we going to do with this woman?*

"Mom, look...how about you let me drive for a few blocks—until you feel more comfortable?" suggested Nick.

After about fifteen minutes of reviewing my options, I reluctantly climbed on and wrapped my arms around what was now almost a man's body and buried my head in his back. As we entered into traffic, he had calm and reassuring words. "Mom, it's fine...we'll be fine. Try to relax. It's really no different from my BMX." He drove perfectly—well, almost— and I was overcome with a realization that he had matured enough to take over in a situation I could not handle. I didn't know if I was proud or sad that our roles were reversing for a moment—that I would have to trust him when he couldn't rely on me. For the next few weeks, the five of us flew around the streets of Chiang Mai, the wind in our faces, getting ourselves where we needed to go, and I am pleased to say we only had about four near-death experiences.

One of the highlights of the trip so far had been the wake of bliss dispersed by Nick's well-worn guitar. Emma often joined him in singing to groups of children, large and small, who had been handed a tough lot in life. Our time with them wasn't a quantifiable gift like so many of GoPhilanthropic's donations, but it made me think about the value and happiness that came from sharing time together. While Nick played, the kids screeched, clapped, smiled, and laughed. We did too. After the shows, there were hugs and photos and more laughing. These were reminders of the special magic that can only be found in the human connection.

We ventured to Laos, to the deeply serene city of Luang Prabang, and settled into a quiet hotel, the rush of the Mekong flowing nearby, banked by terraced gardens of bright lettuces and purple flowers. Mountainous and green, rich with fertile fields, and dotted with ancient temples, French colonial architecture, and baguettes, it was a place you felt you could settle down for a long nap and never quite need to wake up. Aged golden temples lined the roads, with rows of young novice monks headed into prayer.

John had to fly home suddenly, his dear Gramma Groves having passed away while we were in Thailand. While she had not been well over the past weeks, it had come as a surprise. She had always been so full of fun, an artist of so many crafts from ikebana to origami. John's grandparents had held a special role in his life, resting that comforting hand on his young shoulder during some tough early years. Gramma had handmade every piece of paper that our wedding invitations were printed on, bright-purple bougainvillea from her own garden embedded on each and every page. Two days after her death, the kids and I unexpectedly ended up at a local paper-making village after having visited some caves along the Mekong. I bought a few items for the girls, and the woman selling them didn't have the correct change for me. In lieu, she gave me a small handmade paper book. I was surprised to see the paper, made thousands of miles from Naples, Florida, was almost identical to the paper Gramma had made for our wedding.

"Maybe it was the local rice whiskey you were offered at the village!" I said to Nick as he stuck his head down the toilet for the tenth time that night. Between bouts to the bathroom, we were considering where he might have picked it up.

"Maybe it's the local ice used in the fruit shakes," he moaned.

We both settled on the cause being a cup of water we had been offered at the home of Sisaveth, a girl that one of our donors had sponsored to go to school through our partners Laos Educational Opportunities Trust (LEOT), a very small and hands-on organization that selected bright young students with a drive to get beyond secondary school, where the government seemed to leave off its duties to educate. We all thought we had been handed cups of tea due to its earthy brownish color. Sisaveth's mother had beamed as she had toured us around her home, a simple, two-roomed concrete structure with an open fire for cooking and a simple hole in the ground for the bathroom. A plastic tub had held the household's water. She had raised seven children in that home, and she radiated incredible warmth and affection, rubbing and patting my back as we walked around. She had been so proud of having a daughter who was now, through

GoPhilanthropic's support, being offered a chance to inch out of the cycle of poverty she had had to accept during her lifetime. Only a short three years later, Sisaveth would be a proud teacher to young children, working in a neat and tidy classroom despite a lack of electricity and basic facilities. She was like a strict mum with a mixture of care and discipline, we would be told.

After meeting Sisaveth's family, we drove into the mountains with LEOT's founder, Alan, and Kheak, another scholarship student funded through the organization. We were off to visit the place where Kheak was raised, the ethnic hill-tribe village of Pou Kao—high up in the mountains surrounding Luang Prabang. Alan explained how, until his recent visit on New Year's, the villagers had never encountered a white person.

"Certainly you will the first American teenager with a guitar," exclaimed Kheak as he loaded the case of beer into the van. "This is cause for celebration! Nick do you drink beer or rice whiskey?"

"Uh, neither. I'm only fourteen," he answered. Kheak laughed out loud as if that was craziest thing he had ever heard. Isabelle tucked herself under Sisaveth's arm as the van weaved its way up the mountainside, and for a strange, fleeting moment, they looked like mother and daughter. They played with each other's hands and touched each other's hair tenderly. Every once in a while, Izzy looked back at me as if to ask me if was OK. While a part of me wished to be Sisaveth for just one moment, it was wonderful to see a sense of happiness and comfort on Izzy's face.

On the way up the steep mountainside, Kheak chatted about life and how with the support of LEOT, he now had a chance to learn and study business management. Years later he would become an air traffic controller at the airport in Luang Prabang. He was deeply thankful for his opportunities and explained how he hoped he would be able to provide for his whole extended family. At some point, the road turned to dirt and became extremely steep and narrow, dropping off on either side, leaving no room for error. Gazing out across the mountains, I didn't see a sign of human existence across the expanse of high green hillsides and slopes until Kheak pointed to a speck of white way up in the distance. "That's my village," he exclaimed. "That's where we are going."

When we arrived and climbed out of the van, I tried to take in what was before me. It was beyond beautiful, as if out of a dream. Meticulously constructed bamboo huts were clustered and linked by carefully brushed pathways lined by fences. Precious little flower heads poked through the fence gates lining the simple huts. Healthy vegetable gardens sat next to well-groomed pens stocked with plump pigs and suckling piglets. Chickens ran wild between high stalks of corn. Children ran everywhere and stopped, wide-eyed, to look at us. Mothers with babies slung on their backs tentatively approached us, then turned to giggle among themselves, hands over their mouths. They stared and pointed at our blond hair. We were a spectacle, but we felt very welcomed.

Emma took my arm as we walked through this exceptionally scenic place, no sounds other than banana leaves slapping in the wind and birds chirping.

"Mom—holy cow, this is so beautiful. You could put me here, and I would be happy for life," she stated.

But Kheak explained that it could either be the most idyllic place when the conditions were right, or it could be a devastatingly harsh existence should the weather turn bad and the crops fail.

"When I was a boy, I had to walk for miles to get water from the bottom of the mountain. It was no fun to get to the top and trip and fall...the water jug rolling down the hillside," he chuckled. When things went right, the village could self-sustain, but it was clear what a delicate and fragile balance this was. In addition, villagers lacked critical information on family planning and health. Education was limited on all fronts—the secondary school was miles and miles away on foot.

We were ushered into a hut, the whole village following and piling in to sit on the floor. Food was brought out for us and laid on a bamboo platform where we were to sit as the guests of honor. They served us heaps of sticky rice in baskets alongside chicken in a rich broth mixed with morning glory and coriander. Beers were cracked and passed, Emma and Nick's glasses filled. Women drank as heartily as the men, and the village elders came and sat next to Nick, staring intently, small grins appearing on their faces as he played his guitar. The group swayed and clapped to the music, and afterward we dug into the meal, the hut filling with easygoing chatter. A young girl was introduced to Alan. Apparently she wanted to pursue her studies beyond secondary school. Pulling out a notebook and paper, he conducted an impromptu interview, asking her questions about her background and her aspirations.

After touring the village's simple primary school, we were brought back to sample the local rice whiskey, held in a small clay pot on the floor, sipped through three thin bamboo straws. We each took a taste or two of the sweet and strong brew before saying our goodbyes and driving back down the mountain to Luang Prabang.

From the banks of the Mekong, we continued on and reunited with John in Hoi An, Vietnam, our home base for the next month. We rented scooters as we had in Thailand, Nick still acting as my driver, and learned the back roads of the scenic ancient town. But on the days where the wind and rain blew hard, and the ocean along China Beach became uninviting and downright angry, Vietnam's scars seem to surface. A heaviness hung in the air, something that I felt I just couldn't shake during our stay. Vietnam was on a fast track to development, investment money pouring in from China and Russia, but much of the rural country still lacked access to basic things.

Our days took on our unique and odd mixture of home-school, music, workouts, trips into town for odd essentials, and GoPhilanthropic's work within the communities. Strangely, time alone had become a rare and precious commodity for any one of us. We were now always within two inches of each other, piled in a bedroom, clutching each other on the back of a bike, or staring at each other from across a table. It was a cozy and comfortable existence peppered with a bit of madness. We met up with Le Ly Hayslip and helped facilitate a mobile library workshop, distributing hundreds of books to a collection of schools and offering training to the teachers who were unaccustomed to using them. One day she took me way into the mountains, to some remote ethnic hill-tribe villages to bring some much-needed supplies to them. I stayed by her side, listening to her words of encouragement as she handed sacks to each family. She then took soap in her hands and demonstrated the importance of hygiene, explaining that many of their sicknesses were preventable using simple measures.

Over the weeks we were introduced to a handful of truly inspirational people, some of whom GoPhilanthropic would develop longstanding relationships with. We met Linda Burn, an Australian expat in her middle years, with long wavy hair and a deep sparkle in her eye. A decade prior, Linda had traveled to Vietnam to learn Buddhist cooking to then later teach once home in Australia. As a part of the trip, she had arranged a private class with a Buddhist nun. During the class Linda noticed three children running around the grounds. The nun explained that the parents of the children had abandoned them. She said that she and their elderly grandmother could care for them, but could no longer afford their school fees. She then begged Linda, while they chopped and prepared food, to adopt them and take them back to Australia.

"As I already had five children, I tried to explain that I couldn't adopt them—instead I promised to help educate them. This was the beginning of what eventually grew into Children's Education Foundation. CEF has grown and now provides educational assistance for minority tribes, for children and grandchildren of lepers, and for children from impoverished farming and fishing communities. We pay for education for boys in dire situations, but we mainly concentrate on the education of females because the strong Confucian and Taoist influences in Vietnamese culture favor the education of males," Linda explained to me as we sipped tea in her small home in Hoi An.

Fifteen years since that fateful decision to help a family of three children, CEF has begun supporting close to two hundred children in Vietnam.

We visited numerous centers and orphanages that provided care for children born with severe defects due to their soil and water being contaminated with the herbicide called Agent Orange (dioxin), which was used by American forces during the war. In one center we encountered children, ages ranging from six days to seventeen years, born with horrible deformities. There were several children to one bed, each one curled up wearing diapers. Tired caretakers went through the motions, spooning food into their mouths. We drove through massive areas still plagued with land minds and learned that leprosy persisted and that those suffering from it were still ostracized and forced to live in communities cut off from everyday life.

From one day to the next, we listened and learned, listened and learned. From my experience so far in building GoPhilanthropic, I knew there were no quick and easy answers or solutions to these problems. But for every ounce of harsh reality we witnessed, we encountered some gem of a program or person lighting the way with energy, hope, and humility. They left a wake of goodness and a feeling that it was the little actions in life that count. I realized that, while we could not change the reality we were witnessing, there was important work to be done within it and no time to lose in taking the steps to join forces.

We ended the trip in Siem Reap, Cambodia, a place that had now become familiar to us. We hung with Leng and the kids at ODA, reconnected with the towering temples, and chaperoned our kids as they sang in bars and restaurants on Pub Street. The weeks in Cambodia flew by rapid fire, and before I knew it, we were packing to head back to France, and later back to our lives in Rochester, New York. Clinging to my last moments sitting by what had become my favorite temple, hidden down a red dirt road away from the tourist track in the countryside outside of Siem Reap, I considered what lessons we might take home with us. Surrounded by the strength of massive, thick tree trucks, ancient stone, and orange monk robes fluttering in the warm breeze, I realized that my life was beginning to feel full. The trip had welded us together as a family of five, something that we had needed but hadn't quite fully achieved until now.

Maybe it had required the weeks of just being together, of a lot of empty moments on dusty roads to just *be*—as unique individuals but also as one family. Beyond this, though, there was a broader feeling of completeness that had to do with being a part of something bigger, something truly beautiful. The work at GoPhilanthropic represented an interlacing of colorful threads on a loom—a bringing together of people like Linda Burn, Alan, and Leng, the children and young adults they nurtured, and all the others who cared about what they were doing who would eventually weave their way into the tapestry. We could all do a little part, share a little something of ourselves, so the weight of the problems didn't simply fall on the shoulders of a few. Yes, if I knew anything so far, the truth I was searching for had to do with the power of coming together. Building our singular, vertical towers would get us nowhere.

24

A Mother's Grip

You are not obliged to complete the work, but
neither are you free to abandon it.
Talmud

The trip had deeply affected all of us in a way that had us look-ing at life like it was more fragile than we could have imagined. Nick decided not to return to high school, instead choosing a distance learning program, an online private school that al-lowed him to work from home while seriously pursuing his music. Emma would make a similar choice the following year, and neither would ever look back on traditional school again. These decisions to would raise eyebrows, both within the fam-ily and among our friends, but we forged on.

Nick realized that his talent brought so much joy that he wanted to build a life around it—and he felt there was no point in wasting time in getting to it. The music industry was almost impossibly difficult to get a foothold into, and so he convinced us that he had better get started. Two weeks after returning home, he lined up for eight hours under the brutal Dallas sun to audition for *The X Factor*'s first season in the United States. We knew that he was good, that he had a sweet demeanor and a love for performing, but I don't think any of us expected him to get such a big fat collective yes from Simon Cowell, L. A. Reid, Paula Abdul, and Nicole Scherzinger on that nerve-wracking audition day. His hair still bleached from the months under the Southeast Asia sun, sporting a cool black shirt and jeans I had picked up for fifteen bucks in the crowded markets of Phnom Penh in Cambodia, he took a leap of faith and sang a portion of a song he had written himself the year before.

From that fateful audition day until the last show that aired months later, we would be thrown into a whirlwind of Hollywood, cameras, and intrusive interviews. I had pictured our months home after getting back from the trip as a settling back into normal life. It would be anything but this. We jumped from the quiet village paths of Cambodia to the glitz and glam of Hollywood within weeks of being back, and I am not sure if any of us had a chance to take a breath. We just rode the wave and held on tight.

Nick ended up being placed in a fabricated group of young individual artists made by Simon Cowell, a *Glee*-type remake that would make it to the top twelve of the show. John took most of the California shifts while I stayed home with the girls, trying to patch together a normal life for them, but it seemed as though that just wasn't meant to be. Nick's group worked side by side with music and television star

Paula Abdul throughout the fall months, leading up to and during the live shows. Eventually his group was eliminated, Nick's face crumpling in despair. Emma and I clutched each other as we watched the broadcast alone from the couch in Rochester. I felt horrible I couldn't be there to comfort him and prayed that his dreams hadn't been crushed.

But he spent no time bemoaning the end of the experience and spent the next two months back in the studio recording his original music. He had been given a taste of what he wanted, and he was more determined than ever to forge on. I was thankful that the trip had provided such grounding lessons for him, and I don't think for one minute he forgot the privilege of the opportunity. He would say on many occasions, "Mom, when I make it in music, I promise to do what I can for GoPhil...I promise I won't forget everything I have seen." And I knew he wouldn't.

Sometime during this madness I received an e-mail from Pascal in India. There was a photo of an empty room attached, void yet full of light. "What do you think?" he wrote. "I think it's time to start the shelter for tots, the little ones."

As I read his brief words, energy shot through my body. "Yes!" I responded, giddy with excitement. "It's magnificent."

I kept the photo of the empty room as my screensaver, a constant reminder of what could be, what was going to be when someone decided to take action. Three months later, I replaced the picture of the empty room with one of the children on the way to school for the first time, sporting fresh backpacks and water bottles. *How quickly a life can change,* I thought. I was thousands of miles away, but they were with me every day, as I made coffee in the morning and as I took the dog for walks or drove to the grocery store.

After hearing about the opening of TARA Tots, I had to see it for myself. A few months later, I awoke to India's characteristic honking of car horns, whistling of distant trains, and the whirling of my overhead fan. Someone next door was playing very loud American pop while running the shower. My South Delhi hotel was perfectly sandwiched between the blocks housing the new TARA Tots shelter and TARA Boys, only a minute's walk from each of their doors. After two cups of shitty Nescafé, I checked my e-mail quickly to see if Pascal had sent word about the day's plans. I was immediately thrown into the painful ups and downs of raising twenty-five vulnerable children. My heart sank as I read his brief e-mail: "morning Lyd. very important—Amit is playing his destiny at Child Welfare Committee, (CWC)."

Damn—not good. Fumbling for the phone, I called him to get more details. Skipping any formal niceties, he began to tell the story of how Amit, ten years old and an only child from an extremely abusive family, had requested not to return to his home for the holidays. On his last visit to see his parents, he returned to TARA with cuts and bruises—his father having beaten him after a drinking binge. The father was now angry that Amit was not coming home and had requested to be seen at the CWC panel, the governmental department that oversees the welfare of children in residential programs. Amit's father now wanted his son back.

Amit would have to express to the CWC board that he did not wish to go home and then face the repercussions from his angry father. Pascal was afraid that the father would demand that his son return home for good, and that the board, who had been fussy with TARA lately, would grant him his wish.

I could hear the fear and frustration in Pascal's voice. He had devoted his entire life and made unbelievable sacrifices for these children, and the thought of losing one after years of providing safety, love, and amazing opportunities was too much to bear. Unfortunately, Amit's story was a common one. While the parents of most of these children had all but turned their backs on them, they often popped in to reclaim them if they felt it could be of benefit to them. The TARA Boys would work their way toward a life they could never have dreamed of—access to the best of Delhi's schools, activities that would prepare them to be wholesome and hard-working additions to the world, and their parents would become well aware of the potential good fortune. We could only pray that they would allow their children to remain in the program long enough to get a foothold in society.

Two of the older boys had recently bid farewell to the home prematurely, and I knew Pascal had felt the blow. Now there was the threat of losing Amit.

"We will know more in a few hours," he said flatly.

I said a few silent prayers for Amit, the boy I had come to know as having such a magnetic spirit and incredible smile, as I headed on foot under the intense summer sun and 115-degree heat to Sadhna Enclave to see the tots. It would be my second trip in six months, and I was eager to see them again.

There wasn't a tourist or a white face in sight. Luckily my years of feeling gawked at, alone, and vulnerable were long gone. I was no longer fazed at the heaps of putrid garbage, rubble, and workers taking naps along the roadside. To me it was a normal yet colorful scene of people going about their daily work—hair being braided for school, morning teas being sipped at neighborhood stalls—life was just being lived in a different context from what we knew.

I strode through the black iron gates set before the concrete building, past a young girl sweeping dusty steps, and up to a door with a tiny sign bearing TARA's signature logo, a young bird beginning to fly despite its little wings. After ringing the bell, I was greeted warmly by Nanny Pushpa. The kids were happy to see a newcomer and recognized my face from my last trip. I had brought my mum on that last trip, and TARA Tots shelter had only been open one week. Pascal had been as frazzled as the arriving kids, and the newly hired nannies had been at a loss to rein in the four children, logically a bit wild and unsettled from having left their mothers and homes. "It's a bit like a wild jungle at the moment," Pascal had confessed. Their behaviors had ranged from hitting to clinging for dear life to passing out from mental and physical exhaustion. They had been covered in lice and infected with worms. They had all been accustomed to having the run of the slums street, or to being locked in a room alone all day, so the concepts of discipline and structure were foreign.

In the following months, two more tots had been welcomed, making a nice round family of six, but the stresses had only seemed to magnify. Problems had included food theft from the kitchen by an unknown employee, constant nanny turnover, grumpy neighbors, the difficulty of getting the tots on a schedule, and more. Despite the hiccups, and only sixteen weeks later, I was now surrounded by six very calm, organized, and engaged little ones. Their English had flourished, they sat quietly for puzzles and reading, they washed their hands before eating, and they sang Barney's "Clean Up" song when playtime was over. They had their health checkups and bone tests to verify their ages and were all enrolled in preschool. Once the license for the shelter was finalized, they would admit more children from the same prostitution slum area in central Delhi, called GB Road. A life at TARA was an incredible fresh start for these children, a very rare chance at breaking the cycle that had trapped their parents.

After hugs and snuggles and giggles, the children continued their playing, soft light coming through the windows. I hesitated to interrupt Manuj, who was sitting before a mess of puzzle pieces looking determined and resolute to finish despite the other tots popping in every two seconds to try a piece here and there. Manuj, only four, had had a terrible time adjusting at the outset. Before TARA, his mother had often left him in a room for nine hours at a time, a small bowl of food placed on the floor, while she had gone out and worked her day. When he had first arrived at TARA, he had been almost manic, talking all of the time and full of naughty behavior. The Manuj I saw now was collected, and my heart sang at the sight of his focused puzzle work.

With Mansi, Pavarti, and Reena swinging from my hands, I took in the rest of the progress and changes. What had been a large blank wall was now covered in painted jungle scenes. A gardener was outside spraying the growth that was now looking tidy, and I immediately thought of how pleased my mum would be. Having a green thumb at heart, she had been concerned about transforming the tots' garden into something pretty. What had been a droopy kumquat tree in the corner of the garden now produced a bounty of fruit from which the nannies were making jam.

Later that day, Pascal had good news. He'd chatted with Amit's mother and father prior to the CWC meeting and convinced the father to not request Amit being pulled out of TARA. Pascal had agreed that, if Amit's father could swear to not drink and beat Amit, Pascal would let Amit go home for four days, on the condition that Amit take a cell phone with him. At dinner that night in Pascal's apartment, as we sipped wine and munched on locally stuffed paranthas, we reflected on TARA's growth over the years. We chatted more into the night about the good news of Amit staying, and I could see the muscles in Pascal's face relax. One more battle won.

I spent mornings with the tots, observing how Jyoti, the young teacher, was coming along, or helping to bathe the children. In the afternoons, I clamored my way up the dark stairs at the TARA Boys home, anxious to see who was hanging around. It was summer holidays, so the boys were enjoying a more relaxed routine. School term had them in a rigorous schedule of yoga, school, more sports, homework, and French classes. Many of the boys were now comfortably trilingual, and the work was paying off. The oldest, Ram, was being courted by a large French corporation seeing great value in a strong work ethic alongside fluency in French, English, and Hindi. I marveled at the opportunities these boys would have available to them in this growing, now cosmopolitan city, compared to where they were headed prior to TARA.

Despite being on break, they were required to complete a half day of "holiday homework," as they said with their sweet Hindi lilt. But today I found a pack of the younger boys playing cards on the floor. I was introduced to sweet Vinesh, the newest addition to the TARA Boys, having only been at the shelter one week. Vinesh suffered from a heart condition that had been improperly treated, causing one side of his body to become underdeveloped. He approached me shyly, with a delicate look, and shook my hand.

We sat on tatty mattresses stacked on the wall, mattresses that in the evenings made up their beds, nine to a small room. Tushar was vying for my attention, standing proudly, speaking loudly in choppy English, the words clearly not coming out as quickly as his thoughts. When I had been here last, he and his brother had been new to TARA and visibly still fragile. The boy I saw before me was proud and full of energy, ready to take on the world. The hours slipped by, and I realized it was time to make it back to my hotel. Exhausted from the day, I ordered some black dal and naan to my room and put the fan on high, sinking into my bed.

The following day, plump little Pavarti was cuddled on my lap, peering out the window of the taxi as it weaved its way through the crazy Delhi traffic. Her head was still full of lice even after undergoing a righteous second scrubbing and treatment the day before. Her hair mixed with mine, and at that moment, I could not have cared less. She was so comfortably situated that I didn't have the heart to move her an inch. The heat was beyond anything I had experienced, the taxi a sweltering sauna. The other tots, Reena, Mansi, Tam, and Manuj, shared the rest of the back seat, screeching and giggling with joy at every passing train and animal. True to Indian form, they were not strapped in and took turns standing, jumping, and wrapping their arms around the driver's seat, teasing him as he snaked in and out through passing rickshaws and dump trucks. Nanny Pushpa chatted in Hindi with the driver, oblivious to the shenanigans in the back, then finally peered over her shoulder. Relieved she had noticed, I was sure she would scold them as my lack of Hindi had me handicapped when it came to discipline. Instead, a huge grin spread across her face. She looked like a proud mother as she watched the tots jump up and down. Against my better judgment, I let my worry go, reminding myself to just take in the moment.

We were on our way to a library for story and craft time. Stopping at a light, we were bombarded with begging children banging on the window, motioning for something to eat. The tots stopped their playing and stared into the faces on the other side of the window. A strange silence swept in, and I witnessed the tots as they sized up the destitute children on the other side of the glass. I knew the look well. I had seen it on Isabelle's face in Southeast Asia. It was a look of both understanding and fleeting empathy yet desperation to distance themselves. Peering out past the begging children, I set my eyes on a family living on the curbside. A small girl caught my eye, for she was the same age as Pavarti, who now sat safely on my lap on her way to a reading session. This girl was gaunt and filthy, everything around her in a decrepit state. Life had offered her seemingly little, and I knew that her future would be more of the same, only perhaps worse.

The taxi was now thick with heat, and I was struck by something intense as I stared at this little girl. Sweat began to drip from my forehead—streams of perspiration ran down my legs. In need of air, I wanted to roll down the window, but I knew there would be no relief—the city's filth would only find its way in. Instead, I forced myself back to the girl, trying to focus on what I was feeling. Was it guilt? Shame? Yes, something of the sort. My brain sifted through my whirling thoughts, trying to pinpoint the source. Who was I to think that we were making any difference at all when there were millions of children living in similar conditions? How could I sit here satisfied as we headed off to story time? I was staring at an incredibly unfortunate girl whom I could do nothing for. How could I feel satisfied?

Then time, as it had done before, stopped. I knew it meant I should listen. As I continued to look at the girl, words swept through my mind—they spoke softly, clearly, through the densely heated air. There were five little beings in the back of this car, five I was blessed to sit with, five who were lucky to be going to the library for story time. Sweat dripped from my back and forehead as Pavarti pushed herself more deeply into my lap, finally nodding off.

Understanding the message clearly, I then wrapped my arms around Pavarti tightly, as if grabbing onto her for dear life. I knew the feeling well. It was that unmistakable mother's grip. A grip that meant you would fight, protect to the bitter end, no matter what it took. *I may not be able to save the girl on the other side of the street today, but I can do something for the children in the back of this car right now.* And that was all I could do. I could continue to put one foot in front of the other, no matter how small those steps felt. GoPhilanthropic wasn't pulling in millions like other foundations, but a simple idea over a pot of paint had sprouted into a plan, and that plan had sprouted into a team. That team had inspired others to listen, and those others now cared about the TARAs of the world. But as the car inched forward into the dense Delhi traffic, I thought about how despite having made some progress, we could still dream of reaching more. If I had learned anything in my lifetime so far, it was the importance of imagining what could be.

25

As It Is Supposed to Be

*Go forth in peace. Be still within yourself and
know that the trail is beautiful.*
Navajo Blessing

Later that day, trying to shake off the weight of the afternoon, I wandered through the local markets of Old Delhi
at dusk. After losing myself in an old bookshop for over
an hour, I stumbled onto an ancient shop of sorts, dis-
playing relics from God-only-knew how long ago—clips,
bangles, wooden bowls, prints of ancient maharajas. It
smelled a combination of lingering incense, dust, spice, and
sandalwood.

There she stood—a small bronze statue of the Hindu
goddess Tara. Slimmer than the image I had found on the
Internet but nonetheless clearly her. Without hesitation
and not wanting to bother with bargaining, I offered the
asking price of three hundred rupees and popped her safely
in my bag.

On the way back to my hotel, I walked through every second of the dream I'd had about her the previous summer.

I had dreamed that our little family was on a sailboat in clear blue waters heading out of a beautiful lagoon. The water glistened magically, casting little tiny sparkles on the water as far as the eye could see. The boat was rich in exotic woods, lined with polished brass. John was at the helm, confident and strong; a look of profound happiness spread across his face as he sailed his family into the distance. Despite the idyllic scene, though, I was full of fear. The children had made their way up the tall mast, and the boat began tipping from side to side in the swells. *John is driving the boat too fast,* I thought; the waters were gradually roughening, and I felt we were all at risk. Wanting to bury my head in a pillow, I descended into the hull of the boat. At the bottom of the stairs, I was surprised to see a woman sitting cross-legged on a bench. Magical sunlight cast a light on the wooden floors beneath her. All of a sudden, the brass railings and the hull looked a hundred times bigger that they had earlier that day. The woman was smiling, reflecting immense joy and a kind of all-knowing wisdom. I was comforted at the sight of her; my instinct was to go up to her and curl up in her heavy-set lap. I knew it would feel so good, so warm and safe—there would be no more need to worry. And so I did.

"Is everything going to be OK?" I asked, gazing up at her glowing face.

Looking down at me, she chuckled softly. Then, stroking my head, she said, "Yes...that and much, much more..."

For weeks following the dream, I had not been able to shake the image of this woman. She had looked like she could have been a female Buddha of some sort. Her laughter, her comfort, her all-knowing spirit had just felt goddesslike. Determined to learn more, I had Googled images, plugging in simple terms for what ran through my mind—*female Buddha, female goddesses and deities.* Astonishingly, within minutes of typing my first terms into that search box, I was staring at a mirror image of the lady in my dream. Reading about her, I was shocked to find her name was Tara. Stunned at the coincidence of her name given my connection to TARA, I continued to dig more.

The goddess Tara was said to be born out of a bodhisattva's tears of compassion. I had had no clue what a bodhisattva was but quickly learned that it referred to someone on the path to awakening, someone searching enlightenment. It is said that the bodhisattva wept as he looked upon the world of suffering beings, and his tears formed a lake in which a lotus sprung up. When the lotus opened, the goddess Tara was revealed. She represented compassion and support for those in pain and suffering.

That night after finding my Tara in the market in Delhi, I lit a candle and placed it next to her. As I gazed into the flame, I thought back to those days sitting on my porch in Orlando, when leaving the life we knew was merely a dream. I gave thanks to Tara and whatever other forces were out there for having given me the strength to act on it, for showing me through the dark back alleys of the world, and for leading me to all of the wonderful people doing such selfless and important work. I thanked her for bringing me to the TARA kids in Delhi.

Drifting off to sleep, comforted with Tara at my side, I realized that at some point during this life pilgrimage, I had stopped searching. I tried to remember that nagging sense of wanting and needing to figure something out, but I couldn't remember what that felt like anymore. Without even being conscious of it, I had replaced it with something much deeper—a sensation that it was OK to just trust that life would unfold as it was meant to unfold. We were at the beginning of building something that would have no end, a renovation that would never be complete. I knew I no longer had to worry. My answers would continue to become clear as I got up each morning, returning to the computer or the airport, to building GoPhilanthropic, to being a mother, a friend, and a wife. Putting one foot in front of the other simply felt right, like I was doing what I was supposed to do. I would continue to swing from feeling like a clueless schoolchild to knowing deep in my heart that it wasn't all that complicated. I just had to continue to follow my life signs. I had learned to trust them.

The final days slipped by, and before I knew it, I was watching the crumbling city streets whiz by as my taxi transported me back to my other world. As I waited to board my last plane home from Detroit to Rochester, I called John and got a familiar scoop of all the goings on—doctors' appointments, homework, song recording, workouts, horses, dinner menus, "minor scratches" on Nick's face from the boxing gym. It brought a smile to my face yet made my head spin a bit—perhaps because of the exhausting back-to-back, eight-hour flights, or perhaps because I was not quite ready for the world back home yet. I was still coming out of a deep sleep filled with the smells of spices, images of mystical deities, and the din of the children's Hindi ringing in my ears.

Epilogue

Sometime during the course of the years it took to write this book, I stumbled on information relating to the word *Zulu*, which I later learned to be a large ethnic tribe of South Africa. Traditionally they were grain farmers and herders, but they underwent years of warfare with Europeans settlers during the nineteenth century, when they lost much of their resources. Intrigued, I found several websites referring to Zulu dreams, which apparently played an important role within Zulu traditions. Dreams about Zulu were thought to be prophetic, representing the principal channel through which ancestors communicated. Some believe these dreams carry important messages describing a course of action for the dreamer. I often thought of John's dream and what hidden life truth had been buried within it. I couldn't separate it from some of our most meaningful life events, such as Isabelle's adoption and the birth of GoPhilanthropic.

In 2013, we moved to Los Angeles to support Nick, and later Emma, in their music careers. I would have never predicted living here in a million years, but I've learned that when life opens doors, you should probably walk through them.

Isabelle is growing into the strong, capable young woman we knew she would be, her courage and determination eclipsing the hardships she encountered so early in life.

The Only Provence business keeps us intimately linked to a place that gave us all so much. Mas de Gancel just underwent its second renovation and is rented to vacationers for the better part of the year. When the tourist season is over, we return as a family, spending our evenings by the fire with friends as we always have, and walking or running the trails that offered me so many of my life epiphanies.

GoPhilanthropic Foundation continues to thrive, developing an active and growing community of people who believe that philanthropy goes way beyond the pocketbook. An organization based on rolling up one's sleeves and fostering partnership, we don't assume we have all the answers, systems, or methods to solve anyone's problems. We simply enter into our relationships with the willingness and the time to help people and programs be the best they can be. Listening continues to be a cornerstone in our work. Many of the founders and programs described in the book— such as Leng (ODA), Anuradha Bhosale (WCRC), Linda Burn (CEF), Pascal Fautrat (TARA), and LEOT continue to be supported by GoPhilanthropic and its donors. We have since identified a host of others doing equally important work in their communities.

I would like to take this moment to say thank you to all those who encouraged me to push through the pains that came alongside piecing this puzzle together. You know who you are, and your words always seemed to come at just the right time. Thank you to Jessica Rabbiner, who forced me to take the "deep dives in the muddy water to pull out the weeds" needed to offer a clear message in the manuscript. Enormous gratitude goes to my family, who rallied on the sidelines throughout the years it took to see the book to fruition. Greatest thanks however, goes to all of the courageous people out there making a difference in the world, only a few of whom are mentioned in this book. They live by a compass of compassion beyond what we can imagine, casting a light on the most important parts of life.

In sum, I'll sign off with what Ted Simon wrote to me after I read his book of adventures around the world: "Glad you enjoyed my experiences...all the best in yours."

GoPhilanthropic Foundation: www.GoPhilanthropic.org
GoPhilanthropic Travel: www.GoPhilanthropicTravel.com
Only Provence Villas: www.OnlyProvence.com
Author Website: www.LydiaDean.com

18847020R00190

Made in the USA
San Bernardino, CA
31 January 2015